'My' Self on Camera

EDINBURGH STUDIES IN EAST ASIAN FILM
Series Editor: Margaret Hillenbrand

Available and forthcoming titles

Independent Chinese Documentary
Dan Edwards

Tanaka Kinuyo
Edited by Irene González-López and Michael Smith

Worldly Desires
Brian Hu

The Cinema of Ozu Yasujiro
Woojeong Joo

Eclipsed Cinema
Dong Hoon Kim

Moving Figures
Corey Kai Nelson Schultz

Memory, Subjectivity and Independent Chinese Cinema
Qi Wang

Hong Kong Neo-Noir
Edited by Esther C. M. Yau and Tony Williams

'My' Self on Camera
Kiki Tianqi Yu

edinburghuniversitypress.com/series/eseaf

'My' Self on Camera

First Person Documentary Practice in an Individualising China

Kiki Tianqi Yu

EDINBURGH
University Press

Edinburgh University Press is one of the leading university presses in the UK. We publish academic books and journals in our selected subject areas across the humanities and social sciences, combining cutting-edge scholarship with high editorial and production values to produce academic works of lasting importance. For more information visit our website: edinburghuniversitypress.com

First published in hardback by Edinburgh University Press 2019

Edinburgh University Press Ltd
The Tun – Holyrood Road
12 (2f) Jackson's Entry
Edinburgh EH8 8PJ

Typeset in 10/13 Chaparral Pro by
IDSUK (DataConnection) Ltd

A CIP record for this book is available from the British Library

ISBN 978 0 7486 9821 9 (hardback)
ISBN 978 1 4744 7412 2 (paperback)
ISBN 978 0 7486 9822 6 (webready PDF)
ISBN 978 1 4744 4210 7 (epub)

Contents

Figures

Main Terms with Chinese Translations

bie, 别, distinction
chaxugeju, 差许格局, differential mode of association
daji, 大己, greater self
dangguo, 党国, the party-state
danmu, 弹幕, 'bullet curtain'; barrage
danwei, 单位, work unit
dawo, 大我, greater I
fa, 法, law
Fulian, 妇联, Women's Federation
geren, 个人, the individual; the personal; one person
gerenhua xiezuo, 个人化写作, individualised writing
geren zhuyi, 个人主义, individualism
geti, 个体, individual
geti hu, 个体户, self-employed
gongde, 公德, public morality
gonggong, 公共, the public
goutong, 沟通, communication
hujibu, 户籍簿, household registration book
hukou, 户口, resident registration
jia, 家, family home
Jiaodian fangtan, 焦点访谈, Focus (investigative TV documentary programme)
jiapu, 家谱, family tree
jiashu yuan, 家属院, family dependents courtyard
jiating lunli, 家庭伦理, family ethics
jiazu, 家族, family clan
jishi, 纪实, documentary (style)
jishi sheying, 纪实摄影, documentary photography
jishi wenxue, 纪实文学, reportage writing or non-fiction documentary literature
jishi zhuyi, 纪实主义, documentarism
jiti, 集体, the collective

kejia (Hakka), 客家, guest families
laojia, 老家, old home
li, 礼, propriety
liang piao, 粮票, grain ration coupons
min, 民, the people
minjian, 民间, public spaces; among the folk
min ren, 民人, individual people
nong erdai, 农二代, second generation peasant
nongjia fan, 农家饭, peasant food or food with a special countryside flavour
qin, 亲, affection
quan, 权, rights
quanli, 权力, power
ren, 仁, benevolence
ren, 人, a person
sangang, 三纲, the three cardinal guides
shengchan dui, 生产队, production team
shenti xiezuo, 身体写作, body writing
shi, 食, food
shikumen, 石库门, stone gate
si, 私, private (or I in ancient Chinese)
side, 私德, private morality
siren, 私人, the private
si sheying, 私摄影, private photography
si xiaoshuo, 私小说, private novel
si yingxiang, 私影像, private image
sushe lou, 宿舍楼, dormitory building
tianxia, 天下, all under heaven
tizhi, 体制, the system
tongju, 同居, living together without marriage
tuantigeju, 团体格局, organisational mode of association
wanghong, 网红, Internet celebrity
Weibo, 微博, mini blog
Weixin, 微信, WeChat – social media application
wo, 我, I
women, 我们, we
womende, 我们的, our
wo yi dai, 我一代, I generation
wuchang, 五常, the five constant virtues
xianchang, 现场, being there; on the spot
xiangchou, 乡愁, nostalgia

xiao, 孝, filiality
xiaoji, 小己, lesser self
xiao jiqi, 小机器, small machine
xiaowo, 小我, lesser I
xin, 信, sincerity; loyalty
xing, 行, transport
xingdong dianying, 行动电影, action cinema
xintiandi, 新天地, new heaven earth
xu, 序, order
yi, 义, brotherhood; righteousness
yi, 衣, clothing
yingxiang xiezuo, 影像写作, image-writing
yinsi wenxue, 隐私文学, privacy literature
zanzhu renkou, 暂住人口, temporary residents
zhi, 智, wisdom
zhibo, 直播, live web-streaming broadcast
zhu, 住, accommodation
zhubo, 主播, leading presenter
zhuguan, 主观, the epistemic subject
zhuti, 主体, the practical subject or agent of practice
ziwo, 自我, self
zizhi, 自治, autonomy
zuwu, 祖屋, the ancestor's house

Names with Chinese Character Translations

List of individuals who are mentioned in the book and quoted authors whose works are published in Chinese.

Ai Weiwei 艾未未
Ai Xiaoming 艾晓明
Ba Jin 巴金
Cai Weilian 蔡威廉
Cao Fei 曹菲
Cui Ying 崔莺
Dai Jianyong 戴建勇
Deng Xiaoping 邓小平
Dong Zhongshu 董仲舒
Fei Xiaotong 费孝通
Feng Mengbo 冯梦波
Feng Yan 冯艳
Feng Youlan 冯友兰
Gao Yihan 高一函
Guo Jing 郭净
Guo Lifen 郭丽芬
Guo Moruo 郭沫若
He Ku 何苦
He Xiangning 何香凝
Hu Jie 胡杰
Hu Shi 胡适
Hu Xinyu 胡新宇
Ji Dan 季丹
Jia Zhangke 贾章柯
Jia Zhitan 贾之坦
Jian Yi 简艺
Jiao Guocheng 焦国成
Li Ning 李凝
Liang Qichao 梁启超
Liang Shuming 梁漱溟
Lu Xinyu 吕新雨
Lu Xun 鲁迅
Mian Mian 棉棉
Mu Zimei 木子美
Nong Ke 农科
Pan Yuliang 潘玉良
Shao Yuzhen 邵玉珍
Shen Congwen 沈从文
Shu Haolun 舒浩伦
Tang Danhong 唐丹鸿
Tang Yunyu 唐蕴玉
Wang Fen 王分
Wang Hai'an 王海安
Wang Hui 汪辉
Wang Jingyuan 王静远
Wang Nanfu 王男栿
Wang Wei 王伟
Wang Xi 王西
Wang Xiaolu 王晓鲁
Wei Hui 卫慧
Wei Xiaobo 魏晓波
Wen Hui 文慧
Wu Haohao 吴昊昊
Wu Wenguang 吴文光

Xiaodong 晓东
Xu Jilin 许纪霖
Xu Tong 徐童
Xu Zhen 徐震
Xue Jianqiang 薛鉴羌
Yan Yunxiang 闫云翔
Yang Dezhen 杨德贞
Yang Fudong 杨福东
Yang Lina 杨荔纳
Yang Pingdao 杨平道
Yao Daimei 姚玳玫
Yin Xiaofeng 尹晓峰
Yu Dafu 郁达夫
Yu Luojin 遇罗锦
Yu Yingshi 余英时
Zhang Ailing (Eileen Zhang) 张爱玲
Zhang Huancai 张焕财
Zhang Jie 张洁
Zhang Mengqi 章梦奇
Zhang Yaxuan 张亚璇
Zhao Liang 赵亮
Zhao Zhao 赵赵
Zhaxi Nima 扎西尼玛
Zhou Hao 周浩
Zhou Shoujuan 周寿元
Zhu Qingsheng 朱青生
Zhuo Ma 卓玛
Zou Xueping 邹雪平

Acknowledgements

During the journey of working on this book over the past decade, I have received tremendous intellectual and emotional support from my mentors, fellow scholars and filmmakers, friends, and surely, families.

My initial research would not be have been possible without CREAM Research Scholarship in the University of Westminster, supported by AHRC. It was my great honour to have Professor Rosie Thomas as my Director of Studies and supervisor, who provided invaluable guidance and encouragement to me as a scholar and a woman. My gratitude also goes to Professor Harriet Evans who always inspire me to rethink my critical examination of China. Respected scholars Joram ten Brink and Katie Hill have also offered me thought-provoking advice in the early stage of this research.

I feel extremely grateful to have had Professor Chris Berry as my supervisor. Chris stimulated and encouraged me through various stages and offered me tremendous guidance and illuminating comments through our regular conversations, on the topics of Chinese cinemas, culture and society at large. I am also grateful to Alisa Lebow, for her initial inspiration on the subject of first person documentary, with whom our passionate discussions have encouraged me to continually explore the subjective cinema outside the so-called western culture, and constantly motivated me in rethinking and theorising the subject. I also offer my gratitude to Professor Georgina Born for her intellectual stimulation and methodological guidance at Cambridge University, where my training as cultural sociologist deepened my passion for ethnographical research and for approaching cinema as cultural practice.

I offer my sincere thanks to Wu Wenguang and Wen Hui, for their kind help during my initial fieldwork in China in 2009 and 2010, for the revitalising conversations at their Caochuangdi Work Station in Beijing, and for allowing me to access their independent film collections; and thanks to all the filmmakers and critics in China whom I have interviewed for this book, who generously shared with me their personal reflections, observations, production notes and screening feedbacks.

Periodical papers and ideas have been presented at various conferences and venues and published in edited collections and journals. I am grateful to Patricia Pisters for inviting me as a keynote at Amsterdam Conference of NECS (European Network for Cinema and Media Studies) in June 2018, where I discussed some key issues raised in this book, which still impel me towards future exploration – especially on theoretical consideration of Western vs non Western paradigm, approaches outside dominating theories in English language film studies, methods in ethnographical research and film practices in evaluating cinema as a culture, and the instant construction of the self on social media *Zhibo* in the post-cinematic era. The exciting discussion with the audience after my presentation was extremely rewarding and encouraged me to continue my investigation.

Chapter 2 was first presented at 'Saving the Private Reel' conference at Cork in 2010, where I was strongly inspired by conversations with Laura Rastaroli and Patricia Zimmermann. An earlier version of this chapter was subsequently published in *Amateur Filmmaking: the Home Movie, the Archive, the Web* (London: Bloomsbury Academic, 2014) co-edited by the inspiring scholar Laura Rastaroli. Chapter 1 was presented at the 'New Generation Chinese Cinema' international conference, which I co-organised with Keith B. Wagner at King's College London in 2011. My conversations with Zhang Zhen, Yomi Braester and Luke Robinson at the conference further developed my thinking. An earlier version of the chapter was published in *China's iGeneration: Cinema and Moving Image Culture for the 21st Century* (London: Bloomsbury Academic, 2014). Chapter 6 was presented at the 'Documentary Now!' 2012 conference in London, where I received very encouraging and constructive feedback from Alisa Lebow and Brian Winston, and at Lau China Institute seminar series of King's College London, invited by Ralph Parfect. An earlier version of this chapter was published on *Studies in Documentary Film* (2015 9:1). Chapters 4 & 5 were presented at AAS Toronto and SCMS Chicago in 2016, where I have benefited significantly from intellectual exchange from scholars working on Taiwan, Hong Kong and Middle Eastern socially and politically engaged film practices, including Bo Zheng, Ting Chun Chun, Evelyn Hsin-Chin Hsieh.

My past four years' experience working in China, at the University of Nottingham Ningbo China (UNNC) and USC-SJTU Institute of Cultural and Creative Industries (ICCI) in Shanghai, offered me great opportunities to deepen my understanding of the changing sense of self in contemporary China, through close observation and day-to-day living experience. I have benefited significantly from conversations with my former colleagues such as David Craig, David Fleming, Paul Gladston, Simon Harrison, Adam Knee, Ben Lee, Paul Martin, David O'Brien, Ivy Zhang and Xiaoling Zhang, who lent me their different perspectives on China, and with my former Dean, Zhang Weimin, and the very helpful team at ICCI for their trust and support. The regular chats with my friends, fellow filmmakers and scholars in China also compel me to examine deeper into this art and cultural practice. Special thanks go to Chen Ping, Cong Feng, Dong Bingfeng, Gao Shiqiang, Gong Siqi, Han Yuchen, Paul Louis, Shi Hantao, Ma Ran, Ma Xiao, Mao Chenyu, Shen Jianwen, Shu Haolun, Situ Jiayi, Sun Hongyun, Tang Weijie, Zhang Xianmin, Zhang Zhen, Zhou Hao, Zhu Jinjiang, Zou Xueping, Wang Chi, Wang Jiuliang, Wang Yinjie, Wen Hui and Xiao Ya. I am also very grateful to institutions such as China Art Academy, OCAT Shanghai, OCAT Beijing, Ray Art Centre and Rock Bund Art Museum, where I have been invited to present different aspects of this ongoing research to local Chinese audiences who gave me indispensable feedback. Some updated ideas, especially in Chapter 8, have resulted from discussions with my students including Fuyang Yiman, Wang Kunlin, Zhang Weijia, Gao Qi and Zeng Ziyi.

It is my great pleasure to work with Edinburgh University Press. A big thank you goes to the series editor Margaret Hillenbrand, who offered insightful feedback on earlier manuscripts. This book would not be in the shape today without endless and patient help from the commissioning editor Gillian Leslie, and the production team of Richard Strachan, Eddie Clark and Rebecca Mackenzie, and copy-editor Sue Dalgleish, who provided me with their excellent professional support.

Finally, I can never express enough gratitude to my dear families, particularly my parents Haibo and Lijun, for your constant encouragement, priceless support and love, and life influence as great artists and beings; my grandparents Shihua, Aiyun and Xiuzheng, for your boundless love; my parents-in-law Pat and Tony, for your living wisdoms, knowledge and deep affections; and my brother Weiqi, cousins and old school friends, for the continuous sharing of joy and sorrow in your lives – the book is to understand individuals in contemporary China as much as to understand our generation. My last and foremost gratefulness goes to my dearest husband Anthony Thomas McKenna, for your love: with you, there are always endless things to talk about intellectually and culturally; from you, I have gained deep confidence and joy being a woman, scholar and filmmaker.

Xiexie, all of you, for the faith you always have in me.

For Haibo, Lijun, Kenna and Celia

Introduction: Action, Amateurness and the Changing Sense of the Individual Self

My interest in first person documentary started in 2008. In autumn 2008, I was given a chance to work as a part-time researcher on a BBC-commissioned documentary production, *China's Capitalist Revolution* (2010), produced by Brook Lapping Productions, London. The film was constructed through interviews with Western politicians, businessmen, scholars and Chinese exiles, as well as rich archival footage and newsreels on China, mostly shot by Western media from the 1950s to the 1990s. Fascinated by how a British professional film crew represents the country I originally come from, I began to shoot reflexive ethnographic videos about the crew and my experience working on this production. With a small amateur digital video (DV) camera, I documented my daily negotiations, as a researcher and ethnographer, with the crew in their editing suite, offices and studios, on the construction of the image of China and its history. Overwhelmed by the clash of values and self-questioning, I also made intensive video diaries in my room near Northwick Park, recording my personal confessions and confusions in response to the making of this BBC documentary. I found that the complexity and difficulty in cultural translation was starkly apparent in the production of this film. Documentary, with its strong visual impact referencing 'reality' for the construction of 'truth', has been used as an important mediator in the discourse of representing the lives and cultures of 'others'.

The central question that I encountered during my experience working on this production was a philosophical and anthropological one: how to position myself and understand my own subjectivity. *Who am I? How have I come to be what I am now?* As the only Chinese person on the crew, my self-identity became a major issue. For the first time I was exposed to a large amount of contradictory archival material on China's recent history. Such material disclosed alternative historical narratives that were new to me. I had discussions with the director, editor and assistant producer on issues about which we in China have been given different views, such as China's socio-political context and cultural conditions in the 1980s and the 1990s. Looking back, I highly appreciate such discussions – I saw my 'self' as split into different parts: the self that had been constructed in China had become more complicated since I came to the UK.

Who am I? Or what is 'myself'? A Chinese person by ethnicity? But what does it mean to be a Chinese person in the contemporary world, especially as I, like many others, constantly shift between different geo-cultural entities? How has culture in the era of Deng Xiaoping's opening up and the continuous economic development and current national revival agenda constructed my sense of self? How could I position myself facing multiple 'cultures' of China and the so-called 'West'? My reflexive ethnographic filming with the crew and my personal confessional videos were edited into a film and screened a couple of times in a private viewing in London. Watching my own first person documentary and discussing the experience with my mentors, colleagues and friends offered me the distance and space to reflect further on my changing sense of self.

I increasingly found it difficult to present the question of how the 'Western' side of myself sees the 'Chinese' side of myself and vice versa, one of my original aims. It is problematic to separate and define what are the Western and Chinese sides. From a post-colonial perspective, the 'Western self' is no longer easily accepted as a voice of authority, facing other cultures. From a post-structuralist view, the 'self' in Western social contexts is understood as fragmented, multiple and always in flux. In the same sense, an essential Chinese culture hardly exists. In addition to early imported cultures such as Buddhism in ancient China, modern China has been continuously influenced by – and merged with – 'imported' cultures since at least the nineteenth century.

Looking at myself, my personal trajectory illustrates the multi-layered culture of contemporary China. Born in the 1980s in central China, which claims to be the heart of ancient Chinese culture, I moved to Shenzhen at the age of nine. As the first Special Economic Zone, Shenzhen developed from a small fishing village with a population of 20,000, to a metropolis of more than 15 million people, emblematic of China's socio-economic transition over the past thirty years. It is the 'city of experiment' for the socialist market economy, openly embracing Western capitalist culture and Chinese migrant culture. Locating Shenzhen in the larger context of post-Mao China, Shenzhen mirrors the overall picture of a contemporary China in the throes of dramatic socio-economic and cultural transformation.

The realisation of the problematic nature of my own social, cultural and politically situated identity urged me to explore the cinematic construction of self in non-fiction film, especially in self-inscriptive first person documentary practice. I made *Memory of Home* (2009), a ten-minute essay film exploring, in a more abstract manner, the inner truth of myself, or my psychological difficulty in positioning the self when facing China's massive urbanisation and my then position in the West. It was also a time when I was exposed to different forms of first person narrative non-fiction films. I was very excited to see Jonas Mekas' film diaries, Chris Marker's *Sunday in Beijing* (1956) and *Sans Soleil* (1989), Marlon Rigg's *Tongues Untied* (1989), Chantal Akerman's *News From Home* (1977), Alan Berliner's *Nobody's Business* and *Intimate Strangers*, Ross McElwee's autobiographical film series, Carol Morley's *The Alcohol Years* (2000), Alisa Lebow's *Treyf* (1998), Trinh-T. Minh-Ha's *Reassemblage* (1982), Sandhya Suri's *I for India* (2005), Japanese-born Korean filmmaker Yong-hi Yang's *Dear Pyongyang* (2005), Japanese filmmaker Hara Kazuo's *Extreme Private Eros: Love Song 1974* (1974), and so on. These films not only offered a diverse range of forms in presenting the self, such as filmic diary, essay film, and the use of performative and amateur home movie elements, but also prompted me to reflect deeper on the nature of the self: how one's personal trajectory, the family, culture and society one is situated within, as well as the political and technological conditions, affect the changing formation of the self and the aesthetics of representing it, one of the key questions in this research.

First Person Documentary Practice in the West

Presenting the filmmakers on camera, Dziga Vertov's *Man with a Movie Camera* (1929) marks a famous and celebrated example of self-inscription and reflectivity in non-fiction film, though certainly not the earliest one. Early amateur films in different parts of the world reveal various levels of self-inscription, accidentally or purposely. In North America and Europe, pointing the camera on oneself has been increasingly consciously practised by artists, filmmakers and ethnographers since the 1960s, a time when crisis in representation in classic social anthropology, a Western culturally rooted subject, became more prominent. The epistemological critique of postmodernism and post-structuralism placed a strong emphasis on the new reflexive ethnography, which presents the ethnographer's own subjectivity. Ethnographers, including visual ethnographers, became more visible, even central in their work, and the authorial voice becomes an auteur voice of one's own, representing an interpretation rather than an 'authoritative' description.

Mary Louise Pratt developed her term 'autoethnography' in her well-acclaimed keynote address 'Arts of the Contact Zone' (1991), focusing on self-representation by 'others' who were previously represented by the Western 'self'. Later, Catherine Russell introduces this term to describe first person filmmaking practice, stating that

> autobiography becomes ethnographic at the point where the film- or videomaker understands his or her personal history to be implicated in larger social formations and historical processes. Identity is no longer a transcendental or essential self that is revealed, but a 'staging of subjectivity' – a representation of the self as a performance. (Russell 1999: 276)

While Russell sees the subject in autoethonography can also be the Western 'self', she makes no critique of Western self-inscription, except in pointing out 'the utopian impulse' of filmmakers who have access to the camera and have mobility and 'remain[s] in many ways couched in modernist, imperialist, and romantic discourse' (1999: 276). Her statements cover films ranging from those by Western, mostly American, independent filmmakers, home-video amateurs, to what she called 'third world' filmmakers, without offering further specific historical, social and cultural contextualisation. Even though the term autoethnography recognises the autobiographical and reflexive voice of the 'others', and emphasises the value of their own documentation, it does not go beyond the 'self and others' binary.

Within the so called 'West', the increasingly visible identity crisis in the 1960s and 1970s, especially in America, pushed forward the autobiographical documentary practice that explores the filmmaker's self-identity. The rise of social movements on civil rights, feminism, gender, ethnicity, sexuality and so on, politicise personal issues and highlight the problematics of identity. Michael Renov recognises, 'in all cases, subjectivity, a grounding in the personal and the experiential, fuelled the engine of political action' (2004: 176–7). This is made even more salient through first person engagement with the camera. 'Film has the power to stop and even reverse time's inexorable passage, providing a powerful tool for the obsessive investigation of the past, autobiography's stock-in-trade' (Renov 2004: 43).

The technological advances in photographic reproduction means, such as the emergence of video and the development of the digital video camera, contributed to what some argue is the narcissistic nature of self-exposure and the rise of private and confessional videomaking. Catherine Russell points out the crucial role that the technology of representation plays in the identification process of the self, arguing that 'autoethnography in film and video is always mediated by technology, and so unlike its written forms, identity will be an effect not only of history and culture but also of the history and culture of technologies of representation' (1999: 281). In the 1970s, the art critic Rosalind Krauss observed that the first generation video apparatus was a medium that 'is capable of recording and transmitting at the same time, producing instant feedback . . . The body of the self is centered between two machines, the camera and the monitor, that re-project the performer's image with the immediacy of a mirror' (Krauss 1976: 52). Similarly, Renov believes that

> video can be seen as a format historically joined to the private and the domestic, a medium capable of supplying inexpensive sync sound images, a vehicle of autobiography in which the reflex gaze of the electronic eye can engender an extended, even obsessive, discourse of the self. (2004: 203)

Such a documentation of the self as moving image is further constructed during the editing, which adds other layers of self in a different temporal space, where the role of the filmmaker as a creative auteur becomes more prominent.

The complexity of the construction of the self as subject in the postmodern context has also been intensively explored by political theorists, cultural theorists and philosophers. Subjectivity is understood as a constructive process, while identity is seen as floating and transitional, filled from those outside us, rather than a complete product. Individual self in the 'second modernity' (Beck and Beck-Gernsheim 2010: xiv) is seen as non-linear, fluid and reflexive (Giddens 1990; Beck 2000; Beck *et al.* 1994). Stuart Hall famously claims that

> rather than speaking of identity as a finished thing, we should speak of identification, and see it as an ongoing process. Identity arises, not so much from the fullness of identity which is already inside us as individuals, but from a lack of wholeness which is 'filled' from outside us, by the ways we imagine ourselves to be seen by others. (1992: 287)

Judith Butler's work (1990, 1993) on gender performativity has also had a strong impact on understanding subjectivity and the construction of the self from a post-structuralist perspective.

Such debates in cultural studies and political sciences have huge influence on the discussions on subjectivity in studies of first person films. Renov regards what he calls 'autobiographic documentaries' or 'filmic autobiography' as 'a site of instability – flux, drift, perpetual revision – rather than coherence' (2004: 19). In her study on first person Jewish documentaries, Alisa Lebow recognises the complexity of the multi-layered self, which

> is a constructed, culturally inscribed, fragmentary, and incomplete narrative that is neither the sole invention of an ideologically autonomous author, nor the collectively overdetermined product of a monolithic culture, but rather is some admixture of these two impossible positions, made even more impossible by the fact that the cultural context is highly heterogeneous and always at some measure of remove. (Lebow 2008: xvi)

What Lebow recognises as the complexities of the making of self are strongly felt by myself.

Within the form of autobiographic or first person documentary, scholars have identified different styles, including the essay film, or the electronic essay, the diary film, the video confession, the epistolary mode, domestic ethnography, the personal web page and the blog (Renov 2008: 44). Renov intensively investigates the confessional feature of such films, which 'in non-hegemonic contexts can be powerful tools for self-understanding as well as for two-way communication, for the forging of human bonds and for emotional recovery' (2004: 215). For Renov, video has played a significant role in transforming Western confessional culture, by changing the power relations in the traditional confession that Foucault identified. He argues that the video camera's immediacy of feedback, and the possibility of operating it by oneself, enable the subject to 'achieve a depth and a nakedness of expression that is difficult to duplicate with a crew or even camera operator present' (2004: 203). This satisfies Foucault's formulation of confession as 'a discourse in which the speaking subject is also the subject of the statement', in which the 'speaking subject' is understood as necessarily and simultaneously being the 'enunciating subject' (Renov and Suderberg 1996: 85).

Developed from Renov's analysis on 'filmic autobiography' (2004), Alisa Lebow prefers to use the term 'first person documentary film', and prominently claims that first person expression always belongs to 'the first person plural', which embeds the history, memory and identity of a much larger entity (Lebow 2008: xv). Such emphasis on the plural or the relational could also be found in the understanding of Chinese personal art practices, including female self-portraits of the 1920s. Zhu states that such self-portraits

> are never simply self pitying, self-loving, self critical, or self praising . . . Even though every artist's experience is unique, personal experience is also a historical status. Because in her personal situation, there are rich relationships with her parents, husband, lover, children, and friends, and also rich connections with her education, belief, aesthetics, and labour. It even implies their changing attitude and consciousness towards sex, fertility, and family. (Author's translation: Zhu 2010: 8–9)

What is more, Lebow recognises that the multi-layered self is not simply transformed into a filmic text, but through a course of self-negotiation.

> Autobiography . . . has the unenviable task of confronting, confounding, and even confirming the assumptions, impressions, and (mis)conceptions about the author's or filmmaker's identificatory positionings. We might even say

> following Foucault and Butler, that it is in the process of negotiating and articulating these perceptions that the autobiography generates the self, which may then be (mis)apprehended as having existed prior to these mediation. (Lebow 2008: xvii)

Having experimented with the making of her own first person documentary, and inspired by Butler's concept of performativity that regards gender identity as an enacted, culturally constructed social process, through repetitions of socially and ideologically rooted acts (Butler 1990), Lebow recognises the ongoing process of first person filmmaking that contributes to the construction of self on camera. It is a process of negotiating cultural, social and gender conventions and political limitations that one is experiencing, while mediating the self through camera. I share Lebow's view on the constructive nature of the filmmaking process itself, which contributes to the 'textual' self that is seen on film.

From the perspective of European auteur cinema, Laura Rascaroli emphasises the authorial feature of what she regards personal cinema, where the filmmaker '"became" an auteur, took up a central position in both textual and extra-textual discourse and reconnected to the experiences of the historic avant-garde, and, learning from the novelties introduced by Italian neorealism, attempted to produce a personal, private, idiosyncratic vision of the world' (2009: 108). Rascaroli explores the theoretical roots of personal cinema and identifies different forms of personal subjective non-fiction. She groups the diary film, the notebook film and the self-portrait film into the category 'personal cinema', and puts the essay film in a separate category, based on 'different textual commitments, and the spectatorial pact they set up', and tracks the literary or artistic origins of essay, diary, self-portrait and notebook, and discusses how their filmic versions developed from the original versions (2009).[1] Rascaroli has inspired me to look into the cultural and aesthetical tradition from which first person films in China are developed.

Japanese 'I Film' and Chinese 'Private Image'

In East Asia, first person narrative, personal documentary or 'I film' first emerged in Japan with its own history. It follows the tradition of the Japanese 'I novel' (*Shi-shosetsu* or *Watakushi-shosetsu*) of the early twentieth century, that depicts an author's mental activities in their personal and private lives, as well as 'I photography' (*Shi shashin*) first practised by Nobuyoshi Araki in the early 1970s, as a significant part of Japan's post-war photographic innovation.

Marked as Japan's Provoke Era, 1960–75,[2] photographic works at this historical moment highlight performative and provocative personal expression, works including those done by Nobuyoshi Araki, Masahisa Fukase, Shomei Tomatsu and Daido Moriyama. The proliferation of Japanese photo and cine cameras after the Second World War encouraged the rise of the amateur photography culture. The economic and political conditions of post-war Japan also urged for more direct social engagement through camera-based art practices, including photography, film and video. Pioneered by Nobuyoshi Araki and Masahisa Fukase, 'I photography' captures or exposes the photographer's personal life in one's own private realm or public space through the personal gaze. Nobuyoshi Araki's photographic diary books *Sentimental Journey* (1971) and *Sentimental Journey 2* (1972–91) consist of snapshots of his own honeymoon till the death of his wife, challenging traditional social documentary photography.

Intertwined with the literary and photographic personal expression in 1970s Japan, Japanese 'I film' also marked a historical turning point from works by Ogawa and Tsuchimoto as public film (Nornes 2002: 64). Such personal documentaries are often discussed within the context of Japanese experimental cinema. Unlike its neighbouring country China, Japanese experimental cinema has been closely engaged with international experimental or *avant-garde* cinema. Suzuki Shiroyasu and Hara Kazuo are often seen as pioneers of personal documentary. Japanese scholar Nada Hisashi regards it as 'self documentary' (*serufu dokyumentarii*) which shares 'a sense of disclosure and personalness' (2005), whereas Markus Nornes prefers to call them 'private film' (*puraibeto firumu*) (2002: 63). The poet and NHK television cameraman Suzuki Shiroyasu's *Impressions of a Sunset* (1975) is a self documentary/amateur home movie made on his second-hand 16mm camera, CineKodak 16. Influenced very much by Jonas Mekas's *Reminiscences of a Journey to Lithuania* (1973), Suzuki filmed his personal life and close ones, and the public spaces, his colleagues and the sunset. Compared to Suzuki, Hara Kazuo is better known to the international audience for the exposure of his extreme private moments on camera. Hara Kazuo's *Extreme Private Eros: Love Song 1974* (*Kyokushiteki erosu: Renka 1974*, 1974) exhibits the filmmaker's private life with his ex-wife, including sexual intercourse.

Photographers and filmmakers such as Nobuyoshi Araki, Masahisa Fukase, Hara Kazuo and Suzuki Shiroyasu stirred up the documentary scene in Japan that was still focusing on the public and the societal. Their photo diaries 'I photography' and filmic diaries 'I film' echoed 'the personal is the political' statement in America, and requested a reconsideration of what is individual, political and ethical in the context of post-war Japan. In the 1990s, Japanese female filmmaker Naomi Kawase started to make private documentaries, such as her trilogy that explores her relationship with her adopted mother, 'grandma': *Katatsumori* (1994), *See the Heaven* (1995) and *Sun on the Horizon* (1996), as well as her later work *Birth/Mother* (2006), questioning her adopted mother when she herself was expecting a baby. Kawase's films have recently received increasing attention from filmmaker communities in the neighbouring regions and countries in Asia.

In China, first person literary essay writing has long been an important form for individual self-expression even in the pre-modern era. Martin Woesler, who traces informal subjective expression in writing, noticed that

> the ancestors of the essay both in China and the West, are notes written in the margins of books, as well as letters and travel notes saved. These notes differed from the canonised literature through its informal style, its expression of individuality and subjectivity, a much earlier document for subjectivity than the first autobiographical Chinese novel, *The Dream of the Red Chamber*. (Woesler 2000: 19–20)

Late Ming (late sixteenth century to 1644) is seen as the golden age of Chinese autobiography writings (Wu 1992; Huang 1995); self-portraits also emerged in this period, as a result of the political and social upheavals which instigated a new awareness of the individual and the emergence of individualism in Chinese philosophy (Vinograd 1992).

During the May Fourth Movement of 1919 to the outbreak of the Sino-Japan war, a group of modern neologisms such as *ziwo* (self, 自我), *geren* (individual, 个人) and *geren zhuyi* (individualism, 个人主义) emerged. Individualism and subjectivism are the most characteristic qualities of Chinese literature of this period (Průšek and Lee 1980; Liu 1995: 80). Many writers started to explore modern autobiographic writings, such as those by Shen Congwen, Ba Jin, Hu Shi, Lu Xun, Yu Dafu and Guo Moruo, and also Zhang Ailing (Eileen Zhang). The self, as Lydia H. Liu argues, is often constituted as a privileged site for the contest over the meaning of modernity in modern literature, *xiandai wenxue*, as 'the production of new ideologies and symbolic systems required a massive reconstruction of subjectivity' (1993a: 104). For Liu, first person fiction, as a mode of writing, 'seems to authenticate the narrating subject but undermines the authority of the narrative voice at the same time' (1993a: 102–3). Writings such as those by Yu Dafu, who were influenced by the Japanese 'I novel', demonstrate the contradiction of a modern man. Related to the rising individualism in China in this period, early modern Chinese self-portraits also emerged, especially those made by the first generation of modern female artists who had received modern Western art training (Yao 2010; Zhu 2010). Painters such as Pan Yuliang, Cai Weiliang, Tang Yunyu and Wang Jingyuan all painted their own images through modern forms of oil painting. Practising Western painting at the time was a way to enter modernity. It also provided them with a different self-conscious approach to self-examination and self-expression.

It is important to note that many modern neologisms in China at the time were translated from Japanese. The English notion of 'subjectivity' was first translated into Japanese as two notions: *shukan* (主观) and *shutai* (主体)[3] with local cultural inscription. While *shukan* indicates the epistemic subject, *shutai* means the practical subject or agent of practice (Naoki Sakai, quoted by Li 2009). The Chinese modern notion of subjectivity is translated from Japanese, and recognises the meaning of 主观, *zhuguan*, the epistemic subject, and 主体, *zhuti*, the practical subject or agent of practice. In addition, modern Japanese forms of first person narrative writing, photographic and filmic practices were also introduced to China at different stages.

In the Japanese language, the pronoun 'I' in 'I film', 'I novel' and 'I photography' is '*watashi*'. In Japanese kanji writing '*watashi*' is written as 私 ('*si*'), a word taken from ancient Chinese, which indicates the pronoun 'I'. However, in modern China, 私 is better known for its meaning of 'private'. When the Japanese form of first person novel, 'I novel', was introduced to China in the 1930s by writers such as Yu Dafu, it was translated as 私小说 (*si xiaoshuo*), 'private novel'. When Japanese 'I photography' was translated in mainland China in the 1980s, it was called 私摄影 (*si sheying*), 'private photography'. When first person documentary, 'self documentary' or 'I film' was first introduced to China in the 2000s, most famously through Hara Kazuo's practice, this first person narrative or self-inscriptive documentary practice took the name 私影像 (*si yingxiang*). Seemingly a direct translation of 'I film', 私影像 in Chinese literally means 'private image'.

During the discursive translingual practice, it is 'the private' in this form of first person narrative writing or documentary that has been highlighted. Often, the private aspect has been over emphasised, and the political and larger collective resonation neglected. First person documentary or 'I film' does not only associate with the private. Though notions of 'private' and 'personal' seem to be interchangeable in some situations, they are also embedded in different connotations. As mentioned earlier, Nornes also translated Japanese self-inscriptive documentary into 'private film' (2002), and focuses on its private-public division, emphasising the overt exposure of the private to a public audience. Nornes focuses on the film texts, and examines how well filmmakers articulate their own subjectivities on camera with the larger socio-political formation. He criticises 'private films' made by younger filmmakers that emerged in the 1990s[4] for being highly self-indulgent in their private space, and lacking public engagement with the outside world like the previous generation did (Nornes 2002: 66–8). However, the act of looking inwards itself deserves much more attention, as well as how the filmmakers come to negotiate a self-representation on camera, even a self-exposure.

The private and public binary blinds us to looking into the much more complicated nature of the self constructed on camera. The larger social conditions which urge the filmmakers to inward examining also deserve attention. In addition, personal documentaries could create emotional resonance among audiences outside the filmmakers personal relations, even though this is difficult to measure. The political, the collective or the plural aspects in first person documentary practice are indeed emphasised in the studies of first person documentaries in the Anglo-European tradition as discussed in the last section (Renov and Suderberg 1996; Renov 2004, 2008; Russell 1999; Lebow 2008, 2012, 2013; Rascaroli 2009). My own interest in this practice comes from my questions on self-identity, the individual and the changing formation of self. Issues surrounding the binary division of the private and the public are one of the dimensions in exploring the notion of the individual. But I do not want to limit my study by using the Chinese term 'private image', which underlines the private and personal nature of this practice. Instead, I choose to use the more neutral term 'first person documentary practice', which does not emphasise the opposition but welcomes blurring intersections between the collective (*jiti*, 集体) and the personal/the individual (*geren*, 个人), the public (*gonggong*, 公共) and the private (*siren*, 私人), the individual (*geti*, 个体) and the party-state (*dangguo*, 党国), and so on. In first person narrative documentary practice, the camera can be used not only to document the filmmakers' own reflections and confessions in their own space, but also to engage and interact with their surroundings and social environments. In fact, before the term 'private image' was used in China in the 2000s, there were already a few explicit demonstrations of first person expression in other forms of art productions and amateur DV filmmaking practice in the 1990s. What is expressed in these works is also a strong link to the collective and the societal from a very personal account.

First Person Expression in Art and the Rise of DV Amateur Filmmaking

After a decade of heated intellectual debates and cultural fever in the 1980s, the general public space for individuals to express their personal feelings and frustrations became very limited from the beginning of the 1990s. Cultural, media and art institutions were still affiliated with the government. The mainstream representations of personal experience had to fall in line with the dominant ideology of maintaining social stability – rather than causing upheaval – especially after the 1989 Tiananmen demonstrations. Amateur video cameras like Hi8 were available in the early 1990s but were only circulated among a small group of artists and filmmakers, such as Zhao Liang, Ji Dan, Hu Jie, Feng Yan and Yang

Fudong.[5] They produced independent works, documenting the socially marginal groups, or friends and communities around them. As part of the early surge of independent filmmaking, such works were produced outside *tizhi* (体制), the system, and the dominant economic and political structure, and were not widely viewed by the public. Among the early independent artists, some have explored their own personal experience or familial trajectories through a first person narration. Here I do not aim to give a thorough history of artworks that are a direct demonstration of artists' self, but would like to share some noteworthy and crucial works that are, however, overlooked.

Wen Hui, a pioneer in contemporary dance and documentary theatre, explores her personal experience and bodily memory through performance. Born in Yunnan in the 1950s, Wen started dancing very young, and went to study at the Beijing Dance Academy in 1985, later going on exchange to New York in the early 1990s. Her first experimental performance on returning from America, was *100 verbs* (1994), with voluntary performances by her friends. The desire to express herself led her to create her second performance *The Toilet* (*Ma Tong*) in 1995, a first person narrative experimental play performed by herself and her then long-term partner Wu Wenguang.[6] In *The Toilet*, Wen and Wu stand on two sides of a toilet on stage, and each narrates at the same time, from their own perspective, their private life – the shared experience of *tongju* (同居), living together without marriage, which was still a big social taboo at the time. Whereas Wen Hui speaks of her personal feelings of being in love, their first sexual experience, pains, frustrations and uncertainties in their relationship, Wu's first person narration is about what society and surrounding families ask him to do, rather than his personal feelings, an interesting gendered difference in revealing the inner self.[7] This performance has been little mentioned in the historiography of Chinese contemporary art, partially due to its very private nature.[8] Nevertheless, it is undeniable that *The Toilet* was the first attempt of a young independent artist couple who try to communicate their personal concerns and private issues with an audience. This performance may have also influenced Wu Wenguang's later impulse in reflective and first person documentary filmmaking.

In 1996, independent artist Feng Mengbo created his first computer-based artwork *My Private Album* (1996), which includes family photos from his grandparents, parents and himself, tape recordings, documents, personal archives, music records, and a screening of his computer-game-like film on a created stage within the frame of this work. Feng states that his original idea was to build an archive of photos and audio tapes of his own family, but he soon realised that it was not only for himself but for all Chinese individuals and families. The creation of this work made him realise how his personal trajectory and family history was embedded in the much larger social entity, but he still wanted to title the work 'mine'. This installation was regarded as the first Chinese computer-based artwork ever and was shown worldwide at Documenta X and other occasions.

From 1996, DV cameras emerged as consumer products which were widely available on the retail market. This easily accessible documenting tool grants individuals more flexibility to choose their own subjects, for self-expression and artistic creation. Apart from Yang Lina and Hu Xinyu, who have been mentioned more often as the first generation of amateur-turned-independent DV documentary filmmakers, Shanghai-based Dai Jianyong (born in 1976) is also part of the urban generation who started to play with DV cameras in their youth.

In 1999, Dai graduated from Shanghai University, majoring in Design, and was working in an Internet company. Having never been trained in photography or filmmaking, Dai picked up a DV camera as an amateur, to document the rising avant-garde art scene in Shanghai, the artists, writers and rock musicians that were around him. He has recorded a large number of mini DV tapes on the loss and desire of youth around the millennium, as well as of his family and himself. In his personal DV footage, there are sequences of Xu Zhen, the artist of 'Made-in Company' who had just started experimenting with art in the beginning of the new century; the popular female writer Mian Mian, whose writings, usually on very private matters of sex and love, employ a first person narration; and many rock bands' performances and art shows in Shanghai. Just like Jonas Mekas – who documented the New York avant-garde art scene in the 1960s and 1970s in his 'film diary' (James 1992), including the life of Andy Warhol, Dali, Lennon, and so on. But unlike Japanese 'I film' maker Suzuki Shiroyasu, who was influenced by Jonas Mekas, Dai has never heard of Jonas Mekas and thinks 'masters' like Mekas are very far from his personal life. Amateur DV cameras provide young individuals like Dai with a way to communicate with the surrounding world. Though Dai has still not organised his footage into a film, his mini DV tapes become a personal archive of him and his generation.

When I first started the research in 2008, first person filmmaking practice in China had only been consciously practised by a small number of filmmakers and DV amateurs. Despite a few filmmakers, as mentioned above, this practice was still largely ignored within the independent filmmaking community. During my fieldwork in winter 2009 and summer 2010, I found more first person narrative documentaries on the filmmakers' own selves and/or their families. In current academic study of Chinese independent cinema, first person documentary is a realm that has been little explored.

Existing studies in Chinese cinema tend to take independent cinema, including documentary, as departing from mainstream cinema. Current scholarship explores how independent documentaries function as personal historiography that challenges mainstream political ideologies and provide an alternative public sphere, such as some book-length studies, *The New Chinese Documentary Film Movement: For the Public Record* (2010), edited by Chris Berry, Xinyu Lu and Lisa Rofel; Luke Robinson's *Independent Chinese Documentary* (2013); Dan Edwards' *Independent Chinese Documentary: Alternative Visions, Alternative Publics* (2014); and some other recent books and articles.[9] The assumptions which see documentary as a propaganda tool for ideological manipulation, or the opposition to provoke social-political change, have long made the grand social-political domain their primary focus.

The aesthetic style of handheld, rough image and unpolished sound gives a strong sense of 'being there', in '*xianchang*' (现场), a word that is frequently used by independent filmmakers such as Wu Wenguang, which is also theorised by Robinson (2013). This style is usually described in Chinese as '*jishi zhuyi*' (纪实主义), which literally means 'documentarism', and the word '*jishi*' (纪实) has been used to describe the reportage writing or non-fiction documentary literature – *jishi wenxue* (纪实文学), and documentary photography – *jishi sheying* (纪实摄影), that became popular in the 1980s. In documentary film, *jishi zhuyi* is heavily influenced by 1960s' Direct Cinema and *cinéma-vérité*, especially through Frederick Wiseman's works and the slow naturalism in Japanese filmmaker Ogawa Shinsuke's works. The focal points of *jishi zhuyi* documentaries are usually the 'Others' – the ordinary, and more often, the socially and geographically marginalised subjects.

Growing out of the culture of DV amateur filmmaking and the larger social context of the flourishing amount of self-expression in arts and literature, as well as the participatory media in the new millennium, the first person documentary practice of turning the camera inwards to explore the self should be seen as a pioneering act in Chinese cinema, if not to mention amateur home movies in the first half of the twentieth century in China. Wang Qi (2014) explores the notion of '*geren*' (the personal/the individual) as a political and aesthetic strategy approaching history and reality in works of what she regards as the 'forsaken generation', a generation who were born in the 1960s and 1970s. Yet Wang does not investigate much personal documentary filmmaking as a socially engaged practice. Emerging in the beginning of the 2000s, first person documentary takes the filmmaker self as a non-fiction real subject. It could be seen as both a critical comment on contemporary socio-political conditions and a challenge to current independent documentaries which primarily focus on representing others.

Theorising First Person Documentary Practice in an Individualising China

This book explores first person digital video (DV) documentary filmmaking practice in mainland China, primarily in the first decade of the twenty-first century (2000 to 2009), under the context of individualising Chinese society. As the individual emerges as an ever more important social figure in China, this mode of independent filmmaking and cultural practice is also growing in significance. I chose the first decade, because since the change to the new leadership of Xi in 2012, the political and social context seems to have entered a new phase. There has been more state interference in public life, re-enlisting individuals to the traditional collectives such as Confucian values of family in the mainstream discourse; in other aspects, individuals have continuously been gaining more autonomy, especially with state encouragement on entrepreneurship. In addition, the technological conditions of participatory media have been continually advancing. Social media systems such as WeChat (微信) (started in 2011) and *zhibo* (直播) live web-streaming broadcast, provide individuals with more ways of self-expression, even live self-performance to an interactive audience. This book focuses on mainland China and excludes first person films made in Hong Kong, Taiwan or other overseas Chinese communities, because their different socio-political, cultural and ideological contexts deserve a different lens of examination. In fact, there are a number of prominent first person documentaries made in Taiwan, Hong Kong, and by overseas Chinese. Though there are some overlapping cultural indications and historical understandings of the notion of the self, issues explored in those films are deeply rooted in their own social contexts.

Combining the approach of cultural ethnography, interview, with textual analysis of the chosen films, this study examines the motivations, key aesthetic features and ethical tensions of presenting self on camera, and the socio-political, cultural, historical and technical conditions surrounding this practice. The majority of the films and filmmakers examined in this book have been little studied or theorised on in English language writing. Filmmakers include Wang Fen, Tang Danhong, Yang Lina, Hu Xinyu, Shu Haolun, Yang Pingdao, Li Ning, Wu Haohao, Xue Jianqiang, Ai Weiwei, Wu Wenguang, Wen Hui, Wei Xiaobo, Zou Xueping, Zhang Mengqi, villager filmmakers such as Jia Zhitan and Shao Yuzhen in the China Villagers Documentary Project, and others.

In first person documentaries, filmmakers point the camera inward to film the self and milieu, through various aesthetic forms of self-inscription, such as the creative use of first person voice-over, revealing the filmmaking process, interacting with the subjects, the use of personal amateur home movie, performance, re-enacted scenes and graphics. Their films suggest a subjective interpretation of a truth, and present the filmmakers' fragmented and multi-layered self in terms of socio-cultural conditions, gender, sexuality, generation or class, which are constantly in flux. Furthermore, these films cannot be simply put into one single category – of autobiography, diary film, amateur home video, essay film, video confession, first person activist, and so on, but are often a mixture of different forms, some more essayistic – with personal commentary, confessional, others include more direct participatory engagement. But in short, they all explicitly express themselves through a first person narration.

The concept of 'first person' has a strong connotation with the *individual self*. Regarding the *individual self* as a key concept, this book investigates both the *film text* as an aesthetic and cultural object that constructs a self-representation, and the *filmmaking practice* as a constructive social invention. The existing studies of first person filmmaking in the English-speaking world predominantly approach the filmic self-representation on the textual level. There has been little exploration of how the socially and culturally grounded notion of self has informed aesthetic and ethical choices in the making of first person films. I conducted semi-structured interviews with nearly all filmmakers studied in this book, to explore in great depth their personal trajectories and their motivations. I also invited them to reflect on their production and screening experience, and have been to some of the screenings myself. This study analyses, on the one hand, how the individual self is represented and constructed through the filmmaker's own camera; on the other hand, during the process of filmmaking, how the maker-self as a privileged subject understands and further constructs his or her own self as an individual, in relation to others, the society and the state.

This book proposes *action* and *amateurness* as two crucial aspects of this practice, in addition to subjectivity, reflexivity and relationality as the key characteristics suggested by Alisa Lebow (2008). In first person filmmaking, the filmmaker as a social agent is given significant focus: he or she is not only positioned in the field of film production, but is also seen as a socially engaged individual, a public citizen with certain social roles positioned within the larger society. Wang Hui argues that since the early 1990s, China has been in an era of 'depoliticised politics',[10] a time that is lacking in 'political debates, political struggle, and social activism around specific political values and their attendant benefits'(2006: 690–1). Scholars and intellectuals, including Wang himself, have urged the search for new forms of political subjectivity. Wang Hui's discussion of depoliticised politics has provided me with a complex understanding of the nature of Chinese society, under the period of study. However, my observations of this group of first person films and filmmaking practice suggest that new political practices do exist.

Filmmakers use DV cameras as a tool for an *action*, to probe broken family relations, negotiate new patents of communication, to break social conventions and stretch traditional social ethics, or even deliberately provoke an issue in public. This is especially in evidence when filmmakers reach out from their familial or personal spaces and confront the established authority or social conventions in public spaces, such as practised by Ai Weiwei and Wu Haohao, and the socially engaged 'China Villagers Documentary Project'. Thus, first person filmmaking in China can be seen as a form of provocative social participation in the 'depoliticised politics' (Wang 2006: 690–1).

Responding to the debates in international documentary film studies, this book proposes that first person documentary filmmaking has gone beyond what Michael Renov concludes as four distinctive functions of documentary: preservation, persuasion, analysis and expressivity (1993: 21). Following Lebow's discussion on the generative force in the filmmaking process, I regard first person filmmaking practice as a performative act, an *action*, through which the self is further constructed. The process of confronting and enraging people, demonstrates a meaningful power of individuals to engage with social constructs. While it shares some similarities with Jean Rouch's participatory *cinéma-vérité*, notably direct participation in an event, and Michael Moore's reflective and performative first person filmmaking in his explicit self-presentation on the spot, it also closely echoes Japanese filmmaker Hara Kazuo's 'action documentary', which forcibly generates action through the camera, to see the 'embarrassing things' that people want to hide, intentionally breaking down the institutionalised ideologies that cause people to feel embarrassment (Hara 2009: 7).

As Wu Haohao addressed directly on camera in his *Kun 1: Action*: 'Avoid the ideal, avoid the self, and avoid action. China, Chinese, Chinese films are especially abnormal, nauseous, secular and degenerate . . . Take immediate action when facing dilemmas in reality. Film should only record those actions.' This highly provocative manifesto illuminates the central concern shared by many first person filmmakers, who not only aim at recording the social reality but also participating, interfering as a subject, mostly a central one.

In addition to action, *amateurness* is also a strong feature shared by these films. Almost all the first person films studied in this book are either made by amateur filmmakers, or through amateur techniques or aesthetics. The rise of the DV filmmaking wave is closely intertwined with amateur filmmaking, as individuals have found DV cameras to be a direct mediator between rapid social transformations and personal expression. However, amateur filmmaking in China still remains largely untapped, partly due to the limited access to home movie cameras before and during Mao's era. As a rising field of study, amateur cinema is a valuable alternative site that expands mainstream cinema history and constructs collective memory and micro histories. Such first person documentaries undoubtedly should be seen as a vital part of amateur cinema in China.

In this book, I focus on *amateurness* as an approach and an aesthetic style. Proactively reaching out through an *action* of communicating with a camera, as discussed earlier, these films also take an amateurish personal manner and an individual position when approaching the reality. Such an approach means technical competency is not the priority and, as a result, these films are presented in an amateur aesthetic style, often with impulsive 'point and shoot' DV footage. These films give vivid evidence of how an individual's personal trajectories form part of a larger vision of China's past and future.

Reflectively, my own position as a researcher and filmmaker is inevitably part of the *individual self* I am observing, hence my own self-reflection in this research, looking at how my background and experience influence my understanding of this practice. By examining first person filmmaking practice, I am also conducting a first person inward examination of a social cultural context in which I myself am apart. In short, this book aims to offer an insightful view on what it means to be an individual in China and in an increasingly globalised world. These films and the filmmaking practice not only reflect some aspects of the revising concept of the individual self, but also further contribute to the changing constitution of the individual subjectivity in contemporary China.

The Changing Notion of the Individual Self: A Historical Perspective

The notion of the first person pronoun 'I' relates to concepts of 'self', 'individual', 'subject', 'subjectivity', 'person' and 'private'. These concepts have all been interpreted differently throughout the course of Chinese history. In this section, I digress from the films and filmmakers, the primary focus of this study, to provide a brief historical overview of the changing notions of 'the self' and 'the individual' in China. The shifting philosophical approaches to such concepts remain impactful in today's China, hence the importance of unpacking the historical contexts.

Historically, intellectual debates on the notion of 'the individual' have been centred around the notion of individual autonomy. The changing formation of the individual indicates a changing degree of autonomy possessed by the individual. How one relates to other individuals, social groups and the state authority have also been a main concern in discussing this shifting notion.

Confucian notions of self had a dominating role in ancient China and still underpin the understandings of self in China today. Dong Zhongshu (董仲舒) (179–104 BC), a Confucian follower, stated that traditional Chinese family ethics were centred around the three cardinal guides (*sangang*, 三纲): the ruler guides the subjects, the father guides the son, and the husband guides the wife; and the five constant virtues (*wuchang*, 五常) of benevolence (*ren*, 仁), brotherhood (*yi*, 义), propriety (*li*, 礼), wisdom (*zhi*, 智) and loyalty (*xin*, 信).[11] This set of ethical codes correspond to five basic social relations (King 1985: 58), which are *qin* (亲, affection) between parent and child; *yi* (义, righteousness) between ruler and subject; *bie* (别, distinction) between husband and wife; *xu* (序, order) between old and young; and *xin* (信, sincerity) between friends. In this understanding, Chinese society is ethical-relations centred (Liang Shuming 梁漱溟 1990: 79–95), or is a 'familistic' society (Parsons, quoted by King 1985: 58), in which the self is situated within familial and quasi-familial relationships.

Through observation of the films studied here, such ethical relations still largely define how one understands oneself or how one aims to break through. In this view, the self in dominant Confucian thought tends to be relational and selfless (Hall and Ames 1998), lacking a sense of individual autonomy as seen in modern Western enlightenment individualism. But the self is perceived to achieve 'a state of moral autonomy' (King 1985: 57), not by going against authority, but by best performing the self within existing social relations.[12] However, such studies on the ancient notion of individual self put too much focus on Confucianism and 'exaggerate the individualist and non-relational aspects of western social thought and common-sense assumptions' (Stockman 2000: 76).

The first generation Chinese sociologist Fei Xiaotong,[13] who emerged in 1920s China, argues that individuals in the West produce their society by applying *tuantigeju* (团体格局), an 'organizational mode of association ' (1992: 62). People create groups which have clear boundaries and define the rights and duties of members. In China, people create their society by applying what Fei calls the logic of *chaxugeju* (差许格局), the 'differential mode of association', where each person has a different web of social relationships, and each network appears different depending on which person is the focus of the web (Stockman 2000: 73). Fei (1992) argues that in this pattern of social relations, the boundary between public and private has never been clear and does not encourage the rise of individual right.[14] Since the late Qing and May Fourth period during the late nineteenth and early twentieth centuries, the possibility of political participation of intellectuals contributed to the debates on the reconfiguration of the individual self (Liu 1993a, 1995; Zarrow 1998). However, even though dominant thought denied the traditional Confucian values, the intellectual framework was still profoundly coloured by state-focused intellectual tradition, which 'defined individuals in terms of inescapable social categories that define their duties towards collectives and society at large' (Svarverud 2010: 195).

In addition to the modern neologism 'subjectivity', which is translated through Japanese, as discussed earlier, and its central role in modern literature that emerged during the May Fourth period, another two modern neologisms are essential to the discussion here: 'individual' and 'autonomy'. The English word 'individual' was in fact first translated into Chinese as a modern legal and collective concept in the Chinese translation of Wheaton's *Elements of International Law* – 万国公法 (*Wanguo gongfa*) published in 1894 (Yin 2011).[15] Instead of being translated as '*geren*' (个人, one person), as used later by May Fourth intellectuals, the word 'individual' was translated as '*min ren*' (民人), in which the word '*ren*' (人, a person) was put after '*min*' (民, the people), a collective political notion (Yin 2011). In other words, the relationship between the modern individual and the state conceived by the intellectuals in this period was still largely in line with the traditional vision of a relational individual conforming to the larger whole, though autonomy has become a key word openly discussed by the early modern intellectuals.

At this time, Liang Qichao (梁启超) reconceptualised the role of people and the concepts of citizenship, *zizhi* (自治), and morality. Liang's notion of *zizhi* is a Chinese translation of 'autonomy'. However, Svarverud argues that Liang's term *zizhi* is different from the Kantian notion of autonomy, which is on the political level.[16] Instead, Liang's notion of *zizhi* should be best translated as 'self-discipline', a kind of self-legislation that man places upon himself (Svarverud 2010: 207). This shares some similarity with the traditional Confucian value of self-cultivation to achieve moral autonomy. In a slightly later period, Gao Yihan's division of individualism on the personal and social levels has received much attention. He notices the contradiction of social obligation and individual autonomy and applies the term *xiaoji* (小己), 'lesser self', for the individual in contrast to the 'greater self', *daji* (大己), visualising the self in society at large (Svarverud 2010: 217), a terminology that maintains a hierarchical order between the individual and the state rather than establishing an antithetical distinction (Liu 1993a: 179–80).

When it comes to Mao's era, the main argument is that in replacing Confucianism, Mao still puts individuals into a collective group, hence giving little autonomy to individuals. New forms of communist collective institutions emerged, such as *danwei* (单位), the work unit in the urban areas, and *shengchan dui* (生产队), the production teams in the rural areas (Pye 1996; Inkeles *et al.* 1997). Household registration book, *hujibu* (户籍簿), and class label were also introduced to give a new collective identity to the individual (Pye 1996: 28–9). In addition, although 'the socialist new men' are empowered to fight against the traditional constraints, the new socialist state asked for a new kind of submission for the construction of a communist state. The new universalistic morality does not totally replace the Confucian ethical relations; in fact, it was transferred into a new kind of personal relations during the Cultural Revolution, one for the good of oneself, rather than the collective benefit that has been promoted by the social state.

The economic reform instigated by Deng Xiaoping in the late 1970s has brought on a remarkable degree of transformation in social structure and ideology. This also resulted in a radical change of the sense of the individual and its social relations. In the intellectual debates and cultural discourse in the 1980s, redefining the notion of the individual self became a major challenge, to make an effort to overcome the crisis of belief, morality and values, which was 'not only the crisis of political ideology or that of collective cultural consciousness, but also as the deeper crisis of self-identity, spiritual estrangement and the senselessness of individual life' (Lin and Galikowski 1999: 144).

Such a historical overview provides a foundation from which we can develop a further and insightful understanding of how the notions of the individual and the self are perceived today.

The Individualisation of Contemporary Chinese Society

In the study of the individual self in post-socialist China, Yan Yunxiang, an influential Chinese sociologist, takes the European individualisation thesis[17] developed by Bauman (2001) and Giddens (1990) as a conceptual tool to examine the social transformation in contemporary China from the perspective of the individual.[18] Examining China's modernity, Wang Hui advocates a multi-interactive worldview on modernity 'as a universal and unified progression' (Wang 2009: 84), rather than seeing China's modernity as entirely different from that of the West, or taking the West as the model to measure others against.[19] From this perspective, the individualisation process in China is understood neither as purely a mirror of nor entirely different from the Western counterpart. As Yan Yunxiang argues,

> although China was still undergoing the modernization process, Chinese society was demonstrating a number of features of individualization in the age of second modernity at the same time as it bore other features of social change that belong to the modern and even pre-modern eras in the West. (2009: xvii)

Yan concludes with four features of contemporary life highlighted in the European individualisation thesis (2009, 2010). The first feature is differentiation and 'disembedment' from external social constraints, cultural traditions and the encompassing categories, such as family, kinship, social classes, ethnic groups, local and national communities. The second feature is what Bauman refers to as a paradoxical phenomenon of 'compulsive and obligatory self-determination' (2000: 32). 'The "disembedded" individuals were prompted and prodded to deploy their new powers and new right to self-determination in the frantic search for "re-embeddedness"' (Bauman 2001: 145). In this process, a set of new social institutions are required to enable and structure individual choices, and provide resources, techniques, security and incentives for individuals to develop their own way of life (Giddens 1990; Lash 1993; Beck and Beck-Gernsheim 2002). Hence the third feature, 'life of one's own through conformity' (Beck and Beck-Gernsheim 2002: 151). The fourth feature is what Beck regards as 'cultural democratisation', the condition of Western individualisation, a step further from the social and political democracy. Yan admits that these features represent the changing nature of social relations in western European societies, and some of them do not exist in contemporary China, such as the third and fourth features.

According to Yan, the decade of the 1990s was the most liberal in China in terms of the phenomenal growth of the private sector, the retreat of the party-state from its previous control over social life, the replacement of the dominance of communist ideology by neoliberalism, and the reformation of life chances and mobility channels that set hundreds of millions of Chinese on the move (2009: xvi). Yan observes that detraditionalisation, or the disembedment of the individual from the former encompassing social categories and traditions, is also a feature of contemporary Chinese society. From the 1970s, the state started institutional reform of 'decollectivisation', or '*songbang*', untying individuals from previous socialist institutions of work units and production teams (Yan 2009). This, on the one hand, creates more social mobility for individuals and increases their autonomy, but also results in new social problems on the other. For example, the *hukou* system is still enacted which creates unequal rural/urban social identities. In addition, the state gradually retreating from the sphere of public life also means the withdrawal of social welfare, such as subsidised housing, which was previously provided by the socialist state (Yan 2010: 18–19). Hence, the new over-commercialised public space is facing moral challenges (Yan 2009). The problems Yan discusses are also visible in the films studied in this book.

Yan's analysis of the decollectivisation process and how it has impacted on the individual self in post-socialist China is of significant value. He points out the 'state-made individualisation', meaning 'the party-state not merely promoting institutional changes, such as through untying individuals, to stimulate incentives, creativity and efficiency from below, but also directs the flow of individualization by soft management of the interplay among the players: the individual, the market, social groups, institutions and global capitalism' (Yan 2009: 289). This depicts the key feature of contemporary Chinese society under individualisation.

Yan (2009) identifies some important features for the individual, including increasing mobility enabled by the party-state through managing institutional change; the emergence of identity politics and the 'I generation'; and the emergence of new types of sociality – which, on the one hand, promote rights assertion movements and public participation, but still lack social trust; on the other hand, meaning that society faces moral challenges and the rise of the ultra-utilitarian. However, Yan's statements about the 'rising individual' and 'the incomplete understanding of individualism' deny the existence of different forms of individual in Chinese history. Nevertheless, Yan Yunxiang's study provides great inspiration for my own exploration on how the changing sense of self is demonstrated through first person documentary practice in contemporary China.

Fives Themes of the Individual Self in First Person Filmmaking Practice

In the context of post-socialist decollectivisation processes, individuals have been set adrift from previous social and ideological institutions. With the digital video camera, the individual filmmakers analysed here explicitly exhibit their subjectivity and raise their personal voice by turning the camera inward on themselves. However, the analysis of these films demonstrates that these filmmakers are not entirely 'disembedded' from traditional and socialist social relations. In fact, they are presented as multi-layered and conflicted, situated in complex and diverse social relationships among family members, between individuals as individuals within society, and between individuals and the state. I observed five themes of the individual self as illustrated through the analyses of these films and the filmmaking practices.

Theme One: the relational sense of self

The first theme that emerged in these films is the relational sense of self, which is especially in evidence in films that explore the self in familial relations and the domestic space. This collective sense of self can be seen as inherited from traditional Confucian family ethics that emphasise relationality and collectiveness, as discussed earlier. Though Confucian family relations have been challenged since the late nineteenth century, the collective sense of self has not been destroyed and has been further emphasised in Mao's China through socialist collectivism. In post-Mao China, the state has enacted a series of top-down policies, such as the open policy, and structural changes, untying individuals from previous social institutions (Yan 2009, 2010). Since the 1990s, marketisation has provided more resources, materials and choices for individuals to develop their own lives. All this has accelerated individual autonomy, to make decisions and to develop their own life paths. It is undeniable that increasing social mobility and autonomy have enabled filmmakers to make films according to their own wills, and to take a reflexive look into themselves in changing familial or public spaces.

However, the decollectivisation in contemporary China is not a thorough process (Yan 2009). The collective family and quasi-family relations still construct an individual's identity to a great extent, highlighting the relationality of autonomy occupied by the individual subject. In addition, some traditional and socialist collective institutions have not entirely disappeared from social life. While the state retreated from public life, it also withdrew certain forms of social welfare from certain groups of individuals, such as medical care for some and subsidised housing. However, new sets of social institutions to provide resources and security were not developed. The *hukou* (household, 户口) system still exists, holding family as the basic unit of society, and continually creating unequal rural/urban social identities. This tension has resulted in inequality, lack of social protection and over-commercialised public spaces. As illustrated in the first person films that explore the familial self, the individuals tend to turn to their family for a sense of connectedness and collectiveness. Though these filmmakers express themselves through a strong authorial voice, they still emphasise their roles as parts of the larger collective, and are concerned with how the changing social and economic context has influenced their family as a collective. In Chapters 1 and 2, the focus on the collective familial is expressed through the strong concern with broken family relations, while in Chapter 3 it is explored through the changing structure and space of '*laojia*' (老家) – old home.

Theme Two: paternal authority and the gendered nature of ethical expectations

The second theme that frequently emerges in these first person documentaries is that of parental authority, or more precisely of paternal authority, and the gendered nature of ethical expectations – male domination. This is shown both in the films that explore the family and the films that present the self in public spaces, in which the elder, especially the senior male characters, also possess a strong paternal authority. Situated in a deep-rooted patriarchal order, these filmmakers consciously try to break it. It is interesting to find that some male filmmakers try to establish their own authority in this attempt, rather than destabilising the power equation altogether.

Existing studies reveal a well-established pattern of resisting paternal authority and the ethics of female obedience since the late nineteenth century. In the early Republican period, new women emerged, openly challenging traditional constraints set on women. In Mao's China the social status of women had largely risen and women gained more power in the domestic space. However, gender hierarchy still existed. Scholars argue that women's familial obligations and obedience have been re-emphasised. Although there has been a renewed proliferation of women's semi-autobiographical writing, such personal expression continues to reinforce the connection between the female, the private and the domestic.

As discussed in the previous section, Chinese society emphasises family ethics, which highlight the central position of the ruler, the father and the husband in social relations. That the father guides the son and the husband guides the wife, are two of the three key cardinal guides of Confucianism. The dominance of paternal authority is explicitly shown in Hu Xinyu's *Family Phobia* (2010), in which Hu's father 'interferes' in every family issue and holds himself as the authority of the family. In another two films, which explore the public self, Xue Jianqiang's *I Beat the Tiger When I Was Young* (2010) and Wu Haohao's *Criticizing China* (2008), the young male filmmakers challenge the 'senior' quasi-father figures in grassroots public spaces.

Paternal power is expressed strongly in three women's films whose investigations of their family relationships nevertheless challenge the authority of the father in different ways. Responding to it is the principle of 'Three Obediences' that govern women. All three women's films, to some extent, illustrate how the Three Obediences still constrain the female figures in the family. The three women filmmakers take the initiative to investigate their own personal family relations, which challenge the obedient role of daughter. However, they do not aim to be 'strong women'. Instead, their filmmaking practice can be seen as a way of active *goutong* (沟通), 'communicative practice' (Evans 2010: 981), longing for connectedness with their parents. This changing role of daughter as a more active communicator also indicates a change in filiality, which is another theme demonstrated in these films, in response to parental authority.

Theme Three: tensions between individual desire and collective family obligations

The third theme appearing in these films concerns tensions between individual desire and collective family obligations, and a re-negotiation of traditional filial duties of different generations. Filiality, *xiao* (孝), the core virtue of Confucian ethics, requests the children to be obedient and supportive of their parents and ancestors. It also influences parental attitudes and expectations of the children, and has a large impact on social-political structures as a way of maintaining social sustainability (Huang 1995). Even though paternal authority has been attacked since the early Republican period, filiality and kinship obligations have not been widely discarded but have even been further promoted as a key virtue of Chinese culture, to be expanded as 'a civic virtue and public morality' (Stockman 2000: 79). In Mao's era, a new kind of universalistic ethics and communist comradeship was established but the logic of obedience was still the central morality – only the respect due to the elder in familial relations was translated into support for the party-state (ibid.). In the post-Mao era, filiality has been re-emphasised strategically by the state as a way of maintaining social sustainability during dramatic economic and social transformation, as filiality becomes the 'primary source of social security for the elderly' (Fong 2006: 127). It is even legitimately stressed that adult children should provide economic support for their elderly parents.[20]

Parental expectations of filial duties also make the parents invest significantly in their children's education, making enormous self-sacrifices (Fong 2006: 127). This is shown in Hu's film *Family Phobia* (2010) in which the first and second generation family members sacrifice their individual desires and suffer themselves to support the younger generation's study. It is a challenge to filiality if the child does not show obedience to his/her parents; however, filiality does not request parents to pay attention to children's opinions, emotions or happiness (Yan, quoted by Evans 2010: 988). In fact, 'parents felt uneasy at how much power children had over them, and devastated when children were not as filial or successful as they should have been' (Fong 2006: 127). Nevertheless, the threat from disobedient children has become more obvious. The decollectivisation process has encouraged the emergence of the 'I generation', '*wo yi dai*' (我一代) (Yan 2009: 280) or the 'me generation' (Elegent 2007), who are exposed to more opportunities to develop their individual lives. These young individuals, born after the late 1970s, and especially those born in the late 1980s and 1990s, grew up in the market economy, and have been influenced by overwhelming neoliberal ways of being, as compared to older generations who experienced socialist collectivism in their youth. Facing increasing individual choices, traditional family obligations are to some extent in conflict with the individuals' personal desires. Hence a renegotiation of the filial duties of different generations is needed to balance individual desire and family obligations.

The three female filmmakers' provocative investigations of their familial relationships seem to have challenged parental authority and the conventional expectations of filial duties. However, I argue that their practice can also be seen as a renegotiation of filial duty. Chinese cultural studies scholar Harriet Evans' study on the changing experiences of the mother–daughter relationships of urban women suggests that 'desires for recognition of the independent emotional self through communicative practice are replacing "traditional" expectations of the younger generation's obedience to parental authority' (Evans 2010: 986). Evans argues that 'this shift also has its part to play in explaining daughters' attempts to renegotiate their sense of filial responsibility to their natal parents alongside, rather than in contradiction to, their own desires for self-fulfilment' (2010: 986). In this sense, the three female filmmaker's practice further generates what Evans regards as 'a new ethics of mutual recognition and exchange between parents and children' (ibid.).

Similarly, films by male filmmakers also illustrate this renegotiation of filial expectations. Unlike the three women filmmakers who challenge their parents through direct face-to-face confrontation, the male filmmakers, like Hu Xinyu and Yang Pingdao, avoid following their parents' expectations. In Hu's *Family Phobia* (2010) and Yang's *My Family Tree* (2008), the elder generation asks the filmmakers to get married and give birth to the new generation, so as to continue the family clan. Rather than explicitly refusing this request, they remain quiet in the films.

Theme Four: individual rights – the changing relationship between the individual and the state

While the first three themes all explore the construction of the self through family relations, the following two themes are concerned with the relationship between the individual and the state, and between individuals as individuals in their own right.

The fourth theme that emerged in these films, especially in those exploring the public selves, is the changing relationship between the individual and the state, and the increasing sense of individual rights. It is noted that in the history of struggle over the moral and political meaning of the self throughout the twentieth century, individual subjects have been encouraged to challenge Confucian constraints; however, it is still the conformity of the individual towards the state that has been emphasised in different historical stages, rather than the individual's rights against that of the state. At the turn of the twentieth century, along with the introduction of the modern Western concept of the individual, ideas of citizenship, individual autonomy and individual rights became key terms openly discussed by early modern intellectuals. However, the interpretation of these words still mirrored the traditional relationship between the individual and the state – that the construction of the individual identity involved a dual task of both self-cultivation and obligation towards the state (Zarrow 1998: 210).

After the Communist Party came into power, a radical transformation of social structures took place. The socialist ideology requests the submission of all individuals as socialist workers to build the new socialist state. 'Every citizen was to be a fellow comrade, engaged in the common task of building a new social order, sharing the same "will" or "ambition" to combine their efforts in the common cause' (Stockman 2000: 81). It is not until the post-Mao era that the concept of individual rights emerges. The decline of socialist institutions and marketisation has resulted in social inequality and uneven distribution of wealth. Although the socialist workplace has not been entirely abolished, it mainly provides social security and resources for individuals who are mainly urban middle-level income earners (Thelle 2004). For the majority of the rural population and laid-off workers, the structural changes mean the loss of state protection in employment, medical care and housing benefit. Hu's *Family Phobia* illustrates how the cut in socialist social benefits affects the lives of Hu's family members, especially his aged parents, who are former socialist workers.

Consequently, individuals through different means start to link the self with a set of rights and raise their voices to ask for legal protection (Yan 2009: 280); hence the rise of rights-assertion, especially through online activism and recent political participation. This marks a major difference in the individual-state relationship, compared to previous eras. Since the late 1990s there has been increasing activist movement in cyberspace, which reflects the rise of a new citizenship asking for equal opportunities, the protection of human rights and the recognition of marginalised social identities (Damm and Thomas 2006; Lagerkvist 2006; Yang 2002, 2003a,b,c, 2006a,b, 2009). In recent years, the sense of new citizenship and human rights has grown and there is a rise in volunteering in social participation and political activism. In Chapters 4 and 5, I explore how two young filmmakers, Wu Haohao and Xue Jianqiang, use filmmaking as a way to provoke critical political debates in public spaces. I will also analyse the political activist participation led by the contemporary artist Ai Weiwei, which is documented in his film *Lao Ma Ti Hua* (*Disturbing the Peace*, 2009). Shu Haolun's film *Nostalgia* (2006) can also be seen as an individual critique of how state-enforced demolition affects the individual interests of Shu's family and the neighbourhood.

However, the number of people who are aware of their rights is still very small. Thelle observes that before the early 2000s many people were still either not well informed about the nature of their rights (having a profound distrust of institutions) or lacked the means to enforce their rights (2004). Yan notes that most people still do not regard their individual rights as ones they were born with but, instead, as ones they have earned themselves: 'The individual has emerged as a key unit in both discourse and action in everyday life, but consciousness of individual rights is based on a Chinese understanding of rights as earned privileges through individual efforts' (Yan 2010: 9). This might be because the state still carries out firm stewardship of its people. What is more, the people's understanding of individual rights in the current era has been largely constructed by historical cultural traditions. Wu Haohao's *Criticizing China* (2008) illustrates how people conceive individual rights based on their past experiences. When individuals implement their rights, or ask for legal protection, they sometimes disrespect others, even infringe on others' rights. This is also shown in Xue Jianqiang's *I Beat the Tiger When I Was Young* (2010). This, therefore, leads to the last key theme that emerges in all these films – the changing relationship between individuals as individuals in their own right.

Theme Five: the changing relationship between individuals as individuals in their own right

The ways that individuals relate to each other in interpersonal interactions outside the domestic space, or the 'new sociality'[21] (Yan 2009), are vividly shown through all first person films studied in this book, hence the fifth theme. Previously unrelated individuals have now developed new groups based on similar personal interests and forms of public participation on and off the Internet. Along with this is the development of *minjian* (民间) public spaces, a kind of non-governmental organised grassroots public space, literally meaning 'among the folk'. Wu Haohao's *Criticizing China* (2008) illustrates one such space – the spontaneously emerged discussion corner in a public park where local residents participate. His own filmmaking is also a way of interacting with these local individuals. The China Villagers Documentary Project itself creates an alternative public space that allows dialogue and communications between village amateur filmmakers and urban intellectual filmmakers. *Minjian* public spaces also see the rise of individual volunteerism, such as political participation in the aftermath of the Sichuan earthquake in May 2008 and the 'public citizen investigation' project led by Ai Weiwei, the starting point of *Lao Ma Ti Hua* (2009).

However, the mixed and sometimes conflicting value systems also problematise interpersonal communications, as demonstrated in these films, and hence there is the decline of social trust. Peng describes six types of distrust: distrust of the market due to faulty goods and bad services; distrust of service providers and strangers; distrust of friends and even relatives; distrust of law enforcement officers; distrust of the law and legal institutions; and distrust of basic moral values (Peng quoted by Yan 2009: 286). This lack of social trust is illustrated in several films analysed here, such as Xue Jianqiang's *Martian Syndrome* (2010), Wu Haohao's *Criticizing China* (2008), Ai Weiwei's *Lao Ma Ti Hua* (2009) and the China Villagers Documentary Project.

The lack of social trust in an open and mobile society sees a strong emotional need for communication and understanding among individuals. Evans argues that 'individual desires for emotional communication are reconstituting the meaning of the subject, self and responsibility in China . . . much more than an effect of changing socio-economic and cultural forces making people more assertive in articulating their emotional needs' (Evans 2010: 982). First person filmmaking practice, in this sense, could be seen as a 'communicative practice', growing out of an eagerness for emotional connection. The camera mediates the interaction as well as documenting how filmmakers communicate with others and the accompanied ethical problems during the interactive process. In the films that explore the familial self, the filmmakers have a strong desire for connectedness with their families, which have undergone a structural and ethical transformation.

This emotional need does not just exist in intimate personal relationships. The films exploring the self in public spaces also demonstrate the individuals' longing for emotional security. In Xue Jianqiang's *Martian Syndrome* (2010) and Wu Haohao's *Kun 1: Action* (2008), both young filmmakers express a strong desire for a more politicised community where they can find emotional and material security, and one that will help them to build and mature their value system in an individualising society. Nevertheless, these films demonstrate that hierarchical relations and gendered expectations still largely exist in interpersonal relations. For example, in *I Beat the Tiger When I Was Young* (2010), when the filmmaker Xue tries to challenge the senior or elder, the language he uses is still in a violent dictatorial and non-negotiable logic that aims to entirely demolish the old, and the initiation of the 'China Villagers Documentary Project' is based on an unconscious hierarchical positioning of urban filmmaker Wu Wenguang.

To sum up, this book understands the individual self in the first decade of twenty-first century China as multiple, conflicting, in a process of moving, and encompassing multi-temporal connotations inherited from the discursive history of changing meanings of the individual. Positioned within the web of forces, the individual in contemporary China has to deal with different and sometimes contradictory socio-political and moral relations. An understanding of these five key themes helps to unpack the socio-political, cultural and historical contexts to investigate the drives and motivations of this practice, as well as their strategies in the making of first person documentary films. Furthermore, they also contribute to an in-depth understanding of how the practice in China is both different from – and similar to – those in other cultural, socio-political and religious entities.

Structure of the Book

This book is organised into two parts with eight chapters. The first part includes three chapters on six first person documentaries that explore the *familial self*, the self in familial relations or in the private space of the family home (*jia*, 家).

They can be seen as what Renov regards as 'domestic ethnography' (2008). Instead of focusing on the *self*, I pay attention to the *familial* as a central site where the first person filmmakers deconstruct their individual selves as part of the family that is in transition.

Chapter 1 explores the changing gendered features of the individual self in China as demonstrated through first person documentaries made by women in the beginning of the twenty-first century. I centre my analysis on Wang Fen's *They Are Not the Only Unhappy Couple* (2000), Yang Lina's *Home Video* (2001) and Tang Danhong's *Nightingale, Not the Only Voice* (2000). Aesthetically and socially pioneering, these women experiment with a new documentary language to express themselves, often arising from a subversive impulse. Their films depart from earlier Chinese independent documentaries in the 1990s, which were mainly made by male filmmakers and tended to highlight the marginalised others. Their practice also challenges the traditional role of women constrained by patriarchal expectations. I argue that these women's work can be seen as a form of 'communicative practice', bridging the communication of two generations. Their practices, however, have received much hostility for being solipsistic when they were first made, suggesting that society still has not fully accepted women who openly challenge parental and patriarchal power.

Chapter 2 focuses on the amateur feature of first person documentary and theorises the amateurness with a close examination of Hu Xinyu and his film *Family Phobia* (2009). Hu Xinyu is among the first generation of amateur DV filmmakers that emerged in China at the dawn of the twenty-first century. I argue that amateur filmmakers take a dual role, as insiders in their own families, but also as outsiders, whose filmmaking constitutes a significant social act, which offers valuable insights on how family relations have been affected in China's rapid socioeconomic transition. I also discuss the reception of Hu's film, exploring how screenings become a site where the filmmaker negotiates questions of privacy, and how it challenges the limits of what is acceptable to present of one's family's life to the public, at a time before social media proliferated.

Chapter 3 discusses first person documentaries that express filmmakers' nostalgia towards *laojia*, the old family-home, through a close reading of two films: Yang Pingdao's *My Family Tree* (*Jiapu*, 2008) and Shu Haolun's *Nostalgia* (*Xiangchou*, 2006). In post-Mao China, during the nationwide urbanisation process, individuals from the countryside had been 'liberated' from the traditional familial collectivism and the former communist mode of collective production, which also meant the nuclearisation of traditional big families. In *My Family Tree*, Yang revisits his village and captures a sense of decline in traditional family patterns and ritual ceremonies. In the urban areas, demolition and reconstruction have caused the relocation of the family home for many urban citizens who previously enjoyed many social welfare benefits. Shu Haolun's *Nostalgia*, narrated through the filmmaker's own voice-over, is a first person critique of urban demolition and neo-liberal consumerism in his home city, Shanghai. While their work expresses the filmmakers' nostalgia toward the old pattern of family and familial space, it also demonstrates a strong sense of social responsibility, with an attempt to understand how individuals' lives have changed in a fast-transforming and highly mobilised modern China.

The second part of the book focuses on the filmmaker self as an individual in public spaces in an individualising society. It concerns how filmmakers search for their social identities as public citizens, carrying their agencies to politicise the space in which they are situated, by using the camera to engage, interact and even provoke others. I include works by two young filmmakers Wu Haohao and Xue Jianqiang, first person activist documentaries made by Ai Weiwei and his studio, and the 'China Villagers Documentary Project' which featured participation by both intellectual filmmakers and the amateur villagers.

Chapters 4 and 5 explore first person action documentary practices by Wu Haohao and Xue Jianqiang. After exploring the meaning of action in 'first person action documentary', I then examine two major themes of their work. First, their films illustrate the absence of community in the individualising cityscape, where young individuals are constrained in their own spaces longing for communication and emotional caring. This is discussed in Chapter 4, which focuses on Wu Haohao's *Kun1: Action* and Xue Jianqiang's *Martian Syndrome.* While the first part of *Kun 1: Action* solely focuses on Wu's isolated self during his university years, Xue's *Martian Syndrome* depicts the difficulties in communication among young individuals, including Xue himself, living in migrant artist ghettos in Beijing's suburbs. Second, they take their cameras to provoke current social conditions in public spaces, especially the *minjian*, grassroots public space, such as the local debating corner in *Criticizing China*, and the independent filmmakers' community in *I Beat the Tiger When I Was Young*. Their practices have provoked intense debates among local critics, filmmakers and scholars, and also expose the problematic 'public self' in interpersonal communication, facing ethical dilemmas. This leads on to the ethics of encountering in their work, which is examined in Chapter 5.

Chapter 6 investigates how filmmakers use cameras as a weapon to intervene in social issues and participate in political events, which I regard as 'camera activism'. Taking a case study of Ai Weiwei's *Disturbing the Peace* (or *Lao Ma Ti Hua*, 2009), I analyse how it produces a shared political subjectivity through action at three levels: the activist movement documented in the film; the filmmaking practice itself as a political act; and the action of disseminating the film online through social networks, creating an audience and mobilising awareness among a much larger group. As I observe, the film also illustrates the performative elements of Ai's public persona as a revolutionary leader, an authority in his own right who is surrounded by his followers and has attracted enormous international attention. It argues that how Ai destabilises his own authority and continuously works as a symbol to raise more political action becomes contested.

Chapter 7 focuses on a group of individuals who I have not yet discussed elsewhere – the socially less empowered, subaltern villagers – through a case study of the 'China Villagers Documentary Project', a socially and community engaged film project. The interaction and power relations between Wu Wenguang, as the project's 'creative instructor', and the village amateur filmmakers are largely ignored in the current studies of this project. Behind the collaboration is how the village amateur filmmakers unconsciously and consciously deconstruct and resist their 'given' social identity as subaltern selves, hence asking, 'whose self is on camera?' Their action of rebelling against the idealised image of themselves portrayed by intellectuals, and questioning the established social relations reflects their effort to reconstruct their identities through the filmmaking process. This project affects the self-understanding of Wu Wenguang, the urban filmmaker and project initiator, as much as that of the villagers. I argue that the value of this socially engaged project, ultimately, is not to see what the villagers self portraits are like, but to see the negotiation process by which both the villagers and Wu have come to understand themselves and each other, and to construct an acceptable self representation.

The final chapter of this book turns the focus to more recent first person documentaries and to the online interactive form of first person expression on *zhibo* – live streaming broadcasts. Since the 2010s, more first person documentaries have emerged, which continue the features of action and amateurness. Though there are a few first person activist documentaries, most of these films focus on the personal conflicted identity of the makers and their familial relations. The changing socio-political context of Xi's leadership and technological conditions in the post-cinematic era have contributed to the proliferation of personal expression, and given rise to '*zhibo*', also interactive live streaming broadcasts, which allow first person expression and performance for personalised, and profitable, entertainment. In this concluding chapter, I discuss the aesthetics of the self as the *presenter-performer* in 'one man *zhibo* shows', where the presenter's body is centralised on a personal screen, reaching to an audience whose interactions are displayed and constantly updated through live chat messages over the streaming screen. *Zhibo*, as an identity technology (Poletti and Rak 2014), is not merely a platform, but a space where the self is constantly in the process of construction. It renews our understanding of self-expression, performativity and communication. The context and ethical dimensions of *zhibo* will also be explored. The tangled relationship between commercial imperatives and self-expression reflects the complexity of the construction of self in the age of social media. Lastly, I propose some possible directions for future research concerning audio-visual first person expression.

Overall, the films and filmmaking practice discussed in this book can be seen as powerful generative forces, through which the self, constituted as multi-layered within multiple spaces, is constantly being (re)constructed. It is believed that studying first person documentary practice in China is vital to an understanding of the emergence of new kinds of individual selves out of the embers of Maoist collectivism. The cinematic highlight of 'I', eye-witnessing, documenting and provoking what happens through the utilisation of the digital camera, positions first person documentary practices as an important part of China's iGeneration cinema culture (Wagner and Yu 2014) that increasingly emphasises individual self-expression, and digital and information technology, under the global experience of individualisation. This practice is not only a significant part of Chinese independent filmmaking, that illuminates – and mirrors – the larger process of the construction of hybrid modern identities in contemporary China, but also reflects an important dimension of contemporary documentary practice around the globe.

Notes

1. Rascaroli explains that in the essay film, the textual commitments and the spectatorial pact are: 'I, the author, am reflecting on a problem, and share my thoughts with you, the spectator'. In a diary film: 'I am recording events that I have witnessed and impressions and emotions I have experienced'. For the notebook: 'I am taking notes of ideas, events, existents for future use'. Finally for the self-portrait: 'I am making a representation of myself' (2009: 15). 'The essay, is always subjective, but is not necessarily autobiographical' (16).
2. Images and manifestos were demonstrated in a magazine called *Provoke*. Even though this only survived for three issues and a book, it created a long lasting legacy and now the word 'Provoke' is used to describe this period, 1960–75.
3. For more, read Yulin Li (2009), *Liminality of Translation: Subjectivity, Ethics and Aesthetics*, Shulin Publications.
4. Apart from a few good ones, Nornes thinks, such as Kawase Naomi's early self-documentary *Embracing (Nitsutsumarete)* (1992), researching for her father, and ObitaniYuri's *Hair Opera (Mohatsu kageki)* (1992).
5. A Beijing-based film critic, Wang Xiaolu, observes in his article 'Zhuti Jianxian'.
6. Wen Hui met Wu Wenguang in 1981; Wu later went to Beijing to join her in 1987. While Wen was expressing herself through dance, Wu was exploring with video cameras. During their more than thirty years relationship, they have created many art works together.

7. *The Toilet* (*Ma Tong*) was first performed in Beijing, then consequently invited to be performed in London, New York and other art centres abroad.
8. It is Wen's third performance, *Dancing with the Migrant Workers*, that is often discussed, circulated and remembered, together with a DV documentary *Dancing with the Migrant Workers* made by Wu Wenguang documenting the making of this performance.
9. It is usually called the 'New Documentary Movement', the idea of a Chinese scholar Lü Xinyu, but it has been constantly questioned by filmmakers themselves who state that it could not be seen as a movement as only a few people were making independent works. Personally, I think the word 'movement' itself is a historically loaded word used by a generation who has experienced mass collective forms of political movement. I have given a more thorough review of current English language academic writings on Chinese documentary in the article 'Documentary', *Journal of Chinese Cinemas*, 10: 1, 2016, http://dx.doi.org/10.1080/17508061.2016.1142727.
10. For Wang, the 'politics' in the term 'depoliticised' are 'a sphere borne of an active subjectivity' (2006: 691).
11. In Dong Zhongshu's 17-volume book, *Chun Qiu Fan Lu* 《春秋繁露》.
12. Wm. Theodore de Bary, an influential sinologist, states that the fundamental aim of Confucianism is 'to be a man among men', which sees the individual not as an isolated being, but with an inborn moral sense, though it does not mean relations alone solely define a man (1970: 149). Instead, the 'Confucian individual exists in a delicate balance with his environment' (1970: 150). In the Ming Dynasty, Wang Yang-ming, one of the most studied Chinese philosophers, is seen to have encouraged the development of individualism in China (Xu 2009) as he focused on the naturality of an individual's mind, which challenged the traditional Confucian believe in the law of heaven and the courtesy. However, de Bary (1970: 153) argues that while Wang admits the self as an active individual, his ideal is based on 'moral self-reformation, and strongly emphasizes a community of interests as opposed to individual differences'.
13. See Fei (1992), *From the Soil: The Foundations of Chinese Society*.
14. Fei states that 'the concept of public was the ambiguous *tianxia* (all under heaven), whereas the state was seen as the emperor's family . . . The state and the public are but additional circles that spread out like the waves from the splash of each person's social influence. Therefore, people must cultivate themselves before they can extend outward. Accordingly, self-restraint has become the most important virtue in social life. The Chinese thus are unable to assert themselves against society to ensure that society does not infringe on their individual right. In fact, the Chinese notion of a differential mode of association does not allow for individual rights to be an issue at all' (1992: 70).
15. Some scholars believe that the modern notion of 'individual' used during the May Fourth 1919 Movement for Enlightenment came into context roughly around 1904 (Liu 1995: 4; Jin and Liu 2009: 47).
16. Svarverud states that autonomy in the Kantian sense points to man's innate disposition and freedom of moral self-legislation based on his pure reason, only limited by the purposiveness of nature directing human morality (2010: 207).

17. Differing from the neoliberalism which rejects social and public intervention in individuals lives and promotes 'self-interested beings' seeking material success, the individualisation thesis understands that public interventions and modern social institutions can also be used to *promote* individual autonomy and self-determination (Howard 2007: 3).
18. Numerous essays in the volume *iChina* (2010) are also dedicated to the examination of the changing notion of the individual in post-socialist China and its individualisation process.
19. Wang argues that 'eurocentrism in the world of knowledge is a kind of universalistic monism, while a pluralistic view of civilization also runs the risk of falling into the trap of essentialism as well, one that sees civilizations – and especially modern civilizations – as systems isolated from one another, each with their own unique essences' (2009: 83).
20. This is in 'article 49 of China's 1982 Constitution, article 15 of the 1980 Marriage Law, article 35 of the 1992 Women's Protection Law, and article 183 of the 1979 Criminal Law'. As Vanessa Fong points out, 'The cultural model of filial duty remained one of the most salient aspects of China's Confucian legacy. Chinese leaders continued to promote this cultural model because it allowed the state to devote its resources to promoting economic growth instead of social security on the assumption that most citizens would rely on their children for nursing care, economic support, and the payment of medical expenses in their old age' (2006: 128–9).
21. Yan states that 'along with the increase of mobility in social scale and geographic scope, more individuals found themselves interacting in public life with other individuals who were either unrelated or total strangers, whereby collective identity and group membership became secondary to individual identity and capacity' (2009: 284).

Chapter 1

Female First Person Documentary Practice: Negotiating Gendered Expectations

> Communication is truth; communication is happiness. To share is our duty; to go down boldly and bring to light those hidden thoughts which are the most diseased; to conceal nothing; to pretend nothing; if we are ignorant to say so; if we love our friends to let them know it.
>
> Virginia Woolf (2003: 64–5)

Within a decade of Deng Xiaoping's Southern Tour in 1992, a new intensification in development of the socialist market economy 'with Chinese characteristics', China's post-Mao reform had also stimulated what the anthropologist Yan Yunxiang observes as an 'individualisation process', in which individuals have been largely untied from previous social institutions, and have gained more space and autonomy to develop their own lifestyle choices (Yan 2009: xxvii). Alongside China's colossal economic boom and rapid mass urbanisation, individuals were quietly transforming their social roles, often in subversive ways. Three amateur women filmmakers pioneered first person filmmaking in the beginning of the twenty-first century, consciously and unconsciously examining and reconstructing their individual subjectivities.

This chapter focuses on these three female filmmakers and their first person films made in 2000 and 2001: *Nightingale, Not the Only Voice* (dir. Tang Danhong, 2000); *They Are Not the Only Unhappy Couple* (dir. Wang Fen, 2000); and *Home Video* (dir. Yang Lina, 2001). As both aesthetic and social pioneers, these women were experimenting with a new documentary language to express their subjectivity and thus depart from earlier Chinese independent documentary practices in the 1990s, for two key reasons. First, unlike many documentaries traditionally made by male filmmakers, the women who made these films highlight a personalised vision of reality by bringing their own intimate familial spaces to wider audiences and reflexively turning themselves into key characters in their own films. Second, their first person documentary practice often arises from a subversive impulse. It departs from the political economy of the mainstream film industry, connecting a new strand of film practices to what is regarded as the iGeneration canon (Wagner and Yu 2014), and at the same time it challenges these filmmakers' traditional roles as women constrained by patriarchal expectations and the burdens of institutional and familial persecution. It is here that they negotiate their position in the still largely male-dominated film world, as well as their personal position as daughters in these families.

Despite little exploration of the private and the familial in non-fiction films historically, especially those made by women, female self-portraits in modern oil painting (Yao 2010; Zhu 2010) and new women's writing emerging in the 1920s have gained deserved attention. After Mao's China, women's personal writings as 'privacy literature' (*yinsi wenxue*, 隐私文学) re-proliferated in the 1980s, however, facing much criticism for the over exposure of personal desires (Wang 2005). During the 1990s, (semi-) autobiographical writing was packaged as 'body writing' (*shenti xiezuo*, 身体写作), a seductive and popular cultural commodity within the ever-growing market-forces and consumption culture.

It is in this context that the earliest Chinese first person filmmakers emerged in the beginning of the 2000s. Interestingly, the first few filmmakers who picked up the mini DV camera for self-expression and familial investigation are also women who play the role of a daughter in their family. Like Hu Xinyu, who will be discussed in the next chapter, they are not trained professional filmmakers but are amateur DV makers. Also focused on the familial aspects of the maker/writer selves, their practice can be deemed as 'DV individualised writing'.

While women's individualised writings are mostly packaged as cultural commodities, the first person DV documentaries made by the female amateur filmmakers were neither sold on the market, nor have they been widely shown to audiences in public spaces. Expressed through personal experiences, such films can be seen as a strong counterpoint to the official representation of family during the social transition, and complementary narratives to their highly commoditised literary counterparts.

These three women demonstrate a strong awareness of being independent individuals eager for self-expression. Performing the role of daughter, however, they do not simply follow the traditional norms of the 'Three Obediences' expected of women, as mentioned in the Introduction. On the contrary, they challenge the image of the obedient daughter, producing a new understanding of a 'parent-daughter' relationship. In her highly influential book *Bodies That Matter*, Judith Butler emphasises the role of repetition in performativity, or performance as perverse citation. For her,

> Performativity cannot be understood outside of a process of iterability, a regularized and constrained repetition of norms. And this repetition is not performed *by* a subject; this repetition is what enables a subject and constitutes the temporal condition for the subject. This iterability implies that 'performance' is not a singular 'act' or event, but a ritualized production, a ritual reiterated under and through constraint, under and through the force of prohibition and taboo, with the threat of ostracism and even death controlling and compelling the shape of the production, but not, I will insist, determining it fully in advance. (Butler 1993: 95)

For the three female filmmakers, even if their iterative performances do not consciously try to break the conventional norms, they do not just perform the socially defined role of daughter either. These three films are all imprinted with a strong authorial voice as the filmmaker and the daughter in the family.

However, their authorial voices do not just speak for themselves but more for the family as a larger collective, in which they themselves are a part. Michael Renov regards the first person self-representations in the familial space as 'domestic ethnography', 'a mode of autobiographical practice that couples self-interrogation with ethnography's concern for the documentation of the lives of others, in particular, family members who serve as a mirror or foil for the self' (Renov 2008: 44). Exploring this further, Lebow regards what she calls 'family autobiographies' as constitutive of the self (2008: 44). Both Renov and Lebow emphasise the documentation of the familial others as to serve the construction of the self, the central focus of the representation. These films, however, illustrate that family ethics still construct the individual self as a relational one. As I discussed in the Introduction, Confucian family ethical relations, which played a dominant role in ancient China, define traditional Chinese society as ethical-relation based, hence the relational self in traditional Chinese culture (Liang 1990). Throughout twentieth-century China, the notion of the individual has been changing through the detraditionalisation process, from the early republican period, the socialist collectivism in Mao's China, and especially since the decollectivisation (*songbang*) process in the post-socialist era. But the traditional and socialist encompassing social categories, such as family, have not been entirely abolished.

Rather than saying these three filmmakers challenge family filial duties, they are indeed trying to re-negotiate familial duties with their parents, not through passive obedience, but through contributing their own understanding and perspectives to the family. On the one hand, it reflects the features of the 'increasing self-interest of the individual', and could be seen as a crucial part of the 'iGeneration' – challenging their 'given' identity and using a new alternative amateur documentation tool – the digital video camera – to negotiate a new way of communication. On the other hand, their practice can be seen as a form of social participation that probes gendered expectations. Nevertheless, these three women's films have not been widely shown to audiences in public spaces outside the independent film communities of the time, and have received criticism for being narcissistic and solipsistic when they were first shown (author's interviews with the filmmakers). The 'film community' is a group who one would expect to have more progressive views on gender. The criticisms they received suggest that the individualising society in China seems not to have fully accepted women who openly challenge parental and patriarchal power. Their position in society and their communicative practices have remained the subject of an ongoing negotiation.

Resisting Gendered Expectations – a Historical Context

The three women filmmakers, Tang Danhong, Yang Lina and Wang Fen, are three individuals among many others who have gained more mobility in the state-initiated decollectivisation process. Both Yang Lina and Wang Fen can be put in the category of the so-called 'I generation' (*wo yi dai*), which refers to individuals who were born after the 1970s and are more concerned with self-realisation and personal happiness than previous generations. These two filmmakers explicitly express their concern with their personal lives in their films, aiming to find out how the unhappy marriages of their parents have influenced the construction of their own selves. Tang Danhong is in a different cohort; her early experience as a poet in the 1980s who was tightly involved in avant-garde writing has contributed to her expressive, reflexive, poetic and essayistic character. As female filmmakers, their strong authorial voice challenges the morality of the 'Three Obediences' that traditionally constrain the role of women, especially the ethic of paternal authority, given their role as daughters in their families.

Born in the 1960s, Tang experienced her youth during the 1980s, when public debates about modernity and the search for roots dominated the cultural scene. Influenced by the cultural debates and literary discourse at the time, Tang developed a strong interest in writing and has published many poems in the underground publications that circulated in the literary community (Zhao 2010). Her works have been regarded as highly personal and self-reflexive (Zuo 2010). In terms of her career, Tang worked for a short period in a university library, a state-owned work unit in the late 1980s, then left and started to work in a private local gallery in Sichuan. In 1994, Tang started to run a bookshop as *geti hu* (self-employed), then worked in a private documentary production company (ibid.).

Born in 1972, Yang Lina was trained as a dancer and worked at the People's Liberation Army Theatre during the 1990s when she was in her twenties (Wu 2010). Meeting her at her home in Beijing, Yang revealed to me that in her early twenties, she could not stand working as a propaganda tool any more. Though at the time she was not very familiar with the term 'ideology', she increasingly felt uncomfortable about being constrained by the political codes, and was eager to express her true self. In the late 1990s, she left the military work unit and went to Beijing to start a new life. The market economy and the new social context allowed her to work as a freelance. From 1996 to 1999, with a small amateur DV camera, Yang made her first amateur documentary, *Old Men* (*Laotou*), observing the daily life of a group of old men in a local Beijing residential area for two years. The handheld amateur observations with close-ups of the daily life of the old people offer a fresh look at China at the end of 1990s. The film won the Merit Prize at the Yamagata Festival, the 'Golden Pigeon' and jury prize at Leipzig Festival. Since then, Yang has received much attention from the domestic media, which regard her as their first amateur DV filmmaker. It is debatable whether Yang is the first to use an amateur DV camera to film in China, but she is definitely the first to get much media attention, especially for being an independent female filmmaker using a mini-DV camera to record the lives of ordinary people at close quarters. Her second film examined here, *Home Video* (2001), is Yang's personal investigation into her parents' divorce and family conflicts.

Wang Fen is the youngest of the three filmmakers. She was born in 1978 when China was just starting its economic reforms. Leaving home at nine years old, she was trained in an acting school (author's interview with Wang, 2010). In contrast to Tang and Yang, Wang has never worked in a state-owned work unit. This is partly because of her profession as an actor, and partly because, when she grew up in the late 1990s, the state did not compulsorily allocate jobs to young people and, therefore, individuals had to rely on finding a job themselves. In my interview with Wang, she reveals that she started to work as an actress in her late teens; however, she changed her mind and wanted to be a director. She then borrowed a video camera and went back to her home town in Jiangxi province, to interview her parents on their problematic marriage (author's interview with Wang, 2010).

Ten years after making her first film, *They Are Not the Only Unhappy Couple*, Wang Fen was sitting with me in a modern restaurant in Wangjing, a recently developed middle-class district in northeast Beijing. Looking out on a set of glitzy modern apartment blocks and newly erected skyscrapers that reflect the country's economic success over the last two decades, we started to chat about personal stories of living through China's dramatic social transitions. Wang recalled the experience of making her inaugural first person documentary in her early twenties, a personal journey that investigated her own parents' unhappy marriage.

> At that time, I was only about twenty-one years old, but already an adult. I was eager to know myself, my emotions, and how I became who I was . . . These were things I did not understand and really wanted to know . . . (Author's interview with Wang, 2010)

It was the desire for self-understanding and parent-child communication that compelled Wang to take a DV camera back home. In writings on autobiographic documentary, Michael Renov points out that this filmmaking practice functions as therapy for self-understanding and self-recovery (2004: 215). Lebow also regards Jewish family autobiographic films as 'filmic repair', which 'go beyond the problem of displacement and loss, attempting to filmically mend a breach within the family created by time, historical events, lack of communication, generation gaps, different beliefs, or the vicissitudes of memory' (2008: 85). Similarly, it is the desire to understand or to help 'repair' broken family relations that urges these three women filmmakers to make their films; though bringing the broken family members together in the same frame is not always successful or sufficient in rebuilding the relationship in reality, it does reflect a kind of wish fulfilment. For Wang Fen, making the film *They Are Not the Only Unhappy Couple* also arose out of her sense of responsibility towards her parents. Having lived outside her home town from a young age, Wang wants to find out the answer to a question that has confused her since she was very young: 'Why are my parents not happy together?' She regards the making of this film as the starting point of her adulthood. 'Before that, it is usually the parents who take care of the children, but through the making of the film, I start to care about them and worry about them' (author's interview with Wang, 2010). In this sense, the making of the film can also be seen as Wang showing filiality to her parents in her own way, rather than simply being an obedient and quiet daughter. As a filmmaker, she believes that the film raises a much wider awareness of the marriage problem, which is not just a personal issue, but reflects a much larger social reality (author's interview with Wang, 2010). However, traditional Confucian family ethical relations still construct women as powerless and voiceless. Women play the role of the daughter and the wife, subject to the father, the husband and the eldest son respectively, which is indicated in the 'Three Obediences' (Wolf 1985). Rather than simply following the conventional ethical norms, these three women inscribed themselves as strong authorial voices in their films, constantly asking questions from behind the camera.

As briefly mentioned in the Introduction, resistance to the ethics of female obedience as a discursive process has gone through various changes in China, dating back to the country's modern individualisation process in the late nineteenth century. During the May Fourth period, modern educated 'new women' elites[1] protested against discriminatory gender attitudes and practices in an attempt to change the perception of women in traditional society. They addressed a new cultural feminism that 'altered the lives and indelibly imprinted the consciousness of the generation of new women who came of age at the time' (Wang, quoted by Dooling 2005: 7). The women's movement not only had influence in urban China, but also had impact among peasants and the working class, 'by focusing on issues relevant to their needs, such as wife beating, divorce for cause, footbinding, and literacy' (Wolf 1985: 14). During this time, the Communist Party also focused on empowering female identity, especially among peasant women; this was to promote the construction of a new sociality identity, rather than to challenge male domination. Even though the Communist Party's promotion of women's liberation was not a thorough process and was needed for national salvation, it was a relatively liberated view on women. However, the nationalist government repressed these 'new women' during the 'New Life Movement' in the 1930s, with the aim of rejecting Western individualism, and promoted traditional Confucian ethics. It saw the image of 'new women' as a challenge to political uniformity and social stability.

After the establishment of the People's Republic of China, gender inequality was strongly countered through a series of legislation. The new Marriage Law was established in 1950, stating that 'men and women enjoyed "equal rights", "equal status in the home", and "equal rights in the possession and management of family property"' (Evans 2008: 11). The law promoted free-choice marriage and ensured sexual equality. As Wolf states, 'the features of the new law that received the greatest attention, both favorable and unfavorable, were the rights of women to demand divorces and the rights of young people to choose their own marriage partners without parental interference' (Wolf 1985: 15). At the same time, women were also encouraged to move outside the familial sphere to enter the productive workforce and were integrated into social production. Official state organisations, such as the Women's Federation or '*Fulian*' (妇联), were funded. These legal changes have to some extent had a positive impact on increasing women's position, especially in the domestic space.

However, as many scholars have argued, the image of the new strong woman was largely used to support the socialist collective ideology, signifying that the Communist Party would liberate the female victims of traditional Chinese feudal society and help them become active members of the proletarian class. In reality, it was far from reaching the aim of gender equality. Margery Wolf argues that the Communist Party failed to bring Chinese women equality with men legally, politically, socially and economically. Therefore, the gendered features of the expectations in patriarchal society still largely remain. During the first Five Year Programme, 'Five Goods' were promoted by the state: 'since the economy was not yet ready to provide full-time employment for women, they should (1) unite with the neighborhood families for mutual aid, (2) do housework well, (3) educate children well, (4) encourage family production, study, and work, and (4) study well themselves' (Wolf 1985: 23).

However, from 1950 to 1980, and particularly during the Cultural Revolution, the Communist Party went to another extreme, whereby a total denial of feminine features was common (Evans 1997: 8), while in many cases the gender hierarchy continued to exist.[2] Nevertheless, the status of women rose significantly in Mao's China when compared to their role in traditional Chinese society.

Even with all the social changes that have accompanied Chinese economic reform since 1980, popular discourse in China still maintains a focus on the importance of women re-emphasising their own familial obligations. As Evans states,

> 'soft and gentle' images of a supportive femininity topped the rankings for desirable wives. Treating love and sex as key constituents of a happy and stable marriage rapidly became crucial criteria of China's new claims to being a 'modern society'. Though these images were sometimes disturbed by others of the 'strong woman' (*nüqiangren*) and the ambitious female entrepreneurs, the dominant popular message is one of a naturalized and emotional female and connotes the attributes of gentleness, sympathy and care. (Evans 2010: 998–9)

Confronting this mainstream discourse, women's personal writings, as 'an act, a negotiation of selves and identities in history' (Wang 2004: 12) re-emerged in the 1980s, championed by writers such as Yu Luojin, who tried to carve out a space for gendered personal voices, repelling conventional gender expectation and exposing personal emotions, desires and sexuality from a women's perspective. These writings, however, have faced strong criticism and been denounced as 'privacy literature' (*yinsi wenxue*).

During the 1990s, public opinion towards personal writing changed with the emerging burgeoning popular culture, marking the age of 'privacy fever' (Wang 2004: 175). The (semi-) autobiographical women's 'individualized writing' [*gerenhua xiezuo*, 个人化写作] (Wedell-Wedellsborg 2010: 174), such as that done by Wei Hui, Mian Mian and Mu Zimei, re-proliferated in this period. However, they were packaged as a seductive popular cultural commodity to satisfy the rapidly globalising market society, as well as the hedonistic and narcissistic consumer culture in China (Wang 2005: 182). Though such personal writing has carved out a space for women's own voices, the mass consumption of it has made women's personal voice subject to market forces, problematising the traditionally oppositional relationships between women's culturally prescribed roles and their newly independent voices, as well as between the private and the public sphere.

Turning the camera inward to explore filmmakers' familial aspects in a fast transforming society, female first person documentaries can be read as 'DV individualised writing'. In all three films, the women filmmakers are 'performing' – but also challenging – the stereotyped 'given' role of the passive obedient daughter. Yang Lina and Wang Fen question their parents' marriage and divorce. Tang Danhong questions her father's aggressive and malevolent behaviour towards her. By reconnecting to their parental history, they are eager to communicate with their parents, actively producing a new understanding of a parent-daughter relationship. It is in this sense that I regard these two women's proactive first person filmmaking about their parents' marriages as a kind of active communication (*goutong*). Their work can also be seen as a mode of 'communicative practice', a term developed from Jürgen Habermas' theory of communicative action and used by Harriet Evans to describe the changing pattern of 'mother-daughter' communication, as daughters of the younger generation long for emotional relatedness with their parents (Evans 2010: 981). The women filmmakers in my study also aim for a reconnection with their parents and are proactively altering the communication pattern they used to have with their elders. Unabashedly rebellious, first person filmmaking by women also serves as a means of social/cultural construction, as they subversively generate a new set of ethics for communication between parents and children, through the medium of the DV camera.

A Strong Authorial Voice and the Multi-layered Self in the Investigation

The three women approach their parents not just from the viewpoint of a daughter, but more as an 'outsider' – an independent individual who shows responsibility towards her family, and re-negotiates the filial duties expected of a daughter. Yang uses handheld point-of-view shots to create a subjective gaze at her parents, and uses off-screen first person voice to lead the narrative. To the contrary, Wang creates a formal 'objective' look and speaks calmly to her parents, trying to maintain her position as an 'outsider'. Tang Danhong, on the other hand, inscribes herself not just as the 'seer' and the 'editor', but also as the subject to be looked at and to be heard on screen. The self-split between the filmed 'past' and the spoken 'now' gives her temporal distance to reflexively examine herself in the past, and in the 'filmed' past.

Home Video and *They Are Not the Only Unhappy Couple*

In *Home Video*, Yang Lina deeply inscribes herself as the '*seer*' (Russell 1999), the 'origin of gaze', and the *speaker*, aiming to dig out what has caused the broken relationship between her divorced parents, and between her father and her brother. She is also the editor, arranging her interviews in a particular way to reflect and communicate her own interpretation. The title '*Home Video*' indicates an amateurish 'look'. Though Yang does not appear on camera, it is clear that this family investigation would not be possible if Yang did not have the courage to do so. Throughout the film, her point-of-view shots, her voice that keeps asking questions from behind the camera, and the way she edits the material together constantly remind us of Yang's existence as the first person filmmaker.

In *Home Video*, Yang's aim is to dig out the unspoken secret involving domestic violence and betrayal that has caused the break between her divorced parents, and between her father and her brother. Yang's role as a family insider enables her camera to enter the private familial space. As the *seer*, she equates her own eyes with the lens of the camera, creates a special subjective look at the subjects, a look that has gone beyond that of a daughter or a sister. As the *speaker* in the film, Yang does not choose to talk to her family in a formal interview setting; neither does she follow the traditional manner of a daughter. Instead, Yang does the interview in a very casual way, constantly speaking from behind the camera, interrogating her parents like an arbiter. When talking to her mother or her father, Yang's camera sometimes looks at them from above. Her voice coming from behind the camera sounds very firm, almost aggressive. Such an 'amateur look' demonstrates a more intimate relationship between the filmmaker and the subjects, and is very different from the conventional fly-on-the-wall observational documentary mode that had a significant impact on earlier Chinese independent documentaries from the 1990s.

The film opens with a medium close-up of Yang's mother lying on the bed in her underwear (see Figure 1.1). Yang's off-screen voice states persistently that: 'I want to make an investigation into the divorce of my parents. If you think it

Figure 1.1 Yang asks her mother to persuade her father in *Home Video* (2001)

is boring or too intrusive, I will stop.' Her voice is the first one we hear in the film, making it clear it is 'I' who is holding the camera and investigating 'my' parents' divorce. Yang then cuts away from these personal interviews and moves to three family members, to compare their different attitudes toward the divorce and its subsequent effects on the whole family. It is interesting to note that her mother seems not care about disclosing the family scandal to the public. In contrast, neither her father nor her brother was willing to participate on camera in the beginning, even though they were on opposite sides in this dispute. After gaining support from her mother, the film cuts to Yang's father lying in bed in a different bedroom. The camera zooms in on his face, as he addresses the camera, 'Your mum has no idea about anything. She's just happy that she's going to be an actress, right?' Yang laughs while replying: 'No way. How can you think of her like that?' It cuts back to the mother looking up at the camera, saying: 'Tell him to think about it carefully.' Then the camera follows the father walking around, while Yang's off-screen voice speaks: 'If you don't agree, I'll keep following you around.' The intercut between Yang's mother and father creates a dialogue between them, bridging the broken family relationship (see Figure 1.2).

Figure 1.2 Interviews with the father, mother and brother are cross-cut in *Home Video* (2001)

While the father's rejection may come from self-censorship or a sense of privacy, feeling ashamed about talking about the secret, the brother refuses to remember as the act of remembering the 'broken past' would hurt them again. The brother sits in a darkened living room facing the camera, saying: 'I cannot support this.' As Yang insists, the brother replies: 'If we all just speak from our own points of view, it will turn into a family war . . . This is not just an average event from our past . . . You are hurting people . . . Stop talking, turn that thing off.' Similarly, the father tries to cover up the lens, asking Yang to stop filming: 'It's best not to do anything that you will regret.' Despite this warning, Yang firmly replies: 'No, I will be very fair.' At this moment, she does not simply act in the role of a daughter, but like a judge, with the ability to make her own independent decision on this issue. Though being challenged by two male figures in the family, Yang does not give up. She even shows how her brother criticises her on camera. When her brother tells Yang 'I think you are a little shameless', Yang does not feel guilty, instead, she admits it and playfully says, from behind the camera, 'Yes, yes, you are right. I'm beginning to feel very shameless.' Nevertheless, the father and the brother finally agree to participate. As their conversation reveals, the violent family history is that the mother had an affair, which was witnessed by Yang's brother, who then later told his father. The father consequently began beating the mother for her infidelity, and they divorced because of these irreconcilable spousal difficulties. The brother, who also witnessed the domestic violence, has had very complicated feelings towards his parents ever since.

Throughout the film, Yang uses this subjective amateur camera eye to lead the narrative. She not only insists on filming the investigation, but also decides to show the mother's and the brother's views to the father, the authority figure of the family. After the interviews, Yang invites the mother and the brother to watch the film together and records their responses. It is the first time we see the mother and the brother together, for them to see what the father thinks. Then, despite Yang's mother's warning not to show the film to her father, Yang insists on doing so. Through investigating the family secret, which turns out to be serious domestic violence, the film ultimately challenges the father, not only through her gesture of interviewing him and letting him tell the story from his memory, but also through using the subjective memories of the mother and the brother to disturb his own judgement. Toward the end, Yang says she hopes the film can bridge the long-term misunderstanding among these three traumatised family members.

Like Yang Lina in her *Home Video*, Wang also edits the material and constructs her parents' confessions according to her own personal interpretation in *They Are Not the Only Unhappy Couple*. In the opening sequence, Wang uses some experimental elements, having her parents perform themselves in fast-forward motion, as we see close-ups of two pairs of hands cutting out phrases like 'marriage', 'love', and 'family' from magazines, then one set of hands throwing the paper cut-outs into a bin, and the other set of hands picking them out of the rubbish. Then the film cuts to an establishing shot, and the camera zooms in and we see a couple standing side by side – they are Wang's parents. In this sequence, Wang introduces us to the relationship of her parents through a performance she directed.

In *They Are Not the Only Unhappy Couple*, Wang's first person influence is articulated strongly through her self-inscription as the 'seer' and the 'editor'. Wang creates a look that is less personal and more objective. In her interview with her parents, Wang puts the camera on a tripod to achieve a stable view, constructing the interview setting in a more formal way. The father and the mother each sits in the middle of the frame in medium close-up, and address the camera directly, rather than looking at Wang behind the camera. The close relationship between Wang's parents and their daughter makes the parents reveal themselves to the camera without much worry. For them, it is more like their daughter's amateur home movie practice than a new mode of documentary filmmaking.

Wang's off-screen voice only appears a few times from behind the camera, speaking in a very calm and unemotional tone, asking questions and exploring the details. She neither argues with her parents loudly nor laughs nor cries with them, as Yang does in her film. It is this less personal 'look' and neutral tone of questioning that reinforce her position as a filmmaker, one who tries to stand outside her own familial relationship. By doing so, she creates a space for her parents to confess, to speak out about their pain, as a way of showing her care and love for them.

Nightingale, Not the Only Voice

In *Nightingale, Not the Only Voice*, Tang Danhong's authorial voice is much more layered than that in Yang's and Wang's films. She presents herself not only as the *seer*, the *speaker*, the *editor*, but also as the *seen*, making the first person voice more conflicted and unstable. The film consists of stories of three people: a male performance artist, Yin Xiaofeng; a female painter artist, Cui Ying; and the last and key character, the filmmaker- poet, Tang Danhong herself. Three people's stories are interwoven with each other, linked together through Tang's first person narration. As Tang's voice-over reveals, she starts to film herself because the other two characters have strongly inspired her:

> I often do not dare to go out without wearing makeup, but the self behind the makeup has given me power to film Yin and Cui, now the same power has made me turn the camera inwards to film myself. I feel Xiaofeng and Cui Ying are parts of me, so I am in fact recording the fragments of myself.

This establishes that the representation of Cui and Yin in the film are reflections of Tang's[3] own self, and urges her to eventually present her own self. The first time she presents herself is in a bathroom scene, where Tang undresses in her bedroom, then goes naked to the bath. The body acts as a material form that indicates openness.

Tang intensively uses voice-over, not just speaking about her past history, but also commenting on herself as presented in the film. In this bathroom scene, the camera observing from above shows Tang lying in the bath quietly. Her voice-over reflects:

> It is almost like a porn movie. I was in fact very sad at the time, but when I saw it during the editing, I cannot see I was sad at all, because I was bumbling. I was like an alien. What happened to me? The camera pointing at me is like a weapon with a sharp eye, I feel ashamed, embarrassed, and try to hide my true feelings and be calm . . .

The split between the *seer* and the *seen* of the self is also a split between a filmed past, and a spoken 'now'. This distance between the self being filmed and the self in the editing gives her space to speak in a highly reflective and self-critical way. The 'performance' of the self as the seen, and the voice-over examining her performance gives a more open demonstration of her inner self in front of the camera.

The self as the 'seen' is shown most in Tang's confessions to her psychologist about her traumatic childhood when her father often beat her. This confessional scene is filmed by Tang's close friend (Wu 2003). The handheld camera presents Tang in extreme close-up, tracing Tang's face and body up and down, observing Tang's facial expressions while she talks to the psychologist. The camera pans to the psychologist, who is sitting opposite Tang, and pans back at Tang, observing Tang in a strikingly aggressive manner. The unstable, highly subjective, close-up shots magnify Tang's unsettled and flustered feelings, making this moment her own space, leaving no room for the viewer to breath.

The most dramatic scene is Tang's face-to-face confrontation with her parents. Her highly provocative questioning brings the uneasy relationship to the foreground. 'Why did you often beat me when I was a child?' Tang's indomitable questioning discloses the 'pre-text' of this problematic relationship, a traumatic collective memory of China's recent history that has impacted on a large population – the ten-year 'Great Proletarian Cultural Revolution' (1966–76). What Tang challenges is beyond the father as the familial authority figure. In this conversation, the camera shows Tang sitting on a chair facing her parents who sit side by side on a sofa. This is intercut with close-ups of Tang and her parents, filmed by a third person.

Tang asks:

> Around 1975, when I forgot to cook for the family, you beat me so badly and asked me to leave. On another occasion, you were so angry that you gave me a knife and asked me to kill you. How can you beat me like that? (Author's translation)

Cutting back to the long shot, the father looks very serious and pained, but does not seem to feel guilty. The mother sitting next to the father explains:

> The mode of education at the time was not right – to beat meant to love. Because your father was treated so badly during the Cultural Revolution, and was labelled as 'right-wing', 'anti-revolution' . . . he felt very depressed, so he had a very high expectation of his child. (Author's translation)

The father is still quiet, saying nothing.

Both Tang and her parents speak in their local Sichuan dialect, which is different from Tang's voice-over and confessions, which are in Chinese Mandarin. The local dialect sounds less formal and more familial, as that is the dialect she was born with. Tang does not speak very aggressively, but in a quiet, calm and low voice. By contrast, her parents' voices sound more harsh.

> The mother continues: 'It is all because of that revolution.'
>
> The father: 'At the time, my single action, and my family's action, would have influenced me . . . Now I don't want to say anything. I have forgotten many things . . . I was under huge pressure that even your mother could not totally understand.'
>
> The mother: 'There was only loyalty at the time, no family ethics [*jiating lunli*, 家庭伦理] at all.'
>
> The father: 'It was all because of the social environment then. I hoped my children could be better than me. You cannot say this without mentioning the history. That's all I want to say.'
>
> The mother continues speaking for the father.
>
> Tang: 'I want to listen to what father says. You have been explaining for him your whole life.'
>
> The father: 'If people say you have made serious mistakes and they have to isolate you, you know, this means asking you to die.'
>
> Tang: 'So in fact it was not you who beat me, it was the powers asking you to die that beat me.'
>
> (Author's translation)

The conversation reaches the culmination of Tang's confrontation. During the Cultural Revolution, class struggle based on the class division of 'the repressed, the repressor, and the liberator', and a new morality of universalism based on comradeship, replaced the traditional ethics of three cardinal guides and five constant virtues. Individuals were all subjected to the socialist state and the party. In these norms, the young no longer needed to respect and show filial obedience to the old, and the wife could rebel against the husband, if the old and the husband belonged to the 'public enemies', the 'bad' class, that is, the descendants of feudal repressors or capitalists.[4] As Tang's mother reveals in the film: 'there was only loyalty at the time, no family ethics at all'. The father, who was the victim of class struggle, still exercised his patriarchal power at home as the father and husband. The criticism and violent treatment he received outside the domestic space, repressed him heavily and brought him both physical and psychological suffering. The private familial space became the only outlet for him to release himself, even though it was in a violent way.

What Tang questions is not so much the traditional parents-children order, which is 'father guides son', but why her father did not follow the family virtues and show affection to his child. 'Why did you beat me?' Tang keeps asking. By making the film, Tang is criticising how different political ideologies have impacted on constructing human relations and how the class struggle and dominant universalistic ethics during the Cultural Revolution have further problematised family relations. Towards the end of this conversation, Tang understands that it is not her father who beat her, as she says to the father 'it was the power asking you to die that beat me'. The film ultimately blames revolutionary socialist ideology during the Cultural Revolution, which repelled traditional family relations and went so far to damage humanity.

Still a Relational Self

The three women filmmakers challenge the traditional obedient image of a daughter with a strong voice. Caring for their parents and for the family, they insist on knowing more about their parental or parent-daughter relations. Within the films, they each construct themselves as an independent woman through cinematic representations. Yang and Wang investigate problematic familial or parental relations that are not directly related to themselves. Tang, on the other hand, investigates an issue that directly relates to her own self, and directly challenges her father as the authority figure.

Despite the strong authorial voice, their filming does not just speak for themselves, but for the sake of family as a larger collective, in which their individual selves are situated. This is the major difference from how Renov understands Western 'domestic ethnography', in which the representation of the familial others serves as a reflection and extension of the self.

In *Home Video*, Yang's interviews with her mother, father and younger brother are shot via a consecutive and cross-cut technique, producing the appearance of a face-to-face conversation of the three, with the central focus on the family (see Figure 1.2). While one person recalls an event, the other two immediately respond. The film reveals that the relationship between the mother and father, as well as the relationship between the father and the son, are in fact strained. Yet Yang is not the only person who cares about the family as a whole. Her mother insists that Yang should not show the film to her father, as it would ruin the relationship among the family members that has just been rebuilt again in recent years. The mother is especially afraid that the younger brother would lose his inheritance from the father. However, in the end, Yang still shows the film to her father. In the last shot of the film, Yang asks what her father thinks. Her father responds by asking his daughter the same question: 'what do *you* think?' Yomi Braester argues that this moment indicates that Yang is the ultimate protagonist of the film (2010: 211). However, as I see it, what Yang cares about most is the family appearing as a collective, which is the central focus of her film. Yang believes that this filmmaking activity has indeed created a chance for the family members to re-examine their relationships, and to engage in a deeper level of communication than they have had in a long time (author's interview with Yang, 2010).

In *They Are Not the Only Unhappy Couple*, Wang's camera focuses on examining the relationship between the husband and the wife. The majority of the film is made of two separate confessional interviews with the mother/wife and the father/husband, cross-cut and organised like a dialogue of the two. The film presents the couple's dissatisfaction towards each other. The father starts with revealing his promiscuity and affairs with other women, followed by the mother saying that, 'I never really trusted him.' The film cuts back to the father complaining about his wife, then back to the mother who is frank about her animosity towards the man she married. The couple speak to the camera, to their daughter, as if they do not realise that these interviews will be shown to the public.

As the conversations continue, we realise that the traditional ethical relationship between husband and wife is seriously strained in Wang's portrait of her family. In Chinese culture, the 'Three Cardinal Guides' request that the husband guides his wife, showing her affection and protecting her from harm, while the 'Three Obediences' request that the wife obeys the husband. Even when socialist ideology replaced traditional family ethics in Mao's China, the new morality of socialist 'commandership' required an equal relationship and mutual respect. However, Wang's parents' confessions to the camera have destroyed the stereotyped image of a good harmonious couple. As the film continues, it reveals that Wang's parents' unhappy marriage might be a result of

China's changing social-political climate during the Maoist era, when the father could not marry another woman because of class differences. In one scene, Wang leaves her father alone with the camera on and asks him to say whatever he wants to say. Her father appears to be a little uncomfortable at first, gazing at the camera, but then he starts to confess:

> On the issue of marriage, I have been tortured my whole life. Why? Because I cannot be with the one I love. The society did not allow it. But the one I don't like at all becomes my real wife, then I do not experience a single happy day ever since . . . .

It is interesting to analyse whom the father is addressing in this segment when he is by himself. Is he addressing his daughter, as he knows that she will eventually watch this? Is he addressing himself, revealing the pain in his heart? Is he addressing other potential viewers and does he know that this confession will be watched by a larger audience? The father reveals that he attributes his unhappy marriage at least partially to the communist class struggle during the Cultural Revolution, when people were grouped strictly according to their class labels and when personal affections toward a member of a different class were not encouraged.

This scene of the father's personal confession stands in sharp contrast with the final scene, in which Wang's parents are standing happily together side-by-side, waving goodbye to the camera. This 'happy together' moment is a conscious performance in front of the camera, which can be read in several ways. Is it a performance directed by Wang, who imposes her own romantic wish on to her parents? Is the performance happening because her parents want to present a happy image when they are together facing the camera, not knowing what each other has said? Or is it actually part of their daily life, as they both reveal that they do not want to divorce, because they wish to give their children a unified family? In all of these possible interpretations, the family members, Wang and her parents – despite their confessions to Wang about each other – still show considerable care for the family as a collective unit.

Ethics of Screening

Filming oneself and one's family is an important self-understanding process. Wang Fen regards the investigation in her film as valuable guidance for her to understand the meaning of marriage. She states that, even if she had not made the film, she would have understood the problem later. The filmmaking accelerated the process, at a time when she had just started a relationship herself (author's interview with Wang, 2010). Now Wang does not choose the traditional path of marriage for herself, but instead has given birth to a son with one of China's most politically outspoken contemporary artists, Ai Weiwei (a married man). It would be an oversimplification to judge Wang's choice of her unconventional unification of partnership as a direct response to her parents' unhappy marriage, but it nevertheless shows her rebellious attitude towards traditional marriage. Tang Danhong values this filmmaking process significantly as an important learning experience in her life (Wu 2003). As for Yang Lina, the criticism she received from her brother and father, as well as from her audience, has made her reflect on her own ethical relations with her family and the audience (author's interview with Yang, 2010).

While writing is a process limited to a space of one's own, at least until publication, these women have moved their process of discovery a step further. By using a DV camera instead of a pen, they create new avenues of communication – reconnecting with their parents on the one hand and directly challenging problematic familial relations and the expectations of women in Chinese society on the other. Their work draws attention to a re-examination of the institution of the family, which has become heavily layered and more complicated in China's period of transition. Their films illustrate the fact that family, as a traditional institution that has historically defined the individual self in an ethical relational society, still plays an important role in the construction of the individual self. Presenting themselves in complex relations, these women still think highly of the family as a collective group, which can provide individuals with a sense of identity and security. However, unlike the May Fourth new women of 1920s China and the post-Mao individual women writers in the 1980s and 1990s, who built up a collective power and social awareness, these three female filmmakers have not yet formed a broader alliance.

In a few screenings of their films, these three women have received strong criticism, being seen as highly transgressive and disrupting conventional Chinese expectations of passive obedient women. Their filmmaking has not only challenged their parents, but also provoked their audience in serious ways, as the highly private issues and personal moments of one's own family are forced upon the audience, whether or not they are prepared for it. Investigating their family problems and presenting them on camera has drawn attention to ethical questions. As Yang's mother says in the film: 'A movie like this will have a huge impact, but it will make us all look very bad, Yang Lina.' In the decade since its completion, *Home Video* has only been shown three times – once at the Leipzig Film Festival in Germany, and twice inside China. Similarly, *They Are Not the Only Unhappy Couple* was first shown at Yamagata International Documentary Film Festival (YIDFF) in Japan, then it was shown twice in Beijing. Wang Fen recalls that some Chinese journalists seriously criticised her as being shameless (author's interview with Wang, 2010). To some extent, such responses reflect the societal taboo regarding public discussion of personal familial issues in contemporary China. Unlike Yang and Wang, Tang only showed her film twice, in private screenings. It was first shown to some of her close friends at 'Bai Ye' (White Night), a locally well-known art and intellectual salon in the south-western city of Chengdu in Sichuan province, where Tang was based. Then in 2003, the film was shown at the first 'Yunfest' – a visual anthropology film festival in China. After that, Tang has talked little about the film in public and just kept it for her own self-understanding.

It cannot be denied that all three filmmakers hoped to make a 'film as a film'. In *Home Video*, Yang's mother's response to Yang's idea of filming the family as 'fashionable' and a 'good topic' somehow also reflects her own intention. As Yang reveals, 'I've been listening to my mother talking about the issue several times, and think maybe I can make a film out of it, and investigate how others think of the issue' (author's interview with Yang, 2010). However, by making a film out of it and showing it to a wider audience, Yang's familial issue is no longer a personal one. The strong criticism these filmmakers received made them question their own motivations. None of them have made similar documentaries since. Wang was funded to make a domestic commercial fiction feature in 2008 before editing some documentaries for Ai Weiwei. Tang married an Israeli and formed her own family, and moved to Israel in 2006. While Yang Lina keeps making documentaries, she has done some commissioned work for foreign broadcasters, and has avoided personal topics until her most recent fiction exploring female sexuality.

Their self-censorship and concern about privacy after making the films says something about the complex construction of the individual self. Gendered expectations of obedience and filiality, as well as family obligations, still play a crucial role in the individual construction of self in contemporary China. While the individualising society of post-reform China has offered these women more autonomy to pursue their selves outside of the traditional familial space, society seems not to have accepted women who openly challenge parental power and their conventional roles as a way to renegotiate the communication patterns between parents and children. It also indicates that society has not yet opened up public spaces for individuals to examine their selves in the context of unstable, uncommunicative familial relations that were, to a great extent, created by the dramatic transitions occurring in society.

To challenge the still highly patriarchal structure of contemporary Chinese society, as well as the patriarchal nature of the independent film world itself, Yang Lina recently finished her debut feature fiction *Longing for the Rain* (2013), which deals openly with women's sexuality by representing the sexual desire of a newly affluent urban middle-class woman. Yang aims to represent the innermost desires and emotions of women living in today's China, a topic that is rarely portrayed even in Chinese independent cinema. The film, according to Yang, was not submitted for censorship and will mainly be shown internationally at film festivals and to a small audience in independent domestic screenings. Touching on a topic that is little represented in Chinese cinema, even by women filmmakers, Yang hammers at the invisible 'taboo' in the still largely patriarchal society. Moving from making documentary to experimenting with fiction forms, Yang may also be looking for a way to avoid the complicated ethics that she once experienced in documentary practice.

Conclusion: More Female First Person Documentary Practice

Following the pioneer women filmmakers Yang Lina, Wang Fen and Tang Danhong, more filmmakers, who will be discussed in the following chapters of this book, explore their private familial issues as well as their engagement in public spaces through a first person approach. These include the amateur filmmaker Hu Xinyu (*The Men* 2001, *My Sister* 2003, and *Family Phobia* 2010) who, arguably, may have started filming the personal around the same time as the female filmmakers already mentioned. In addition, more women filmmakers have picked up their camera to make personal documentaries on themselves and their own families. For example, a Beijing Film Academy graduate Liu Jiayin has made two award-winning first person docu-dramas, *Oxhide I* (2005) and *Oxhide II* (2009), with family members playing themselves. Similarly, Song Fang's *Memories Look at Me* (2012) also portrays her and her parents in their domestic setting, as they casually unearth shared memories on their past mundane family life. Like the three films already studied here, the films by Liu and Song are also dialogue based, and the conversations are usually non-scripted. Nevertheless, it is worth noting that Liu's and Song's parent–daughter conversations, no matter how casual they seem or spontaneously provoked, are all carefully staged for the purpose of filming, as if a communication between the two generations is only possible through deliberate arrangement. Another woman's first person film that deals with generational communication is Zhang Mengqi's *Self Portrait: Three Women* (2010), which explores different values of love and marriage among Zhang's grandmother, mother and herself. Differing from the other dialogue-based productions, this film includes elements of on-stage performance, as the filmmaker/dancer Zhang uses her own body as a communicative tool, performing in front of the camera as a way to communicate with her mother, and herself.

Apart from these urban female filmmakers, a couple of subaltern class women have also been introduced to DV filmmaking. They take the camera both as a communicative tool and a constructive engine to build a new identity. Guo Lifen's *My Name is Fenfen* (2008) documents her personal experience as a rural-to-urban migrant worker in China's nationwide urbanisation and decollectivisation process. Familial conflicts, especially her challenge to patriarchal authority, are inevitably part of her transitional life. Shao Yuzheng, one of the amateur villager filmmakers in the 'China Villagers Documentary Project', which I will discuss in Chapter 7, has also made documentaries through her first person vision since 2005. Unlike other female filmmakers who predominantly focus on familial issues or their personal emotions, Shao is more like an independent journalist, keeping a record of the daily events in her village, and even documents her own interaction and confrontation with the state media and the rule of law.[5] By doing so, Shao has not only challenged the stereotypical image of the peasant class, but also the image of an illiterate domestic peasant woman, who is usually seen as having little interaction with the public and wider society.

In all these films, the construction of self, especially as regards the gendered features of a woman, has been further complicated by a society that is undertaking a dramatic decollectivisation, urbanisation and marketisation. While these women filmmakers raise their strong authorial voice, confronting the conventional expectations of women, they still care about the family as a collective unit. Articulating different devices of cinematic representations to inscribe themselves, these women filmmakers are searching for a new voice, and new ways to communicate with their families and society. The complicated and problematic family relations explored in the films also reflect the multi-layered and still largely relational dynamics in wider socio-political spaces in China today.

Notes

1. The 'new women' figures included journalists, novelists, playwrights, poets and critics, such as Ding Ling, Bing Xin, Xiao Hong, Qiu Jin and Zhang Ailing (Eileen Zhang).
2. Wolf analyses the reasons why gender equality was not achieved in Mao's China. 'Although sexual equality as a principle has not been vacated, it has been set aside at each economic downturn or show of rural resistance without recognition that such casual treatment will in time devalue a principle until it is but a hollow slogan. I do not think this was a conscious effort on the part of CCP to keep women subordinated, but rather a consistent failing on the part of an all-male leadership to perceive their own sexist assumptions.' For more, see Margery Wolf (1985), *Revolution Postponed*, Stanford: Stanford University Press, p. 26.

3. Author's translation.
4. There are many autobiographical books that tell real-life stories through a first person narrative of how personal lives were affected by the Cultural Revolution and how family ties and friendships were sundered by class struggle. Examples include *Born Red* by a former Red Guard Gao Yan, *Son of the Revolution* by Liang Heng and Judith Shapiro, *Wild Swans* by Jung Chang and *Spider Eaters* by Rae Yang.
5. Locally well known as a village filmmaker, Shao has attracted journalists to come to interview her. When state journalists ask her to play in some enacted scene and rehearse the conversation, she uses the small camera in her hand and documents her direct confrontation with the state journalists for their highly constructed, and unrealistic, ideal image of Chinese peasants.

Chapter 2

Amateurness and an Inward Gaze at Home

> Usually the amateur is defined as an immature state of the artist: someone who cannot – or will not – achieve the mastery of a profession. But in the field of photographic practice, it is the amateur, on the contrary, who is the assumption of the professional: for it is he who stands closer to the *noeme* of Photography.
>
> Roland Barthes (1999: 98–9)

The family portrait is a quasi-ritualistic practice producing memories of family gatherings and smiling faces. The process of sitting, chatting, laughing, arguing, fades away with the sound of a shutter clicking. The rows and tears that are part of everyday family life are forgotten or hidden. In *Family Phobia* (2010), Hu Xinyu, however, offers those tearful real-life dramas in his own extended family through his nearly decade-long first person 'gazing' at home, assisted by his amateur DV camera.

The film is compiled from Hu's home videos starting from a family gathering during the 2003 Chinese Spring Festival. As an amateur and independent filmmaker who is passionate about recording life with a DV camera, Hu is conscious of documenting every minute of his family life, but without a clear idea initially of what kind of film he wants to make. The film records the mundane everyday life of Hu's parents, sisters and brother, and nephew and nieces, in a small state-subsidised flat in Xuqing, a third-tier post-industrial city in Shanxi Province, north China.

Hu Xinyu is among the first group of amateur DV filmmakers to emerge in China at the dawn of the twenty-first century. He received no professional training in filmmaking, and works as a music teacher in a provincial college. He was introduced to the field of filmmaking through being an actor in Jia Zhangke's film *Unknown Pleasures* (2002), which recruited some non-professional actors. Working with a small crew filming on video, he realised that filmmaking did not require high level qualifications; therefore he bought a DV camera and started filming his close friends and family (author's interview with Hu, 2010).

Nearly all the first person films studied in this book are made by amateur techniques or with amateur aesthetics, if not all by amateur filmmakers. That is the case for many documentaries made in China that are recognised as 'independent' from mainstream political ideology. However, instead of focusing on the changing meaning of independence in Chinese documentary practice, I focus on *amateurness* as an approach and an aesthetic style. In this chapter, I first explain how I conceive the meaning of amateurness in first person documentary practice and its significance in contemporary China. Then attention is given to *Family Phobia* (2010), on Hu's practice, the film text itself and the screening of it. These together demonstrate a conflicting sense of the self of the filmmaker.

Theorising the Amateurness: an Aesthetic Choice and Ideological Positioning

Internationally, amateur cinema, facilitated by the evolution of consumer-level moving image cameras such as 16mm, 8mm, 9.5mm Super 8, video camcorders and digital video cameras, mobile cameras and Go-Pros, has increasingly become a valuable alternative site for multi-disciplinary exploration, in film studies, cultural studies, memory studies, media archaeology and broader historiography (Zimmermann 1995; Ishizuka and Zimmermann 2008; Moran 2002; Rascaroli 2009; Rascaroli *et al.* 2014; Motrescu-Mayes 2014). Theorising amateur filmmaking, Zimmermann sees amateur cinema as a plurality of practices including 'home movies, surveillance, narratives, experimental works, travelogues, documentaries, industrials, hobbies, sites for emergent subjectivities' (2008b: 275). For Zimmermann, the major difference between amateur and professional is whether it functions as an exchange commodity, as amateur films are produced 'outside of exchange values' (2008a: 9). Similarly, the experimental filmmaker Stan Brakhage also argues that the 'amateur' means not 'working for money, fame or power' (cited by Rascaroli 2014: 231).

The lines between amateur and professional become more and more blurry in the digital era when it is difficult to judge whether an amateur film is completely without a monetary value. Amateur videos, or user-generated moving image content, uploaded online could generate profit for social media sites through stream viewing. Amateur footage could also be used as citizen journalism providing alternative news sources. The development of digital technology makes amateur production and distribution tools more professional and professional tools more easily accessible. Pointing to a distinction between the home movie and the amateur film, Liz Czach takes 'home movie' as those unedited, with no apparent genre and produced through casual leisure with a 'point and shoot' aesthetic (2014: 30), whereas amateur films are often carefully crafted through well planned pre-production and post-production, with aesthetical ambition, can be identified as in a certain genre, and are authored (2014: 30–1).

Amateur could be recognised in many ways: (1) the personal motivations for creation, for love or passion, as the word 'amateur' first developed from the Latin meaning 'lover of'; (2) the filmmaker's background – whether the filmmaker has undertaken professional training; (3) the source of funding – whether the films go through professional fund-raising process, such as through TV commissioning or film festival markets, or through self-funding; (4) the level of professional environment and equipment support; and (5) how the maker identifies his or herself, that is, one's self identification as an amateur or a professional.

The amateur aspect of the first person documentaries studied here could fit into one or more of these categories. However, I recognise amateurness first as an *aesthetic* choice, personal and subversive, often incorporating impulsive 'point and shoot' material and even deliberate technical inadequacy. Such aesthetic choices reflect the filmmakers' ideological self-positioning – a personal view on everyday life and on one's self 'from below'. These films are produced with amateur aesthetics, sometimes because of financial and technological limitations, and sometimes as a deliberate aesthetic choice, to demonstrate the very personal – *geren* – angle on the social reality and one's self.

In the previous chapter, three female filmmakers' works present apparent technical inefficiency, which gives a sense of urgency in their provocative action of family investigation. In this chapter, Hu Xinyu's *Family Phobia* is constructed through a 'point and shoot' style with his own family. In the next chapter, the banker-turned-filmmaker Shu Haolun intercuts re-enacted home-movie 'look' personal memories in *Nostalgia* (2006) and Yang Pingdao travels in southern China with a small domestic-use DV camera hanging around his neck, searching for his *(My) Family Tree* (2008). The amateurness becomes more explicit as a subversive visual style, either deliberate or 'default' given the filmmakers background: Xue Jianqiang is a second generation migrant worker and a self-trained amateur, the peasant filmmaker in the 'China Villagers Documentary Project' (2005–9) praised for being a 'peasant auteur'.

The amateurness as an aesthetic choice and ideological position in these films is grounded within the social cultural contexts and technical conditions in the late 1990s and early 2000s, as discussed in the Introduction. For filmmakers, amateur filmmaking after the 2000s can be seen as a form of individual empowerment. The popularity of consumer DV cameras signifies the change of representational power from the hands of experienced professionals to those of individuals. It enables the makers to get closer to their subjects and their own subjectivities in a less hierarchal sense, as usually the amateur filmmaker is also one of 'them', the documented. While the professional camera '*da jiqi*' used by the state media represents the social 'reality' from an official perspective, the DV camera as '*xiao jiqi*' (small machine, 小机器) provides a view from a personal lens of grassroots everyday life.

In one of my evening conversations with Wu Wenguang during my summer visit to Caochangdi in 2010, Wu emphasised that filming with *xiao jiqi* was like 'writing with a pen', taking reference from Astruc's *caméra-stylo* (1948); Wu saw the DV camera as *xiao jiqi* allowing individuals to work with more flexibility and reflexivity (author's interview with Wu, 2010). Throughout the years I have had periodical conversations and exchanges with Wu on the concepts of first person documentary, essay film and subjective cinema. In the Chinese publication of Laura Rascaroli's *Personal Camera: Subjective Cinema and the Essay Film*, I translate what anglophone and European filmmakers and scholars regard as 'essay film' as '*sanwen dianying*' (散文电影) in Chinese. Reflecting on 'essay film', Wu uses 'image-writing' – *yingxiang xiezuo* (影像写作) – to describe his more recent practice, such as in the making of *Treatment* (2010) and *Investigating the Father* (2016). Wu compares filmmakers to writers, emphasising the personal mode of writing – on one's own – and for him, this should also be available in filmmaking. What Wu regards as 'image-writing', in my understanding, is a personal mode of reflexive essayistic creation through moving image.

The aesthetic style and ideological positioning of amateurness in this practice allows filmmakers personal expression and self-discovery, and it also allows socio-political intervention. Jia Zhangke advocates amateur filmmaking as carrying a spirit of democracy, believing that 'access to cinema is conceived of as a human right – that is, a privilege that should be universal' (Jaffee 2006: 83). This echoes the debates among scholars of amateur cinema studies (Odin 2008), who believe amateur film gives 'voice to the politically, ethnically, and socially excluded, revive the productive capacities swallowed up by globalization and consumerism, and restore creativity and freedom' (Odin 2008: 266). Nevertheless, even though amateurness carries more freedom, making a film does not necessarily mean anyone will watch it. The channels of distribution are not democratic even if access to equipment is.

In her insightful study on amateur DV documentary filmmaking in post 1990s China, Yiman Wang values the closeness of the DV camera to the material reality that offers a 'truth-value' so brutal that it challenges conventional documentary ethics, but also could 'burn' and 'wound' the filmmakers who document it (2005). Whereas Wang sees amateur documentarians' self-defined authorial status not as activist but simply as a *witness* with limited knowledge and little power to change reality, I argue that amateur filmmakers are not just witness but active participants and decision-makers in their own construction of 'cinematic truth'. Wang fails to see the filmmakers' choice-making and negotiation with themselves during the filming and editing. Even if it is just to show the cruel reality to challenge documentary ethics, the very decision of inclusion is an active and conscious one. First person documentary practice, which turns the camera on the self, manifests the active choice more explicitly, given the very nature of representing or even performing the self.

Lastly, the amateurness in first person documentary practice provides valuable sources of micro-history to understanding changing conceptions of the individual self. Cuevas believes that documentaries of 'little people' in their everyday life provide valuable details that enable us to understand history differently, to see from a different scale and to study new types of historical knowledge, to study 'history from below' (Cuevas 2014: 140). It also allows us to re-evaluate the national cinema culture. Whereas Zimmermann regards amateur filmmaking as a counterweight to the history of dominant mainstream cinemas, including highly commercialised and government-controlled cinemas (2008a), Liz Czach (2002, 2014) argues that amateur films should also be valued as 'an important part of a country's visual heritage' (2014: 27). In recent years, Chinese official media and official documentary film festivals have frequently used Chilean documentary filmmaker Patricio Guzmán's statement 'a nation without documentary is like a family without an album' to emphasise the value of documentary as cultural heritage.[1] Often neglected in the official media discourse, personal documentaries should also be seen as a crucial and indispensable volume of China's 'family album'. This is especially true at a time when state-approved documentaries are still largely conforming to state ideology and mainstream historiography. The amateurness in this practice provides a micro-view of contemporary China via a private lens. These filmmakers look at everyday life 'as it is happening', keeping evidence of the personal lives of individuals who would be forced into silence by official historiography in the future. First person documentary becomes a valuable site for micro-history construction, to understand contemporary China and Chinese individuals through a 'view from below', from the self, on the self, a site where the reconfigurations of the meaning of individual self are constantly at play.

Family Phobia : a Dual Self in between the Insider and the Outsider

Family Phobia (*Jiating Kongju*, 2010) presents a micro-history of China's economic rise through the changes in the filmmaker's three-generation family in a small city, from 2003 to 2010. It is the third personal documentary by Hu Xinyu, after *The Men* (2003) and *My Sister* (2008). All his films present his private or domestic space in extreme close-up, which has created intensive ethical debates. *The Men* (2003) documents his own private life with some bachelor friends, including their open criticism of women – which made some female audiences leave the screening when it was shown at Yunfest in 2005. In *My Sister* (2008), Hu follows his third elder sister to America where she lives with her white husband in a house in a typical middle-class suburban residential area.

As 'an inwards gaze at home', Hu's personal digital-camera eye quietly and closely observes the everyday life of his big family. His camera does not shy away from intimate and often embarrassing moments. The film is full of family quarrels and dramas, in which Hu himself inevitably gets caught. It is argued that in the traditional family structure, containing strong hierarchical traits and where the father figure is usually the camera man and the origin of the gaze, home movies usually document the holidays and happy moments (Odin 2014: 19), whereas 'in the new family structure where hierarchical constraints have weakened, the family is now presented "as it is"; of course with happy moments, but now also with all its moments of pettiness and all its instances of rivalry and conflict, which are inevitably a part of every group dynamic' (ibid.). Hu Xinyu documents from the perspective of the youngest son, brother and uncle. As an insider of the family, Hu captures the lives of his relatives with great intimacy. His camera acts as a fly *in* his family spaces, travelling free and documenting everything he wants without facing rejection (see Figure 2.1). However, Hu's vision on his own family is not the pure insider's 'look', but the inward gaze of a relatively autonomous individual who plays other

Figure 2.1 Hu's family eating together in a small flat

social roles in the society; thus, he plays a dual role in filming his own family. In *Family Phobia*, Hu often distances himself from his family's lives, consciously examining them as an outsider. His camera offers valuable insights on how family structures and relations have been affected by China's rapid socioeconomic transition, and on individuals' desires to be reconnected to the traditional institution of family.

The family space in *Family Phobia* that Hu observes has not changed through the years. It is the external spatial changes and the changes of individuals' values that make the unchangeable familial space seem inappropriate. The familial space Hu so intensively films is a sixty square-metre flat belonging to his eighty-year-old parents. It is located in a former socialist state-subsidised apartment building area, *jiashu yuan* (family dependents courtyard, 家属院), where the staff members of state-owned work units used to live, before the modern apartments of commercial real estate took over the cityscape. The hall and stairways in the former socialist apartment buildings are presented as being very dark and dirty, with cheap advertisements messily pasted on the walls, a mark of the decline of socialist collectivism. Hu's personal amateur camera travels around the public spaces in the family dependents courtyard; the handheld aesthetics, with his voice sometimes speaking from behind the camera to his family members walking beside him, offers an immersive feeling of how it is like living there.

Decollectivisation has greatly encouraged the social mobility of individuals and liberated them from the previous social institutions, such as state-subsidised work units, which have been gradually transformed into more private enterprises. This has been accompanied by the gradual privatisation of China's housing market since the late 1990s (Fong 2006: 28). The film shows the cityscape full of demolition of the old and the construction of new commercial and residential space. When Hu's elder brother comes back home, Hu follows him to revisit the old residential areas and public places they used to pass by every day in their childhood; they find that many of these places have been knocked down. In a long shot, Hu's brother stands in the streets, looking around but finding nothing familiar. However, not all the socialist state-subsidised apartment buildings have been destroyed. Hu's parents have been living in their small flat for a long time and this family space has not changed during Hu's seven years of filming (see Figure 2.2). Hu observes the generational conflicts in this domestic space that is closely identified with the former socialist period and the transition from a planned to a market economy.

During the Chinese New Year period, when Hu films most intensively, the small flat is full of family members from three generations, twelve people in total. Spring Festival is precisely the kind of time when family photographs and home movies are supposed to capture happy moments, like those I mentioned

Figure 2.2 The apartment building where Hu's parents' flat is located in *Family Phobia* (2009)

in the beginning of this chapter. Yet, in this instance, the amateur aesthetic and approach take us deeper and closer into a world we would not ordinarily see – the world behind the pretence of posed photographs. In Hu's film, the small flat does not offer much space; the second and third generation family members, growing up in a changing society, have different views on individuals, family and nation. The old socialist familial space seems to be inappropriate for the family members, who are themselves changing in a transforming society.

Zimmermann states that 'amateur films map the private sphere from the point of view of the participants, collapsing the borders between subject and object' (2008b: 278). Hu is both the documenter and the documented at the same time, the 'seer' (the origin of the camera gaze) and the 'seen' (the 'body image' of the film) (Russell 1999: 277). Most of the time, the camera 'eye' and the 'I' quietly observe the family, almost from a third person perspective. The camera eye either stays in a corner, observing what happens through a long shot, or moves around following the characters through point-of-view shots. It magnifies Hu's 'outsider' identity, who consciously documents the triviality of family lives from extreme proximity. In some scenes, the closeness to the blood and bones offered by the amateur aesthetic of Hu's first person documentary make the audience uncomfortable to view such private details of his family.

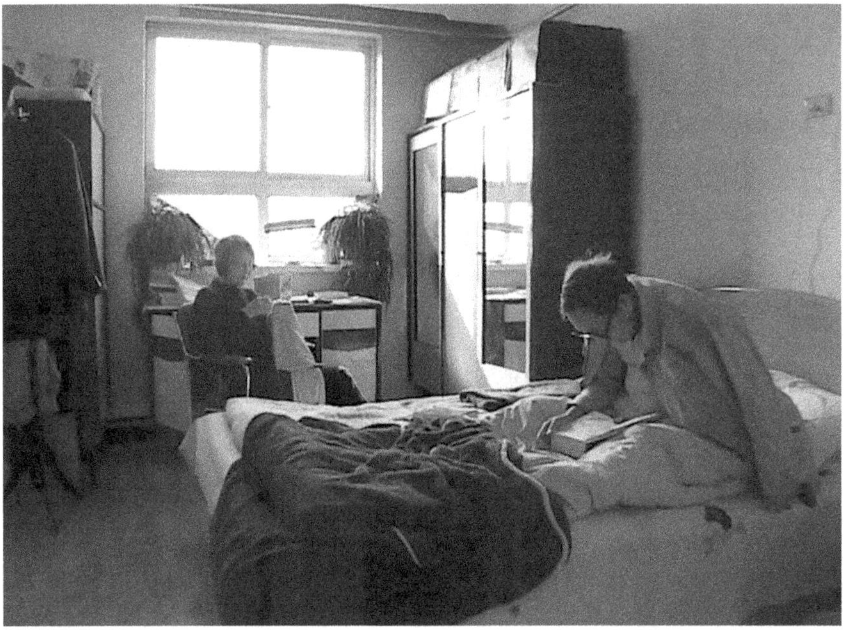

Figure 2.3 Hu's mother and father in their bedroom

At this moment, amateurism connects to voyeurism, putting the audience in a position of spying on someone's family.

After an opening sequence with the sound of a morning radio programme, the film starts with a long shot in the bedroom, presenting Hu's father standing by the bed in the middle of the frame. He tries to wake up his grandson, who is still sleeping though it is already eight o'clock. It is followed by a sequence observing Hu's old parents' daily lives in the small flat (see Figure 2.3), such as a long shot of the father sitting on a stool while the mother is cutting his hair, and close-ups of the mother administering eye-drops to the father who is lying on the bed. In the first half of the film, before Hu's brother returns home from the USA, most shots are filmed in the interior familial space or the residential area where the flat is located.

However, it is precisely his identity as an 'insider', the youngest son in the family, which gives him the proximity to film some very intimate and emotional moments without any hint of rejection or intentional performance. His family members do not really care about being filmed, though they do not really know why Hu films them. In a sequence when Hu follows his father across the street, his father shouts at him: 'Watch the cars! What's the use in recording this!' (see Figure 2.4) The family members take playing with DV as Hu's hobby – a 'useless' hobby that cannot get him more money or a wife (author's interview with Hu, 2010), the two things the family cares most about Hu having.

Figure 2.4 Hu's father asks what Hu is doing with the camera

The conflicts of the dual self captured by Hu indicate the tension between traditional familial obligations and individual self-realisation of the younger generations, reflecting the changing mentality behind China's fast individualising society. Hu's family obligation for the parents is to get married and give birth to the next generation. Hu's situation of being nearly forty years old but still without a proper girlfriend to marry is constantly pointed out by his mother, who seems to be very worried. In a couple of scenes, Hu's mother speaks to Hu who is behind the camera about her worry about him being single. Once, the mother speaks to him in front of the camera, 'This year you must solve your personal problem of marriage, otherwise mama is under too much pressure.' In another scene, the mother stands directly facing the camera, telling Hu her ideal image of a good wife for him. Hu deliberately walks from behind the camera to enter the frame, standing side by side with his mother. His mother does not notice his deliberate gesture of exposing himself on camera, so she still tries to 'educate' him about what kind of wife he should get, and Hu presents himself as a speechless child being educated by his parent. Near the end of the film, Hu's 'personal issue' is raised again. Two of Hu's sisters mention that it really worries the old parents and Hu should think seriously about it. Only the third sister from American supports him in not getting married for marriage's sake.

When the self is seen through a camera eye, exposed to the audience from the view of a third person, the public self of the filmmaker is also quietly observing his own 'familial' self trapped in the family obligation of giving birth to the next generation. Throughout the film, Hu does not reveal his personal opinion on his own 'personal issues' – in fact on most family issues. His quietness suggests his unimportance in the family as an individual in his own right, though ironically, his marriage is important to the family as a collective whole.

Phobia of the Family: Documenting the Intimate, the Forbidden and the Unpleasant

One striking feature that differentiates *Family Phobia* from many other amateur home movies is the brutal exposure of family conflicts and dramas. The idealised projections, such as smiling faces and joyful moments, wedding ceremonies and birthdays, tend to dominate home-movie-based filmstrips. For example, home-movie footage collected by the Hungarian filmmaker Péter Forgács in *The Maelstrom* (1997) portray the cheerful moments of the Netherlander Jewish family during the Second World War before they were sent to Auschwitz. In Michelle Citron's *Daughter Rite* (1980), stereotyped home-movie fragments of the happy moments between mother and daughter are contrasted with the first person voice-over narration, revealing inner feelings of the emotional distance between the two. Rarely are home movies like Andrew Jarecki's *Capturing the Friedmans* (2003), in which family disputes were recorded solely for private viewing, given public airing.

The title of Hu's work, *Family Phobia*, immediately suggests the filmmaker's anxieties and ambivalence around ideas of family and home. Hu's consciousness of being a filmmaker creates a sense of distance between him and his own family. Gazing inward at his own familial space, Hu captures the generational clash and private disputes which are closely identified with the former socialist period and the consequences of the transition from a planned to a market economy. Such private documentation contributes a valuable micro-history to understand the still largely patriarchal structure and problems of a typical multigenerational Chinese family.

The conflicts revealed by Hu's personal camera are not rare occurrences, but reflect an important feature of interpersonal relationships in contemporary China: the coexistence of different generations with distinctive ideologies and ethical values, formed by varying and sometimes contradictory socio-political structures that emerged at different periods in twentieth-century China. This phenomenon has made interpersonal communication difficult. Hu observes these conflicts as they occur in front of his camera, without giving much judgement, but sometimes he himself is unavoidably caught up in them.

In *Family Phobia*, the eldest generation, the 'grandparents', are Hu's parents; the second-generation family members are Hu and his brother and sisters, born between the late 1950s and early 1970s; and the youngest generation is represented by Hu's nephew and niece, born in the late 1980s and 1990s. The conflicts centre on daily family lives, from *yi* (衣), *shi* (食), *zhu* (住) and *xing* (行) (clothing, food, accommodation and transport), education, career, and marriage, through to international relations. These concerns reflect contrasting perceptions of an individual's freedom, and family and nation as collectives, also mirroring the larger changes in social structures in China of this period.

It is not difficult to notice that, as the eldest generation, the retired grandfather – Hu's father – is seen as the authority figure in the family, intervening in nearly every family issue (see Figure 2.5). He firmly holds the family together as a collective whole, insisting that one should study and modernise oneself in order to make a contribution to the state. His voice is the first one heard in the film – when he stands by the bed asking his grandson to wake up and recite English. His voice is also the one heard most throughout the film; in contrast, we hardly hear the youngest generation speak, despite many of the conflicts being

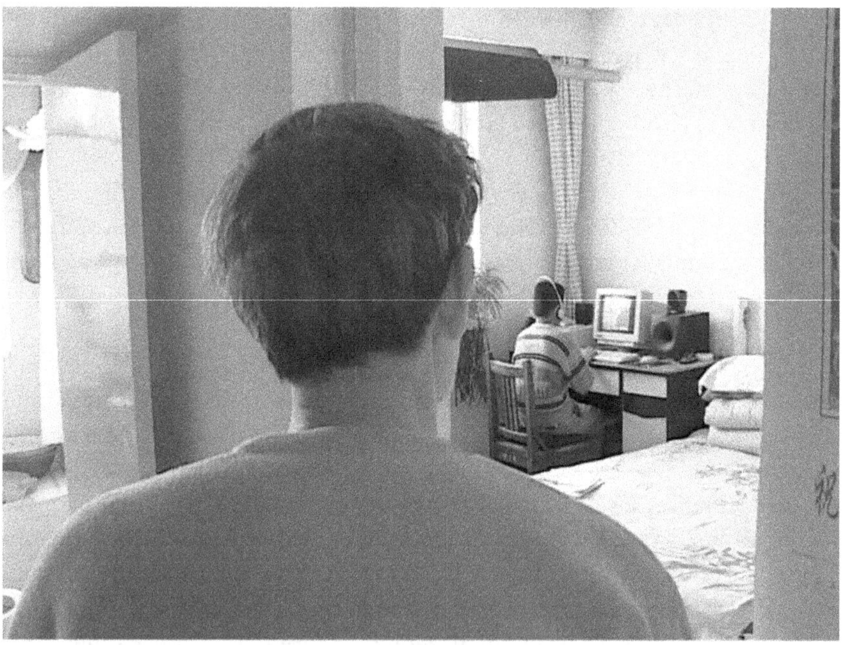

Figure 2.5 The grandfather tells his grandson Chaochao not to play computer games any more

provoked by their 'improper' behaviour or resistance to orders. This youngest generation lives in a time when China's economy has started to grow and they have experienced a much richer material life, when the general ideology has moved from socialist collectivism to individualism, the so-called hedonism of a market economy.

As the 'man of the house', the father also interferes in the lives of the second generation. Arguments usually take place at the dining table, presented in long shots framed by the camera in a corner. At these moments, Hu also presents himself as 'seen', sitting with the family. Just like other sequences, the family members have their discussions as if the camera were not there. Such conversations are not just about personal issues but also about their conflicting beliefs in the nation. In one dining-table scene to welcome Hu's third sister back from the United States to visit the family, the father is in the middle while the children are sitting around him. As the conversation unfolds, Hu's third sister shouts loudly that Tibet should be an independent state. The father seems very angry and insists that Tibet is historically part of China. Whereas the politics surrounding Tibet are a very sensitive topic of debate in public spaces in China, there is more freedom to discuss such a flashpoint in private familial space. Within a family, different views on this issue are usually held by different generations, as revealed in Hu's personal camera. In this scene, Hu's sister insists in her opinion, yelling in front of her father that her parents have been totally brainwashed by the Communist Party. Having lived outside this familial space and formed her own family with an American husband in the United States, Hu's third sister does not follow the traditional codes of behaviour of an obedient daughter and openly challenges her father. Displaying this family debate on camera, Hu makes no personal judgement of his father's socialist ideology or his sister's beliefs in Western democracy.

However, this conflict leads to a larger fight between father and daughter that results in the father's refusal to recognise her. At this moment, Hu also gets involved. Towards the end of the film, a long shot shows Hu and his sister sitting side by side on the sofa in the living room, the voice of the father coming from outside the frame, shouting at the sister. The fight is still going on. Hu says to his sister: 'I have chosen not to fight with them for several years, just to be keep the peace.' However, as the father continues to shout at them, Hu cannot stay quiet any longer and standing up, positioned in the centre of the frame, he rebukes his father 'You are the Mao Zedong in this family!' (see Figure 2.6). It is the first time that Hu candidly challenges the family authority. The father, however, responds from outside the frame and criticises Hu's filming: 'Today I carried 35kg of stuff and you were just filming me!' This argument depicted in *Family Phobia* opens up a larger debate about the ethical position of the filmmaker: the choices one

Figure 2.6 Hu stands up and shouts at his father outside the frame in *Family Phobia* (2009)

makes on what kind of personal life to film, and how much of it to be shown to the public. At this moment, Hu does not respond to his father's comment; instead, he chooses to stop the scene here, leaving the discussion unsolved, and giving room for the audience to judge or for himself to reflect.

The Tension between the Individual and the State

The film also presents the importance of an individual to their family, which is affected by the changing relationship between individuals and the modern state in the ongoing decollectivisation process. The lack of social protection from the state in the current era is in stark contrast to the social benefits offered by Mao's government, such as housing, insurance and job allocation. On the one hand, this has put increasing pressure on individuals, but it has also led to a strengthening of the ties between individuals and their families, on the other. As one takes from the family in terms of security, he or she is also expected to give back to the family members, especially to the elderly. Hu's personal camerawork shows that when Hu's parents are alone, the eighty-year-old couple's conversations are centred on the rising price of domestic appliances and medication. In one scene, Hu observes his father in extreme close-up talking on the phone to Hu's third sister in America. The moment he mentions healthcare, he suddenly breaks down, remembering that when he was ill in 1994 he realised that if he could not afford to pay for the hospital, the hospital would not provide any treatment: 'I was there spitting blood and they just ignored me! They only treat you when you have paid. What sort of country is this! It only serves rich people.' In these moments, Hu does not speak from behind the camera. He just stands there, observing the emotional moments and insecure feelings of his aged parents. His quietness also suggests his powerlessness to provide his old parents with a better life, and implicitly seems to confirm his father's critique that amateur filmmaking is a useless hobby that will not provide him with economic power.

Housing is another issue that reflects the changing relationship between the state and the individual. In one sequence, Hu follows his father to visit his second sister. The sister also lives in an old apartment for socialist workers. Walking into the apartment building, the camera passes by a dark corridor on the ground floor, where cheap advertisement posters are messily stuck on the dirty walls. Hu consciously asks the father from behind the camera: 'What a shabby and dirty building! Who built it?' The father, climbing up the stairs, says to him that 'They (the Housing Administration) built it for the grassroots, but they never live here themselves. They have better houses elsewhere . . . Being an official now is like doing business. They first buy a position, and then others give them money.' What the father reveals reflects the changing relationship between the individual, the civil worker and the state. While in the socialist past, the government provided apartment buildings for its socialist workers, now the buildings have been used as commodities to rent to individuals who cannot afford to buy the modern apartments developed by the real estate developers.

Towards the end of the film, Hu's niece accompanies her grandparents (Hu's parents) to visit a spacious modern apartment that they intend to buy. It seems that in the national transition, the old familial space of the small socialist flat is no longer big enough for all individuals in the family. The film does not reveal whether the family has moved to the new flat, but the long shot of the grandparents and the granddaughter walking hand-in-hand back toward the camera, indicates that the family continues as a collective.

By consciously observing his familial space, Hu documents the generational conflicts between the first generation and the second, and between both of these and the third generation, which are caused by the problematic familial relations that have become twisted with the conflicting political ideologies. It reveals how traditional family relations have largely constrained attempts by individuals in contemporary China to develop their own individualities. However, Hu's personal documentation of his own family also reveals the changing relations between the individual and the state. The amateurness of his film helps to reveal such history 'from below', bringing immediacy and an immersive approach that would not be obtained from official documentation or documentation by a professional filmmaker of someone else's family. What Hu's camera also shows is that the family as a collective institution is still the place where individuals find their selves and security, despite the conflicting and problematic family relations.

Screening Privacy to the Public: Pushing Ethical Boundaries

While in an individualising China affordable DV cameras have given rise to this new personal and family activity, amateur filmmaking is not limited to the domestic space; as noted, it is also connected to the wider independent cinema culture in China. As well as the conflicts captured on camera, Hu's own filmmaking practice also mirrors his dilemma of being between family obligations and individual (self) realisation. Filmmaking fulfils Hu's personal passion, but his conscious inward gaze at home also makes his documentaries recognisable to the independent cinema scene in China. Even though Hu did not initially have a clear idea of what kind of film he wanted to make from his personal home videos, he has to make decisions on what to include and what to cut out when he edits the film as an independent work. The negotiation of ethical issues is a prominent aspect of amateur documentary; the exhibition of amateur film on one's family problematises the border between the private and the public, and pushes the boundary of how much to present of one's private life to the audience.

In my interview with Hu (2010), he did not make it clear whether his family knows that he has shown the film at a public viewing, but admitted that

> I would not show this film to them [Hu's family], as they would think this is nothing, not an achievement at all. They would think 'you should at least ask me to dress up properly for your camera'. They think that art should be beautiful and shining. (Author's interview, but Hu, 2010)

This revealing observation makes it clear that when Hu's family members know that they are being filmed, they do not know what it is for. Constructing the film as a sample representation of a family in the transitional China, Hu has made his insider's identity as a member of his own family secondary, something to be examined by the audience and by his self as the filmmaker. Nevertheless, an inward gaze at home from amateur eyes is more than just a self-reflection. By screening it to the public, it has become a social practice of exercising one's identity as an independent filmmaker, or a public citizen, to negotiate with both family ethics and public social responsibilities.

Audiences' responses to amateur personal documentaries, as discussed in the last chapter, also reflect people's perception of individuals in public and private. Through the years, Hu has experienced a shifting attitude towards his films. His first amateur independent documentary, *The Men* (*Nanren*, 2003), observes the very intimate emotional and sexual lives of himself and two male friends, as well as their direct, frank and uncensored comments about women. When it was shown in independent film festivals in China, the film received strong criticism, especially among female audiences, for its provocative language and sexist behaviour towards women (author's interview with Hu, 2010). Hu's second film, *My Sister* (*Wode Jiejie*, 2006), observes the family life of his third sister in a typical suburban American middle-class environment. Similarly, it received criticism both from the audience and from his sister, who said she will take him to court if Hu shows it to the public. Having seen the film in a filmmaker friend's collection, it appears to me that Hu's personal camera eye is often peeping or 'zooming in', almost like a stranger breaking into his sister's private domestic space. When I spoke with other filmmakers and some members of the audience about these two films, some were very critical of Hu's overt exposure of his family members' privacy; they felt Hu trapped the audience in a very uncomfortable position.

While some criticise Hu, Wu Wenguang, who advocates personal documentaries or 'private image',[2] has been encouraging Hu to keep producing personal documentaries of his family (author's interview with Hu, 2010).[3] Since 2010, and especially between 2010 and 2012, more screenings of personal documentaries have been shown to audiences at independent film screening events in China. These include the China Villagers Documentary Project started in 2005 and the artist/dancer Li Ning's *Tape* (2009), which is similar to Hu Xinyu's *Family Phobia* in its uncovering of Li's own problematic relationship with his wife, and his dilemma of being split between family obligation as a husband/father and his pursuit of artistic expression. Wu Wenguang's *Treatment* (2010) is about Wu's personal confession and memory of his mother and, in *Investment of the Father* (2016), Wu investigates the personal trajectory of his father and his relationship with him. Such films keep challenging viewers' perception and idealised imaginings of family. They also disturb the ethical expectation that comes with documentary filmmaking. However, the increasing self-expression through mainstream media and social media has made audiences more used to the exposure of intimate private lives. In this context, Hu's *Family Phobia* did not face the same criticism as Hu's other two films. It should also be noted that Hu is quite selective about where his films are shown inside mainland China, even though he is eager to define himself as one of the earliest filmmakers making such private images. Hu's concern, however, is less about the ethics of presenting his family to the public, but more about political sensitivity, as the dining-table debates on Taiwan and Tibet could bring trouble to his family (author's interview with Hu, 2010).

In my interview with Zhang Yaxuan (2010), a Beijing-based independent film critic, she commented on the unlimited exposure of personal issues, which reflects the current imbalance in Chinese society.

> Every society needs to leave an exit point for individual personal expression. But in China, this exit has been so small for a long time. The public space has been so strong that it represses the growth of personal space. For a long time personal emotion cannot be openly expressed . . . Therefore, when there is an opportunity of expressing oneself through DV camera, things are disclosed without a limit. One cannot say it is not good, as no one can give a simple moral judgment.

Zhang's observations on the unbalanced development of the public and the private spaces and the accompanying ethics in contemporary China are certainly valid. The overt exposure of private family conflicts and prohibitions can be seen as a critical response to the mainstream and official documentation of family imaginary. However, instead of simply concluding that such amateur first person documentary filmmaking practice is ethically problematic, it could be argued that this practice opens up critical and timely debates on how one interacts with others in the private domain, as well as revealing one's privacy to the public. Yan (2009) regards social interactions among strangers, who are outside familial relations or other social groups, as new types of sociality.

> Along with the increase of mobility in social scale and geographic scope, more individuals found themselves interacting in public life with other individuals who were either unrelated or total strangers, whereby collective identity and group membership became secondary to individual identity and capacity. (Yan 2009: 284)

When a person points the camera at close family members and their self, then displays the camera-mediated personal images to a public audience, the filmmaker as an individual bears the ethical responsibility of how they communicate with the filmed subjects, as well as with the audience. In other words, first person documentary filmmaking practice that takes amateurness as an aesthetic strategy and ideological position reflects and leads us to face a new challenge in the rapidly individualising society: that is, how one interacts with other individuals as an independent individual equipped with the mediating tool of an amateur DV camera and how one perceives the power of representation when filming the self. This will be further explored in Chapters 4 and 5.

Notes

1. It has been used by the Guangzhou International Documentary Festival, and media coverage of many other documentary events.
2. I have discussed the notion of 'private image' in the Introduction.
3. Also see Hu and Wu's personal email exchanges, published in *Author Film*, Special Issue on First Person Documentary and Private Image, March 2016.

Chapter 3

Nostalgia Toward *Laojia*: Old Home as an Imagined Past

> At first glance, nostalgia is a longing for a place, but actually it is a yearning for a different time – the tie of our childhood, the slower rhythms of our dreams. In a broader sense, nostalgia is a rebellion against the modern idea of time, the time of history and progress.
>
> Svetlana Boym (2001: xv)

The decollectivisation process (Yan 2009, 2010) has encouraged social mobility in the rural population, resulting in a large amount of migration from rural areas to the south-east coastal cities for employment, especially since the late 1990s. As individuals from the countryside have been 'liberated' from the former socialist mode of collective production, it also has meant the nuclearisation of traditional big families (Yan 2009: xxiv) and the decline of familial collectivism. The notion of *laojia*, 'old home', one's birthplace or one's ancestors' home, has become more prominent psychologically, indicating a strong sense of roots and collectiveness that links all family members together. Traditionally, it constructs an individual's sense of self as part of a collective whole. The existence of *laojia* signifies the continuity of a family clan. In this chapter, I discuss two documentaries that express the filmmakers' nostalgia towards *laojia*, Yang Pingdao's *My Family Tree* (2008) and Shu Haolun's *Nostalgia* (2006). Presented through both filmmakers' personal camera eyes, *laojia* has been disrupted and reshaped by the accelerated urbanisation since the new millennium. *Laojia* has become a space associated with a certain period of time that is almost impossible to go back to.

In *My Family Tree*, Yang Pingdao revisits his hometown, a small village in Guangdong province, capturing a sense of decline in the traditional family and the rise of nuclearised small families in his own family clan. In the urban areas, demolition and reconstruction have caused the relocation of family homes for many citizens who previously enjoyed social welfare benefits, including the public housing of Mao's era. *Nostalgia* is Shu Haolun's first person memoir of his childhood and a vanishing lifestyle in Dazhongli, a '*shikumen*' (literally meaning 'stone gate', 石库门) style residential area in Shanghai. *Shikumen* is a kind of tenement building constructed in the colonial era from the 1920s to the 1940s in Shanghai, especially referring to the carved stone pillars and archways that adorn these houses. Like many other local *shikumen* areas, Dazhongli (大中里) was facing demolition under Shanghai's new urban planning scheme when the film was made in 2006. Homes of many generations of local residents would be redeveloped into commercial districts with modern bars, fashion shops or skyscrapers like the famous Shanghai '*xintiandi*' ('new heaven earth', 新天地), used by international tourists and foreign expats, as well as the domestic nouveau riche.

Both films demonstrate individuals' resistance to breaking away from *laojia*, the 'old home'. Their first person documentation signals the sense of crisis and loss, when *laojia* has been dramatically interrupted by state-initiated urbanisation. The changing economic and technological environments, most obviously the rise in digital technologies and participatory media, have opened up more spaces for individuals to express themselves in. With a personal camera in their hands, Yang and Shu are purposely recording their families as the time passes by, keeping evidence of the individual lives that are forced to be silent by the official historiography. By doing so, they are intentionally keeping a personal family historiography, inscribing themselves as central characters, in an attempt to understand how individuals' lives and their family home have changed in a rapidly transforming modern society.

For Shu Haolun, the filmmaking practice is a return to the old familial space and community, which he moved out of when he went to university in the 1990s. *Nostalgia* was shot during Shu's holiday back in China in 2005, when he was studying filmmaking in the USA. Being afraid that the old home would have disappeared next time he came back, he immediately picked up a camera and revisited Dazhongli, nostalgic about a vanishing communal lifestyle which had constructed his sense of self. For most families in the community, only the older generation (such as Shu's grandmother) were still living there, but the old house still represents the familial centre that binds the whole family together.

In the summer of 2010, I visited Shu in Shanghai in his shared studio space in a small creative arts cluster, which gathers together many small studios or creative companies. He told me that

> since the film was made, Dazhongli area has been demolished. Families in the community were forced to move out, and were relocated to several marginal places in suburban Shanghai . . . The urbanisation has a huge impact on family.

> In the Chinese tradition, no matter whether in cities or rural areas, there is a concept of '*laojia*', usually the place where the grandparents live. Dazhongli was the '*laojia*' to many families. The demolition of this area has in fact destroyed the '*laojia*' concept for the local residents. (Author's interview with Shu, 2010)

For the local residents, the demolition of old houses not only means the loss of a family centre or an old lifestyle they have lived all their lifetime, it also means the loss of benefits and the convenience of living in central Shanghai. After the demolition, many households have been relocated to the suburbs of the city, indicating a loss of privileges that the local Shanghainese used to have. Shu Haolun records the last moment before the demolition of his old family house and residential community in urban Shanghai.

For Yang Pingdao, the making of *My Family Tree* is a personal journey of going back to his home village, which he left at a young age to study and then to work. As the title *Jiapu* (*Family Tree*) suggests, it covers a *jia zu* (family clan, 家族) as a much larger collective whole, with a history of where it came from, its traditions and transformation. The film, four hours and thirty-eight minutes long, tells the history and current situation of the family in seven parts: (1) The old family house; (2) My grandpa and grandma; (3) My uncles and aunts; (4) Far away from hometown; (5) Go back for the spring festival; (6) My father's 'last-home'; and (7) My brother gets married.

Yang's personal view shows that it is not the family conflicts, as shown in Hu's film, but the physical distances between family members that indicate the structural change in the family. *Zuwu* (祖屋), the family ancestral house in the small village, is inevitably declining, representing the weakening of the family collective root. This is not because exterior forces have demolished the ancient village, but because the younger generations have been gradually migrating to industrial towns and cities, and forming their own small families. However, the extended family clan still works as an 'imagined community', to borrow Benedict Anderson's words (1983), that emotionally links all the family members together. The family has now spread out in different cities and towns inside and outside China. From the end of 2007 to the spring of 2008, Yang visits more than twenty family members of four generations living in different places. For Yang, the filmmaking practice is a process of reconnecting to 'his people' as a '*nong erdai*' (农二代, which literally means 'second generation peasant') from the 'outside', where he was just about to start a career as a filmmaker; a young migrant individual trying to survive in the massive and expanding urban net.

Not just about family communication, this style of filmmaking is also a significant social practice that provides valuable materials for understanding the changing sense of self among individuals who face a rapid transition of familial space. As an impulsive longing for the old pattern of family home. Their practice also reflects an anxiety to 're-embed' or re-inscribe the individual self back into the traditional institution of family home, turning back to the *laojia* for social security and identity construction.

'Second Generation Peasant' Revisits *Laojia* – an Imagined Community: *My Family Tree*

In *My Family Tree*, Yang presents himself as a member of a large family, yet no longer a pure insider of his village, but also a migrant who is drifting around in the cities. Like many other *nong erdai*, Yang was born in the small village in Guangzhou province and has since moved to towns and cities for schooling. First, he went to the nearby city of Yangchun for secondary schooling; then he went to the province capital for university and worked there for a few years. Later he went to the capital, Beijing, to studying filmmaking.

Nong erdai refers to young Chinese who were born in peasant families in rural China and/or whose parents also work as migrant workers in urban cities. However, though these younger generation individuals can work in the city, their *hukou* (户口, resident registration) are still bound to their hometown villages, hence, they are classed as temporary residents (*zanzhu renkou*, 暂住人口) in the cities. When I interviewed Yang Pingdao in 2010, Yang had just moved back to the small city of Yangchun near his home village, to start a small video production company. He shared with me his reflection on being a *nong erdai*. Such an identity made him feel unsettled in Beijing, which attracts millions of migrant individuals from all parts of China searching for their dreams.

The film was made during Yang's final year as a postgraduate film student in Beijing. Yang reveals that his intention was to use his extended family as an example to mirror China's urbanisation at large.

> In my life so far, I have been constantly moving, from the rural toward the urban. Living independently outside home, I have been thinking about many issues related to the rural and its urbanisation. And I also constantly think about what my big family has been going through. Some family members have migrated to Hong Kong, some even go to the States. At the time it was 2007 and 2008 and the government was paying increasing attention to rural development. I want to make a critique on it through my own family. (Author's interview with Yang, 2010)

Therefore, Yang records his family, not just to understand the relationship between himself and his family, but also the relationship between his family and the nationwide urbanisation.

My Family Tree demonstrates the nuclearisation process of family as has happened in many other societies. Yang's family members have left *zuwu*, the ancestor's house, and moved away from their home village to industrialised towns and cities. *Zuwu* is gradually losing its traditional role as the physical centre of the family's activities but still serves as an 'imagined community' that links the small nuclearised families together. Individuals still play their familial roles as a relational self in a family collective community. The filmmaker Yang himself, as a son in the family, carries the responsibility to give rise to the new generation.

Yang Pingdao takes the camera as an extension of his own eyes, presenting himself constantly shifting between public spaces and private familial spaces. His self as a young migrant individual is established in the very beginning of the film. The film starts with a few long shots of the Beijing train station at dawn, a bustling public space full of traffic and restless migrants. As the music starts, it cuts to a point-of-view shot of Yang walking up an escalator among many others (see Figure 3.1). Yang's camera captures people with emotionless faces, carrying luggage and busy going back home, or to their next destination. Yang's first person narration appears as subtitles: 'My brother just has a daughter born in the mid-night, but neither my mother, brother, nor myself is at home. And the father was died eight years ago [sic].'[1] While the moving image presents a public space

Figure 3.1 The point-of-view shot of Yang walking among other individual strangers in *My Family Tree* (2008)

full of strangers travelling around, the subtitle speaks of the very personal and private familial issues of the filmmaker, the birth of a new family member. This is similar to Chantal Akerman's *News From Home* (1976), in which Akerman, reading her mother's personal letters to her, is played over the images of public spaces in 1970s New York. The two elements, the moving image and the subtitles in *My Family Tree*, split Yang into two selves: one self is connected to the transforming Chinese urban landscape that is increasingly occupied by migrants, the other is connected to the home, where Yang comes from and is going to.

Then it cuts to Yang's point-of-view shot through the window of the train: moving landscape, mountains and rivers, the industrial towns and remote villages. The train takes Yang back to his village where his family *zuwu* is located. The next scene, a shot slowly panning from top to bottom, presents piles of ancestors' monuments on a table (see Figure 3.2). The title *Jiapu* (*My Family Tree*, 家谱) appears. The monuments fade into an old family portrait, in which rows of family members stand together facing the camera. In the photo, Yang is a young boy standing among them.

The first part of the film 'The old family house' starts. The black screen fades into a couple of long shots of a newly constructed highway, reaching the small village. An off-screen voice of an old man tells the family history in local Hakka dialect. Then it cuts to the old man, Yang's grandfather, sitting in the living room of an old house talking to Yang from behind the camera. He is giving an oral history of how their ancestor arrived more than three hundred years ago from northern China, to develop this place and establish this village for their family.

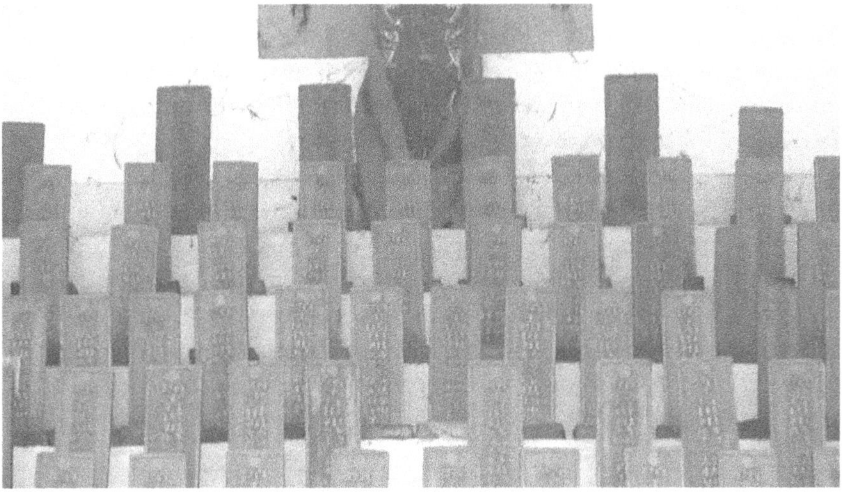

Figure 3.2 The shot of ancestors' monuments is followed by a family portrait

Yang's family is regarded as Hakka or, in Mandarin, '*kejia*' (客家), which literally means 'guest families'. It refers to Han Chinese who moved from the north or central China to southern China. It also means Chinese people who migrated overseas, such as to Southeast Asia or other countries, in different stages of history. For generations, Yang's extended family has been living closely in this village as an agricultural family. During the socialist period, the *hukou* house registration system forced the rural population to stay in the countryside. Since the economic reforms, the state has loosened its control over the rural population and Yang's family has been experiencing a rural to urban migration. Since his father's generation, many family members have moved out to towns and cities seeking work. Yang Pingdao himself left at a young age. This has seriously changed the previous family structure.

Like Hu Xinyu, who I discussed in the last chapter, Yang is playing a dual role as a family documenter and an independent filmmaker. Rather than just playing the 'fly on the wall' within his family space, Yang consciously uses his personal camera to interview family members and record the oral history. He puts the camera at the level of his chest, so the grandfather can have eye contact with Yang behind the camera, rather than talking and performing to the camera. Yang, as a younger generation member of the family, is receiving knowledge of the family ancestors from the elder, so the history of the family clan can be passed on.

As observed by Yang's camera, family traditions are fading away in this transition, especially through the decline of *zuwu*, the family ancestor's house, where his grandparents still live in the film. The domestic space of the ancestral house is dark and quiet, with a few pieces of old furniture. While interviewing his grandfather, Yang pans his camera to observe the old house in its current condition – large cracks in the damp walls, a long stick holding up the thatched roof, the incense burners, the farming tools, the ruins of collapsed walls. Traditional firewood is still used for cooking. The TV next to the grandfather seems to be the only link to the outside world. While the grandfather is telling the family history, the TV is switched on, showing the news, commercials and TV dramas, bringing a sense of contemporaneity into this space.

Yang's family's *zuwu* is presented as the core of his family, which is often mentioned in his conversations with other family members (see Figure 3.3). The old people are concerned that if their old house becomes too dilapidated it could collapse one day, and then the traditions would get lost. In the older generation's view, a good condition of the ancestral house means the prosperity and continuity of the family as a collective whole. They regard it as the origin of a family; one should always remember it and come back to it.

In one scene, an old man, Yang grandfather's brother, is lying on a shabby bed covered by an old mosquito net. The room is very dark; we hear the old man talking in a very low voice to Yang, asking him if his old house will collapse, as

Figure 3.3 Yang's grandmother standing in the living room

it always leaks when it rains. 'It needs to be repaired,' mutters the old man. In another scene, the camera pans around the village, observing the small muddy village road and houses; it captures an old lady holding a big umbrella. She tells Yang, slowly and quietly in the local dialect, that her old house leaks when it rains. In part two, Yang has a long conversation with his grandmother, who is also lying on the bed covered with a mosquito net. The camera observes his grandmother, nattering quietly and recalling every family member. She says that one should come back to the old house when one is dying.

Yang's camera travels around in the domestic space of the villagers. The old houses in the village all seem very dark and in a state of decline. The public spaces of the village in Yang's eyes are almost empty. While the traditional houses still occupy the scenery, they are no longer fully occupied by villagers. As Yang's camera shows, only old people, young children and women are in the village, reflecting a typical 'left behind elder' and 'left behind children' phenomenon that has raised much public and governmental attention in recent years. Several family members mention that their children have gone to the cities for work. Yang's father died some years ago and his mother has remarried again in Hong Kong. In the village, Yang captures a few women villagers passing by, greeting Yang in their local dialect, 'Pingdao, you are still taking pictures?' They are not sure whether Yang is taking photos or filming, but are happy to see him coming back from the outside and injecting some liveliness into the sleeping village.

Before Yang leaves the village, a long shot shows the old houses standing quietly in the rain in the distance. The subtitles come up again,

Figure 3.4 The old house

> My grandfather told me that a lot of people come back to build their old house when they've earned enough money in the city. He told me to rebuild the old house when I have enough money. He said, even if nobody goes back to live there, it's still our ancestor's place, it shouldn't be so ragged. (See Figure 3.4)

Like many younger generation Chinese, Yang says he does not totally believe the traditional family customs, but he still pays respect to them, as they are part of his roots (author's interview with Yang, 2010).

While urbanisation has brought social mobility to rural populations, it also has the inevitable cost of a decline of the traditional family space and its central role in life. In contrast to todays' China which, under Xi's leadership, has sought to re-emphasise 'traditional' Chinese values and festivals, when I met Yang in 2010 there was a feeling of decline in the importance of tradition among the public.

In the film, after visiting his home village, Yang is on the road again. His personal camera is travelling and drifting around in public spaces in order to visit his family members who have moved to other places. Taking buses, trains and boats, Yang travels to different parts of China, from neighbouring towns to nearby cities in Guangdong province. Yang stops by to visit family members then is on the road again, to Hong Kong and Chongqing in southwest China. The public spaces observed through Yang's camera are full of moving migrants. The sounds of traffic, construction sites and street pop music fill up the restless public spaces, where endless economic development is taking place. On the trip following his brother's wife to Chongqing, Yang's handheld camera captures close-ups of migrant porters or labourers waiting for customers, moving cruisers on the

Figure 3.5 The migrant individuals captured by Yang's personal camera in *My Family Tree* (2008)

Yangtze River, Chinese flags on the sails, and bridges. He also captures a middle-aged man, an entertainer, singing loudly with a microphone on the street at night. In another city, Shaoguan, when he visits his brother, Yang observes migrant workers sitting on the floor individually or in groups, waiting to be picked up for work (see Figure 3.5). The lack of human voices indicates the lack of inter-personal communication.

These public spaces are presented in high contrast to Yang's familial spaces, which are usually filled with endless conversations, children crying or family eating together. Though Yang's film shows that his 'old home' is declining, it still plays a crucial role in constructing Yang's sense of self as a 'second generation peasant'. For young migrant workers, 'the high mobility, unpredictable employment and emphasis on individual choice among young migrant workers have not done away with the family as a unit of life meanings' (Hansan and Pang, quoted by Yan 2010: 20). Yang's journey shows how small families are spreading out into the vast expanding urban net, as separate growing cells, with individuals developing their own families. But the extended family with a network of relatives and blood connections becomes, to borrow Benedict Anderson's term, an 'imagined community'. While Anderson originally used this term to describe the modern nation, family, unlike national values, is not 'imagined',[2] but passed on generation by generation, as discussed in the Introduction. However, the life of a migrant can perhaps make it feel that way.

Born in rural China and growing up in urban cities, Yang neither breaks away from his familial self as a rural person, nor does he try to rebel against tradition.

As depicted in the opening sequence, when Yang walks in the restless public space of a train station, it is the family news from far away that gives him a sense of belonging and brings him back home. Though the extended family is not physically present as a strong prosperous community any more, it still emotionally links the family members together. Going back to his old home and visiting relatives' small families, with a camera in his hands, becomes a practice of drawing the boundary of his 'imagined community'. Touching the limit of the private and the public, he knits the widely spread small nuclear families together. This is not done to exclude others from his family, but to circle them together as an island, to build a handle for them to catch onto in the flood of individuals.

The continuity of the family is one of the most important messages delivered through this film. Though Yang himself is not married yet, the film starts with the birth of a new family member, his brother's child, and ends with Yang doing traditional worship to his dead father, followed by the marriage of his brother (his brother has a baby first then gets married). It signifies the rearrangement and continuity of the family, as one member dies and a new member arrives, and the family tree continues to grow.

Like Hu Xinyu, Yang as a son is also burdened with the task of fathering the new generation to continue the familial clan. During Yang's journey visiting relatives' families, several family members ask Yang whether he has a girlfriend. In the ten-minute conversation with Yang's grandma, the old lady tells Yang what kind of girl he should take as wife. 'You don't want to get married, then I might not be able to see the grandchild, but if only I can see you having a wife, I will be happy . . . Please note, an ordinary looking girl would be good . . .' When Yang visits his mother, who is taking care of his brother's child in the city of Yangchun near the village, the mother also worries about Yang's marriage and asks him just to find a normal girl. They do not require outstanding characteristics in the woman, nor do they care if Yang can find his true love, as long as she can give birth to the Yang family and keep the family harmonious, still a gendered expectation of women.

In my interview with him, Yang reveals that though he has been living outside the family home on his own for a while, not many family members seem to care about his personal achievements: 'Usually I bring back money to the elderly when I come to visit. They normally just ask me how much I can earn. They do not really care what I am doing, as long as I can make a living and bring wealth back to the family' (author's interview with Yang, 2010). It seems, for family members, it is still how one can contribute to the family as a whole that matters, rather than individual achievement.

As a filmmaker, Yang uses his first person experience to illustrate his family responsibilities to the audience, the demands he receives to get married and have children. While the sense of self and individual desire has changed along with the dramatic social transformation, traditional family values still act to enforce a collective sense onto individuals. Yang's revisit to his *laojia* through the camera confronts such matters for the viewer – matters and conflicts that resonate with many living in contemporary China.

Visiting the Unvisitable, Touching the Untouchable: *Nostalgia*

While *My Family Tree* illustrates the transition of the filmmaker's family structures as a result of urbanisation on a national scale, in *Nostalgia* state-enforced demolition has a very prominent and radical impact on the filmmaker Shu Haolun's old house and community.

The film begins with Shu's voice-over, with English subtitles written in the middle of the frame, speaking that 'My grandmother called me one day saying that our old house in Dazhongli would be demolished soon'.[3] While Shu speaks, the camera shows news articles from a local newspaper, then it fades into a long shot overlooking the *shikumen* area – a large block of old houses. Shu continues to speak: 'Although demolishment [sic] in my city Shanghai is very common, I cannot feel common anymore at that moment, because our old house is in Dazhongli. It hits home, our old house.' The camera gradually tilts up, revealing that the old community is now surrounded by modern skyscrapers (see Figure 3.6). He continues

Figure 3.6 The old houses are shown surrounded by skyscrapers in *Nostalgia* (2006)

speaking: 'Now what I could do is that I take my camera to Dazhongli, which hasn't became [sic] skyscraper yet. I want to "write" my nostalgia through lens.' Then the title *Xiangchou* (*Nostalgia*, 乡愁) appears on screen.

This opening sequence establishes the film with a very personal and critical tone. Shu starts from the position of an individual coming from the outside, revisiting his old family house and the neighbouring community. The urgency of the demolition that is about to hit his own home compels him to take a camera and start filming. The government project to turn this residential area in central Shanghai into a modern commercial area, with huge economic profits, impacts Shu's individual interests and his family's interests. This destruction also indicates the loss of a communal lifestyle, as facilitated by the *shikumen* style of residence. Mostly built in the first half of the twentieth century in wartime Shanghai, *shikumen* are blocks of two- or three-floor houses connected together, with rooms within a house usually owned separately by individual families. The hallways and staircases are shared public spaces for cooking, hanging washing and collective gathering, creating a unique community. In the current neo-liberal society, such a communal lifestyle is largely missing. In this sense, Shu's nostalgia is not just for the physical form of the old house itself, but also the communal lifestyle and community relations in socialist China. The word 'nostalgia' originally comes from the Greek '*nostos*' ('return home') and '*algos*' ('pain'), together meaning 'homesickness'. 'Home' in this sense, is not just a place, but a past era. As Boym suggests, nostalgia is not only a longing for a space but also for a time (2001).

The first person filmmaker Shu is inscribed as multi-layered, constructed through two cameras. One camera is held by a professional cameraman, what I regard here as 'the third person camera', capturing Shu as the *seen*, who engages closely with local residents or talks directly to the camera as a presenter. The other camera is held by Shu himself, 'the first person camera', presenting his own personal observations of his people in the community. The two cameras depict Shu as an insider within his family, as well as a part of the collective community of Dazhongli. Usually the third person camera describes Shu's interaction and reactions while, through Shu's first person camera, his grandmother and neighbours talk directly to him. Shu's identity as someone who grew up there makes the local residents less sensitive to his camera, as he is part of 'them'. Shu also talks from behind the camera to his own community in Shanghai dialect. When he reflexively comments from his position as someone going *back* to there, and when he talks to the third person camera, he speaks the official Chinese Mandarin. These are the moments when Shu's identity as an 'outsider' is felt more strongly.

After the opening sequence, the film cuts to a medium shot of an old lady (later found to be Shu's grandmother) holding a piece of paper. Shu's voice

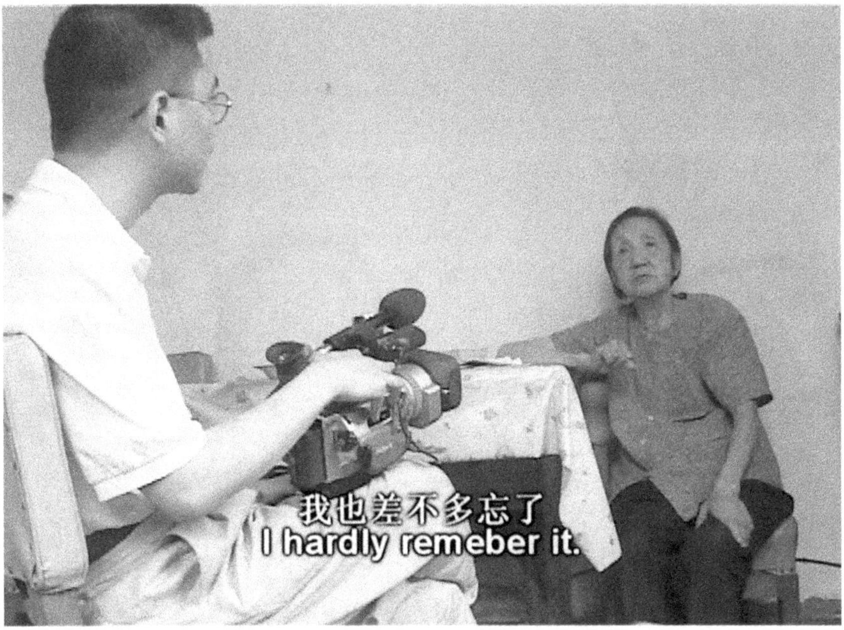

Figure 3.7 Shu interviewing his grandmother in *Nostalgia* (2006)

speaking Shanghai dialect comes from behind the camera, chatting with the old lady. Then it cuts to a long shot taken from the third person camera, presenting Shu holding a camera facing the old lady, and saying that 'I finish (adjusting white balance)'. Then it cuts to Shu chatting to his grandmother at the table with a camera in his hands (see Figure 3.7). Shu's voice-over appears, stating how his grandparents first arrived in Shanghai and settled down in this old house in the 1930s. His conversation with his grandmother also reveals that Shu was born in this old house and experienced his childhood and adolescence in this open community.

During their conversation, the film presents some old family photos of the grandparents in the 1930s, and a childhood photo of Shu and his brother standing in the local public hallway. The photo is dissolved into a shot of the hallway in the present. Through Shu's first person camera eye, we see neighbouring families living very close to each other, sharing communal spaces and participating in group activities. A montage of the life in *shikumen* shows the neighbours preparing food, hanging their laundry in the public hallway and playing mahjong together (see Figure 3.8).

Like Hu Xinyu and Yang Pingdao, Shu's first person self is never introduced as an isolated individual, but is always in relation to others – family members,

Figure 3.8 Shu's grandmother playing mahjong with the neighbours in *Nostalgia* (2006)

friends and neighbours. The third person camera captures Shu wandering around in the open hallways of the *shikumen* with acquaintances passing by and greeting him. Shu also tells stories to the third person camera of his family and neighbours. At these moments, Shu's self is no longer a pure insider, but a mediator, connecting the local to the audience, the outside world.

It is interesting to note that the characters in the film are not introduced by name, but through their positions in the neighbourhood, as how they remember each other. When Shu chats with neighbours about the past, they casually mention Shu's familial stories, as if everyone's life in Dazhongli is intertwined with each other. In one scene, the third person camera captures Shu walking into a house of a neighbouring family, greeting an old lady sitting at the window eating lunch. Then it cuts to Shu's first person close-up view of the old lady facing the camera. While Shu's voice in the film is chatting with the old lady in the Shanghai dialect, his voice-over gradually emerges, introducing this old lady to the audience: 'this is our neighbour, grandma of Yu's family, who is such a good cook that I often came to eat here when I was small, following the smell of food'. In return, this old lady tells to Shu's camera her memory of Shu's father and aunts when they were very young (see Figure 3.9).

Figure 3.9 Shu's old neighbour, the lady grandma Yu, in *Nostalgia* (2006)

Through these conversations about their common memories and experiences, the film presents the audience with a circle, a network of relations. The first person 'I' does not only stand for the singular 'I', but also speaks as a representative of this circle, who tells the story of 'us', the collective of selves living in this area. Lebow claims that first person expression always belongs to 'the first person plural', as 'every autobiography engages the embodied knowledge, memory, history, and identity of much larger entities than the self' (Lebow 2008: xv). In this film, Shu's individual self is aligned with the larger collective identity, 'the first person plural' of the neighbourhood, constructed through the *shikumen* architectural space and sharing many common life experiences and memories.

In representing the first person plural of the local community, Shu shows a strong nostalgia for a disappearing Shanghai lifestyle, especially under socialist collectivism. To connect with the past, he reconstructs some black-and-white enacted scenes, and has a boy play his childhood and a teenager play his adolescence. In one scene, the young Shu goes to school with his neighbours, passing the local breakfast shop. Then Shu's voice-over introduces this breakfast shop, which he went to almost every day when he was a child, a type of breakfast shop common in *shikumen* areas in Shanghai in the 1970s and 1980s. He also uses some archival footage showing how people used to queue up in the morning, buying breakfast for their family with '*liang piao*' ('grain ration coupons', 粮票), a special food currency distributed in Mao's era.

The film evinces nostalgia for a period when the sense of 'we' rather than 'I' was felt more strongly, when the communal collective interest rather than personal interest was given more attention. Shu states that 'people who have lived through the 1980s in China have all experienced the collective and communal lifestyle. Therefore, people often have the dream to change the world, feeling that everyone has the obligation to help others, to change the reality' (Shu, interviewed in Xu 2008). In one sequence, Shu walks to the old neighbourhood committee house. He tells the third person camera that this used to be the local residential office which maintained the public order of the neighbourhood and organised community activities in Mao's time. Shu also reveals that in the 1980s, when TV sets were still very expensive and not every family could afford to buy one, people in the neighbourhood used to gather here and watch TV together in the public hallway. In fact, this is an experience shared by many Chinese in both urban and rural areas in the 1980s, when China had just begun its period of economic reform.

Showing nostalgia for the socialist past, the film also inserts some old TV programmes of the 1980s. One is a children's choir singing, 'We are so happy'.[4] Even though the song could be regarded as a piece of socialist propaganda, it also shows something that has largely disappeared in the current society – the collective notion of 'we', 'us', 'our'. Another enacted scene is a school memory. After a scene in the classroom where pupils are reading a Chinese text on Lei Feng, a socialist hero who submitted himself to the collective, the school bell rings. It then cuts to a long shot of the school yard, where a school staff member is sweeping the floor while a loud-speaker is saying 'Our education policy must enable everyone who receives an education to develop morally, intellectually and physically, to become a worker with socialist consciousness and culture'. This slogan reflects an idealised individual identity that was pursued by people under Mao's socialist China. Then the film cuts to how the schoolyard looks nowadays. However, he finds out that the primary school has disappeared and the high school has now turned into the office of a real-estate developer. As Shu's voice-over says later in the film 'this area would soon turn into a picturesque postcard, visited by the foreign tourists'. Shu's experience is commonly shared by many living in contemporary China: while memories of the past are still vivid in people's mind, the physical places that have constructed their life experiences are nevertheless disappearing.

Shu's first person filmmaking expresses a strong nostalgia toward home and a vanishing lifestyle, which constructed his own self, but has become an imagined past. It could also be seen as an important political comment of a public citizen who openly makes a personal critique of the changing ideology and the worship of materialism. Throughout the film, Shu's reflective voice-over presents him as a rights-conscious individual with strong social responsibility. Having experienced a childhood with a socialist education, and witnessing the increasing commercialisation of the market economy, Shu cannot stay quiet. He narrates his childhood memories, comments on issues that occurred during his revisit, and also expresses his critical view of the highly commercialised public space and neo-liberal culture in the beginning of twenty-first-century China, or 'the pervasive worship of modernization and profit-seeking' (Berry and Rofel 2010b: 140).

Towards the end of the film, clips have been inserted from a Shanghai promotional video made by the famous filmmaker Zhang Yimou for the bid of World Expo 2010. The video depicts a modern, fashionable Shanghai as a flourishing metropolitan city in East Asia. His voice-over comments over the image: 'Do people truly worship these skyscrapers? I doubt it. Do the times really drive everyone to chase so-called fashion, pursue the so-called modern, and love the neon lights at night? I don't believe it.'

The experiences of Shu's family and community are caused by the irresistible forces of the state and market transforming the individual's life. Shu's disappointment also reflects the lack of social protection for individuals, as discussed by Yan Yunxiang (2009: 280). And in the case of Shu's family, this is not just a loss of social welfare like in Hu Xinyu's family, but a loss of their old familial space and neighbourhood, and the convenience of living in central Shanghai. Shu comments in an interview:

> Zhang Yimou spent eight million RMB (approximately £800,000) to make this commercial but I think it is very stupid. It shows people waving their arms in front of the Oriental Pearl – from the worship of leader in the past to the worship of capital, money in contemporary China . . . (Shu, interviewed in Xu 2008)

The tension between the brutal demolition enacted by governmental and commercial powers and the existence of individuals' familial space has been expressed by many others through different means. Some have also used a camera to demonstrate their position. For example, in *Meishi Street* (2007), the directors Cao Fei and Ou Ning invite the subject, a local Beijing resident Zhang Jinli, to film his own resistance to the demolition that hits his home. The substantial first person footage he filmed is used in the documentary. Zhang's public side as a rights-conscious individual stands out eminently, to fight for the interests of himself and his family. In the next chapter, I will discuss in more detail the public self in first person documentary practice in contemporary China.

Conclusion

Observing how family traditions face decline as members move out to the urban areas, Yang Pingdao's film demonstrates that family has regained its importance as an imagined community within which individuals find security and a sense of belonging. Shu Haolun invokes the nostalgia for a family lifestyle constructed by the *shikumen* communal residential places, as well as the period of socialist collectivism. He also explicitly criticises the inhuman demolition and widespread materialism. Both filmmakers are in between their family and the public spaces. In the next three chapters, I will explore how individuals construct their selves in public spaces on camera, and the accompanying ethics of encountering.

Unlike Hu's *Family Phobia*, which has not had much public exposure, both *Nostalgia* and *My Family Tree* have been screened several times domestically and received positive responses in different ways. Even though Shu explicitly expresses his critique of the governmental project of demolition and the mainstream worship of capital, the film has not been banned by officials. On the contrary, it has been well received not only by foreign media, but also by state-sponsored domestic media. The domestic media mainly focus on how the film captures the details of local people's lives in indigenous *shikumen* architectural buildings.[5]

In my interview with Yang, he told me that the film had been entered in the competition at Yunfest in 2009. Four judges from mainland China thought very highly of the film; the fifth judge from Taiwan said such personal films about one's family were very common in Taiwan, and though the film horizontally documents the current lives of a large number of family members in different places, it does not have a vertical observation across a long time period (author's interview with Yang, 2010). Nevertheless, the film received the 'Special Jury Prize' at Yunfest and overall has been well received in local independent film communities. However, because of its length (more than three hours) it has not been shown much to wider audiences (ibid.).

Since his visit to his extended family in *My Family Tree*, Yang has got married, formed his own small family and has a baby daughter. Since then, he has made another first person film, *The River of Life* (2012), merging documentary with fiction, and in which Yang performs himself with his newly wed wife and their new-born baby in front of the camera. Structured around the death of Yang's grandmother, Yang's own small nuclear family presents their personal life for the audience, mostly from the bedroom. Just like *My Family Tree*, *The River of Life* also has an amateurish look, due to the roughness of the image and loosely structured editing. The obvious performance of the filmmaker self suggests a conscious response to the idea of autobiographic film and family drama. However, the use of first person here becomes a deliberate choice, reflecting a narcissistic self-obsession with wanting to be a film auteur, desperate to establish a kind of directorial style, rather than the spontaneous self-driven documentary practice of the earlier film, *My Family Tree.*

Notes

1. The English translation is from subtitles of the film.
2. Yan Yunxiang also mentions family as 'imagined community' in the Introduction to *iChina* (2010: 20).
3. The English translation of the dialogue in *Nostalgia* is from the subtitles.
4. When I invited the director Shu to show this film at a campus film festival at UNNC, a few students sang along to this song, as it evokes nostalgia among the wider audience.
5. For example, a local Shanghai TV channel (*dongfang weishi*, 东方卫视, or Dragon TV) praises the film for its detailed description of local Shanghai lives in *shikumen*.

Chapter 4

First Person Action Documentary Practice: Longing for a More Politicised Space

> 'In the beginning was the camera.' I try to forcibly generate action with the camera. I try to wrench it into existence. With deliberate force.
>
> Hara Kazuo (2009: 7)

Outside of the domestic space and family relations, I am eager to see how individuals stand alone, in their own space or in the public spaces. In a transitioning society that destabilises conventional social and ethical norms, how do individuals interact with others: strangers, friends, colleagues, fellows, the older and the younger, women and men, in multiple public spaces? In my second fieldtrip to China in spring and summer 2010, I did notice an increasing number of young individuals using cameras to approach others, and to document their own fragmented and almost suffocating personal lives in their own private spaces.

Wu Haohao and Xue Jianqiang are two young filmmakers that stand out from the crowd, making some noise in the independent film community. Whereas all the first person films analysed here carry a certain level of reflexivity and performativity, and emphasise authorship through the use of voice-over, direct physical appearance on camera, or through an amateur home video aesthetic, Wu Haohao and Xue Jianqiang put their role as 'author-performer' more explicitly in their films. Influenced by the practice of the Japanese filmmaker Hara Kazuo, both filmmakers term their practice as 'action documentary'. Apart from the conventional documentary action of recording the reality, the action taken by this form of performative first person documentary foregrounds provoking, interacting and interrogating, and places these interrogations at the centre of the films. Their practices are the outcome of their almost indulgent self-exploration in the individualising China, and their consequent active reaching out from their personal space, crying for communication and recognition. Recognised as being very different from previous independent filmmakers in China, the two have provoked intense debates among local critics, filmmakers and scholars. Through their 'action documentary' practice, they express a strong desire for a community, a more public space where they can find emotional resonation, social acceptance and societal engagement in the beginning of their adulthood.

This chapter first theorises on so-called 'action documentary cinema', then it explores in detail Wu Haohao's *Kun1: Action* (2008) and Xue Jianqiang's *Martian Syndrome* (2010), in which the two filmmakers turn their personal camera inwards to film their individual spaces and the absence of community in the individualising cityscape. Improvisations, roughness, long takes of unpredicted accidents dominate Wu's and Xue's action documentary cinema. Both films exude a feeling of loss in China's neo-liberal period, a time when younger generation individuals have experienced much more freedom and autonomy to develop their own lives in the increasingly commercialised and globalised environment. What accompany this, however, are a loss of social protection and an emotional sense of security and belonging. In their films, young individuals are presented as degenerate and decadent, such as the hysterical young migrant artists in Xue's *Martian Syndrome* and the dissolute university students in Wu's *Kun 1: Action*, lacking understanding and connection to society. There is little description of public spaces in their films, but extensive focus on the inner feelings of the filmmakers and other subjects. Their language tends to be fragmented and incoherent, just like the visual language of the films, jumbled and non-linear. Through their filmmaking practice, Wu and Xue are desperate to reach out, giving a hammer-blow to society with their personal camera.

The following chapter continues the discussion of first person action documentary and examines the ethics of encountering in the practice of these two filmmakers. In *Criticizing China* (2008), the then university student Wu explicitly puts himself as the 'performer' and disturbs a public debating corner where old people gather and talk about politics. In *I Beat the Tiger When I Was Young* (2010), the former migrant-worker Xue uses his camera to provoke the hierarchy of the independent filmmaker community. Whereas both filmmakers boldly address their own political subjectivity with a strong desire to break the conventional institutional and ideological forces that have constrained them, their films also illustrate new but problematic ways of how individuals interact with each other in *minjian* grassroots public spaces, and also the changing relationship between individuals and the state. I argue that their action documentary practice should also be seen as an experiment investigating the changing sense of self in a society that has been undergoing dramatic social and ethical reconfiguration.

Theorising Action Documentary Practice

Motivation: alienation, provocation

Born in regional areas, Wu Haohao and Xue Jianqiang have gone to larger cities such as Chongqing and Beijing to develop their own lives. Since the economic transition to the neo-liberal model, the retreat of the state from public life has left young individuals to develop their own biographies and careers – though since 2012, the Xi leadership has witnessed the growing interference of the state in public life again, especially in cultural and political life. The young individuals have gained more freedom but have also lost the lifelines that had been available for previous generations, such as the *danwei* (the work unit), a lifelong work place in the cities that also offered social benefits, like housing and medical care. In the highly marketised and commercialised public space, individuals find no one to rely on but their own selves.

Both Wu Haohao (born 1986) and Xue Jianqiang (born 1984) belong to the so-called 'post-80s generation', a popular social label which refers to the cohort who were born in the 1980s and which grew up during the economic reforms. They are also part of the emerging 'iGeneration' of filmmakers, who's concerns are more about individuals' personal lives in the individualising China, and often practice with Internet media. Both filmmakers revealed that they do not have a close relationship with their family, and were also very rebellious when in the education system (author's interviews with Wu and Xue, 2010). Xue skipped classes at school and finally left at the age of fifteen. He then started working in different places as a young migrant labourer, waiter, assistant hairdresser, and so on. Wu was sent to a remote village for high school by his parents during his late teens, then he went to university in a southwest city, Chongqing. Though Wu eventually finished university, he attended few classes, spent most of the time on his own and lived off campus (author's interviews, 2010).

Both filmmakers are influenced by the Japanese filmmaker Hara, who also terms his practice as 'action documentary'. Hara's documentary method is highly aggressive, forcibly generating action through the camera, to see the 'embarrassing things' that people want to hide and intentionally breaking down the institutionalised ideologies that cause people to feel embarrassment (Hara 2009: 7). By doing so, he expresses a strong eagerness for social change in the environment he inhabits. As Hara states, 'In the sixties and seventies, there was a feeling that if the individual did not cause change, nothing would change. At the time, I wanted to make a movie, and I was wondering how I could make a statement for change' (Hara, quoted by Nornes 2003: 147).

Similarly, these two young filmmakers are keen to reach out of their personal space, eager to communicate with their subjects or even to provoke their subjects to get their responses. When I interviewed Wu Haohao in a university campus in Beijing, he told me that 'we are so poor, but not in terms of materials – though we are not rich either. We are poor because we desperately need communication and emotional care' (author's interview with Wu, 2010). They not only document their provocation but also their critical reflections on their filmmaking. Wu told me that during his university years he had watched nearly all Hara's documentaries. He is heavily influenced by Hara, stating 'Hara's films are full of lethal [sic.]. I was energised by him and wanted to do something similar. Filmmaker's like Hara also includes Michael Moore' (author's interview, 2010). Even though Wu mentioned that he was not aware of Hara's term 'action documentary', he also labels his practice as '*xingdong dianying*' (行动电影), which literally means 'action cinema'. He sees action as a reaction to repression, as a symbol and a statement.

The titles of many of Wu Haohao's films start with the verb 'criticising' and connect this with a noun, such as *Criticizing China*, *Criticizing University*; others explicitly have the word 'action' in the title, such as the series *Kun x: Action*. He takes the name 'Kun', the girl he first fell in love with in adolescence, to represent a primitive passion. For Wu, 'action' means direct confrontation with current social constraints and conventions through interacting with his subjects. His approach is to actively engage with others, in order to get direct interaction with people. As he explains:

> I do not have the money or resources to travel around to make films like some other filmmakers. Even my camera was borrowed from others. I know some interesting people through friends or on the Internet. I introduce myself to them as a filmmaker, who would like to film them . . . In some way, the camera is a medium for me to get to know about other people and interact with them. (Author's interview, 2010)

Inspired by Wu Haohao, Xue Jianqiang also labels his filmmaking practice as 'action filmmaking'[1] and regards it as a communication tool. With no institutional training in filmmaking, the amateur filmmaker Xue approaches the camera playfully and sees documentary as no longer holding an aura of mystery that constructs the truth (author's interview with Xue, 2010). Xue states that 'the older generation (of Chinese documentary filmmakers) is too serious about documentary. They worship documentary for its privileged relationship with reality. But for me, everyone can make a documentary, as everyone can access the camera. It is just a daily practice' (ibid). He sees his filmmaking as a haphazard activity in real life, neither staged nor prepared. The small camera in his hands simply records unplanned interactions with people in his daily life, and brings the audience into his world – the independent film community – where most of his daily activities take place.

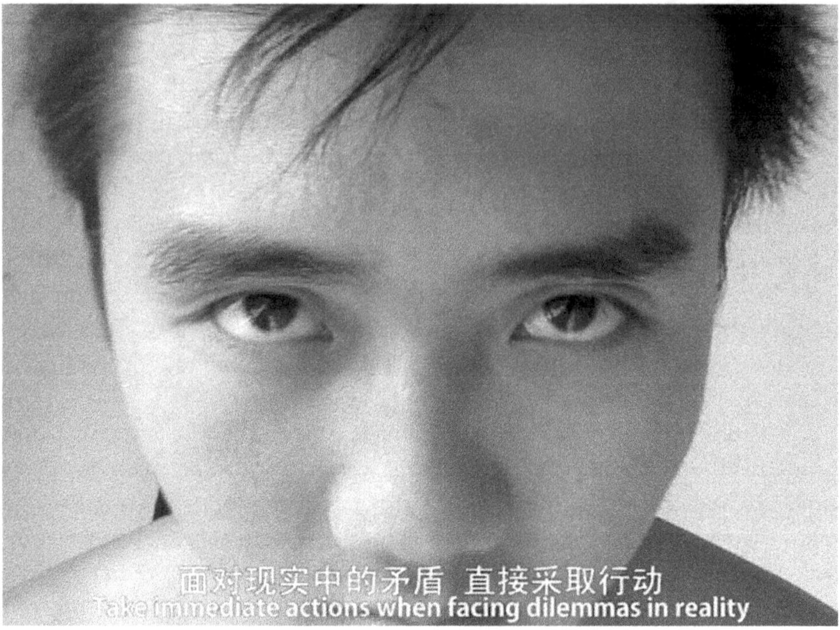

Figure 4.1 Wu Haohao staring at the camera in close-up in *Kun 1: Action*

These two filmmakers not only document their provocation but also offer their critical reflections on their filming practice in the film, as what Stella Bruzzi called part of 'a film's ongoing dialectical analysis' (2013: 50). As Stella Bruzzi states: 'What author-performer-based documentaries reiterate are the twin notions that a documentary is its own document and that the interventionist documentary film-maker is a fluid entity defined and redefined by every context in which he or she appears' (2013: 50). Wu's agenda is explicitly expressed in his films. In *Kun 1: Action*, Wu Haohao states straightforwardly to the camera: 'Take immediate action when facing dilemmas in reality. Film should only record those actions' (see Figure 4.1). Similarly, *Criticizing China* opens with an extreme close-up of Wu's face, as he stares at the camera and his first person narration sharply states:

> I need to intervene into people's lives any day [sic]. In fact, I am nervous of going into the crowd, to communicate, to fight with people, and record it. This personality of mine is cultivated in the environment that I've grown up, and those lousy Chinese people in this environment [sic]. But I am eager to do so, I need to rescue, and express my love. This is my struggle.

This statement shows that his main aim is to provoke people, to join their discussion and to disrupt an established social order and the ideologies that cultivate people's mindset.

Such action is also highly political, grounded in the context of depoliticised public spaces in China. Both filmmakers criticise previous Chinese independent filmmakers, who were highly influenced by 'Direct Cinema', for not directly engaging with society.[2] Instead, they eagerly interact with society, and do not like the fact that it is the older generation who control the world. They are rebellious young men who are not happy with the standard institutionalised society practice of competing to go to good schools, good universities, then get a good job and live the normal life. Wu Haohao believes that is not the only way of living and he is eager to do something different (author's interview, 2010). With a personal DV camera, they are eager to experiment, to adventure, to reach out of their lonely space, to break conventional social and ethical norms so as to better understand the self.

Action and aesthetics: doubly in the present

Unlike filmmakers discussed in previous chapters, who use the camera to investigate unspoken family histories or to revisit an 'untouchable' past, Wu Haohao and Xue Jianqiang actively use the camera to document their lives as they are happening 'now', as well as the 'now' of filming, the process of their filmmaking action. The action of collecting the unpredicted daily material as it is happening, as an ongoing practice, can be seen as what David E. James regards 'film diary', 'the practice of filming regularly, of producing footage of one's life' (James, quoted by Rascaroli 2009: 128). Wu's *Kun 1: Action* is an accumulation of fragmented video diaries of Wu's life during his four-year university period; *Criticizing China* documents Wu's interaction with his subjects over a couple of days. Xue constantly holds his camera, documenting his deliberate or unpredicted interactions in everyday life.

Comparing diary with autobiography in her book *The Personal Camera*, Rascaroli emphasises the contemporaneity of the diary format, stating that 'Diary obeys at least two rules: it must say "I" and it must say "now"' (Rascaroli 2009: 119).

> Composed at a short distance from the events, diaries produce an effect of immediacy . . . Such immediacy distinguishes the temporality of the diary from that of other autobiographical writing: while the autobiographer, in an attempt to dominate time, imposes a teleological design on contingency and inscribes a profound meaning onto disconnected events (a meaning that

> often resembles a narrative of predestination), the diarist adapts and surrenders to the unpredictable and variable rhythm imposed by the everyday. (2009: 119–20)

The 'now' in action documentary practice or film diary is doubly in the present: the present in filming and the present in editing. Laura Rascaroli also identifies editing and post-production as important stages that 'make a diary out of a set of audiovisual "notes"' (2009: 130). She argues that 'the filmic diary is twice in the present: it offers both the "now" of the recorded images, and the "now" of the reflection and commentary on them' (2009: 119).

Wu Haohao's films reflect this double present. Not only does he present fragments of his daily life as visual diary, he also presents the 'now' of the editing, the second stage of action, when he reflexively looks back at himself during the filming process. In both *Kun 1: Action* and *Criticizing China*, Wu presents himself in the action of interacting with people, and the action of editing and reflexive thinking. Commenting on the making of *Criticizing China,* Wu revealed that he had been observing the local public debates for a couple of weeks. He then decided to film them, thinking this was a very good phenomenon that reflected public speech in *minjian* spaces (author's interview, 2010).

In Xue's films, the filmmaker Xue as a central subject is always on the move, holding a small amateur DV camera in his hand, recording his interaction with others at extremely close range. Xue uses long takes that document whole events or conversations without cuts. The images he records are usually very shaky and are not well composed. In both of his films analysed in this book, he presents some random life sequences in the beginning and the end of the films, without much link to his main action. This roughness of the images and the randomness of the opening and ending sequences not only give his films a strong amateurish look, but also indicate that he is in the 'middle' of his activities, while filming is just to record this. As the filmmaker Guo Xizhi comments on him in *I Beat the Tiger When I Was Young*, Xue uses the camera almost like a microphone, rather than as a moving image recorder.

The concept of action documentary is not just limited to the practice of Wu Haohao and Xue Jianqiang. Ai Weiwei's documentaries, which will be examined in Chapter 6, are also regarded by some as 'action documentaries' (author's interview with Wu Wenguang, 2010). Ai dedicates himself to the action of investigating legal and political issues, and the activity of filmmaking is part of his political activism to challenge the dominant institutions. Ai Weiwei regards the self in itself as a medium that is only produced through the action of self-expression. I will discuss more of Ai's practice in Chapter 6.

For self-understanding

While the 'I' is produced through action and self-expression, action documentary in return helps to understand the self. For Hara, his filmmaking practice comes out of an eagerness to find his self.

> There is something unknown with in me that leads me to unfamiliar places, and perhaps I'm afraid of that. But I do have a very strong desire to find out what that is, and when I make a documentary film, I'm not doing it for social justice, or to organise the masses, or to expound some theme, or anything except to discover that question mark within me. Therefore, although I use my camera to shoot my subjects, I'm also carrying the camera toward the inside of myself, and going further and deeper within. (Hara, quoted by Nornes 2009: xiv)

Similarly, Wu's and Xue's action is also a way for them to reflexively look at their own selves. Action documentary filmmaking became an important part of Wu's life journey, especially when he was in transition from adolescence to adulthood. Wu reveals that during his university period he read many Western political philosophers and watched much world cinema, from which he developed his own ideas of filmmaking as action (author's interview with Wu, 2010).

> In China most people want a similar life: going to good school, good university, then finding a good job and living their whole life like that. What I do may seem a bit adventurous. Sometimes I choose to attack people first and then see their reaction. I want to give them a chance to think about things differently. I am eager to communicate with people. When I am communicating with others, I am also giving myself a chance to know more. (Author's interview, 2010)

In Wu Haohao's films, he exhibits himself explicitly, not shy in showing his naked body and sexual intercourse. Xue also insists that documentary film should function for self-understanding, as he constantly mentions in *I Beat the Tiger When I Was Young*. In the film, Xue not only reveals the whole process of his 'attack', but also people's response to him on camera. This is coherent to his agenda that documentary should function for self-healing and self-criticism. Around 2009 and 2010, there were increasing debates in China's independent filmmaker community on how filmmakers should position themselves in relation to their subjects and the audience.[3] Xue revealed that he did not agree with the current observational style that dominated the majority of Chinese independent new documentaries (author's interview, 2010). As a newcomer, Xue believes that filmmaking is ultimately for self-understanding. In the following part, I will illustrate first person action documentary practice in greater detail through examining Wu Haohao's *Kun 1: Action* and Xue Jianqiang's *Martian Syndrome*.

Performing the Self, Taking Action and Longing for a Sense of Community in *Kun 1: Action*

Kun 1: Action does not have a linear narrative. It is constructed through fragments of Wu's long-term video diaries or filmic 'body writing', a term originally used to describe women's individualised writing that takes one's own body as 'the innermost, deepest and most intimate parts of life for exploration and reflection'. The film consists of six parts, which cover different stages of Wu's life during his university period in Chongqing, titled: 'University Lives', 'Dream of China', 'Action Film', 'Love', 'Long Live Chairman Mao' and 'New Communist Party'. The first three parts focus on his university life in dormitories and classroom, and demonstrate his ideas about filmmaking. The later three parts show his actual practice of what he regards as 'action documentary', his interactions and conversations with friends outside university, and his political action or performance.

Kun 1: Action starts with the action of editing, as Wu's voice-over emerges from the background music, stating his location: 'Song Zhuang district, a suburb of Beijing'. Five different shots describe this place: the village street, a house yard and a room. People familiar with independent film and art in China would know that Song Zhuang is a grassroots community for independent artists. Then the camera enters the room, a long shot showing that Wu is sitting in front of a computer. It is followed by a medium close-up of Wu staring at the computer, while his voice-over continues: 'action: editing the movie'. The title appears on the black screen: 'Kun 1: Action'.

In the first half of *Kun 1: Action*, Wu presents his physical body and his isolated personal space in a highly narcissistic and almost self-indulgent manner. After the opening, the film starts with Part One, University Lives, presenting fragments of his university period in the city of Chongqing, southwest China. Wu presents three years of his university life through three shots, in which we see his naked upper body or a fully naked body. Wu gradually exposes his body more explicitly in his university dormitory, looking at the camera or displaying his body for the camera. Over the image, Wu's voice-over criticises himself and the environment he is living in: 'Year one, year two, year three. Masturbation all over my body. The world and myself. Weak will, looked down by myself.' He does not like to speak in a full sentence, but fragmented words. The nude dominates the scenery and sets up a solitary feeling that permeates the overall tone of the film. He shows himself taking a shower, singing the international song, presenting himself as a passive, daydreaming, degenerate youth. In my interview with him, Wu reveals that when he was taking such video diaries he did not have a particular purpose (author's interview, 2010). These materials are his experiments, evidence of how he gradually forms his worldview, and also how he forms the idea of 'action documentary'.

The body as a material form of self has been intensively shown on camera. Yet Wu obsessively filming his own body is not just a 'private event' that is limited to himself.[4] Exhibited through his personal camera, Wu's private space has become a public site where the self has become a 'public self' performing to the imagined audience, what Berry regards as the 'electronic elsewhere' (2010). Wu uses his body to indicate a relation of self to the world. His obsession with revealing his naked body in a narcissistic way reflects the limitation of his actions in the physical world. In several shots, he presents himself half-naked standing on the balcony (see Figure 4.2). The space in which Wu is situated, as later revealed through his personal camera, is a standard four-person university dorm in a typical '*sushe lou*' (宿舍楼), dormitory building. The camera pans to the left, revealing that what surrounds this building are similar concrete blocks of buildings intensively erected, filling up the cityscape and breaking the grey sky into pieces. Small balconies and windows are like little drawers inserted into the buildings. Wu is imprisoned in one of these 'drawers', while his voice-over states that the city is like 'a morbid congregational zone'.

Wu presents the cityscape as full of concrete buildings and emotionless people, staring at his camera. After a series of shots of people in public spaces, it cuts to a shot of him sitting at a desk in front of the camera, writing, then gazing into the viewfinder, then looking straight into the camera – where, by extension, he is looking at us, the audience. The voice-over states: 'when you look at yourself, you will understand yourself and this world'. Wu's self is separated through his role as the gazer, and being gazed at. Such a dual role is further complicated by a temporal distance. While the 'I' in the filming is gazing at the self narcissistically through the camera lens, the 'I' in the editing stage also looks back at the self in the past. Wu's self fills up the film in a suffocating way:

Figure 4.2 Wu stands in the small balcony of his university dormitory looking outside in *Kun 1: Action* (2008)

his body occupies his room, his camera lens and his personal computer screen, while his voice-over keeps commenting on his self. Such concentration on one's own body forges an isolation that enhances the solitude. It also demonstrates his eagerness to break the isolation and to reach the outside world when his voice-over comments that 'through examining the world, I know myself better'. Through gazing, being gazed at, and re-viewing in the editing process, Wu tries to deconstruct himself and to understand himself and his relationship with his surroundings.

Wu's first person voice-over constantly reminds us of the existence of another time, the stage of editing. In the section 'Dream of China', he presents himself imitating a shot of Fay Wong in Wang Kaiwei's *Chongking Express* – he shoots himself half-naked sitting in front of the computer, singing the song *California* and day dreaming. It then cuts to the same shot on a computer screen, then back to him singing and wondering in his rented room. His voice-over states: 'California and Chongqing, China and USA, China's California, USA's Chongqing. The world becomes a nation. There is no limitation. Communism's ideal.'

While editing offers him a space to look at himself again, the computer also connects to the virtual space through which he can communicate with others. Such a space has no spatial limitation, which is in high contrast to the isolated physical reality in which he exists. Again, his face and naked shoulder are shown in close-up, facing the camera. His voice-over states: 'Time is shown in every passing moment. In this passing moment, we think, meditate, self-criticize and act.'

In analysing individualised women's writings, Wedell-Wedellsborg argues that

> We may also interpret the seclusion of the protagonist as a longing for a different kind of community from that available to her, and her subsequent breakdown as that of a self without embedding it in some sort of collective . . . What is left is the imagined community to which the text repeatedly – implicitly as well as explicitly – refers: that of writing. (Wedell-Wedellsborg 2010: 176–7)

Similarly, Wu's seclusion can also be seen as a longing for a more 'politicised' community in which he can reach out and have direct interaction with others. Wu revealed to me that after year one, he did not attend class anymore. No one in the university shared interests with him, so he did not like to hang out with anyone from there. He lived outside campus on his own and only returned to take exams so to get a degree, which was what his parents cared about (author's interview with Wu, 2010). Living on his own, Wu expresses a strong loneliness and also a desire to communicate with others, but not those who follow a conventional life route. While the practice of writing happens in one's own space, the act of filmmaking does not limit one to one's own space. Filmmaking is a practice that enables the maker to approach and interact with other individuals. After obsessively looking at the self, Wu takes his camera outside his personal space, to interact with others.

His desire for action is a reaction to his limitations – a desire to break through the boundaries. A long take shows Wu walking in a long dark corridor of a university dormitory, back and forth, paying homage to the last scene in Jean Rouch and Edgar Morin's classic *cinéma-vérité* production, *Chronicle of a Summer*. While Wu is walking, his voice-over continues: 'only actions are able to break through those boundaries. Now our lives have been so decadent. An acting force and its counterforce interact with each other perfectly.' This scene transits Wu's personal space to the outside world. It is also a scene where he explicitly demonstrates his agenda of action filmmaking.

In the second half of the film, Wu presents himself as a young avant-garde filmmaker and experiments with various ways of communicating with others, looking for what life, dreams and love mean to them. Taking the role of a psychiatrist, Wu asks his subjects to confess to his camera, speaking out about their emotion, pain and confusion, about love, life and sex. Wu's camera acts as a window through which the subjects disclose themselves. For example, in a ten-minute-long sequence, a university girl confesses her love story to Wu's camera in an extreme close-up shot. Collecting individual confessions mostly in the subjects' own individual spaces, the film reflects a desire for communication among a larger group of young individuals. While Wu asks others to confess their private inner feelings to his camera, his voice-over constantly comments on these people. He also enacts some performances to demonstrate his agenda, and asks the characters he engages with to perform in front of his camera. For example, he presents a man enacting the gesture of holding a camera (see Figure 4.3), like a mirror of Wu himself filming others. Breaking from conventional observational style, his performative authorship is also demonstrated from the use of archival materials and various film techniques, such as slow motion, repetition or fast forwards.

Wu's filmic body writing is not just limited to filming his own body, but also the bodies of others, and his sexual intercourse with them. In the section

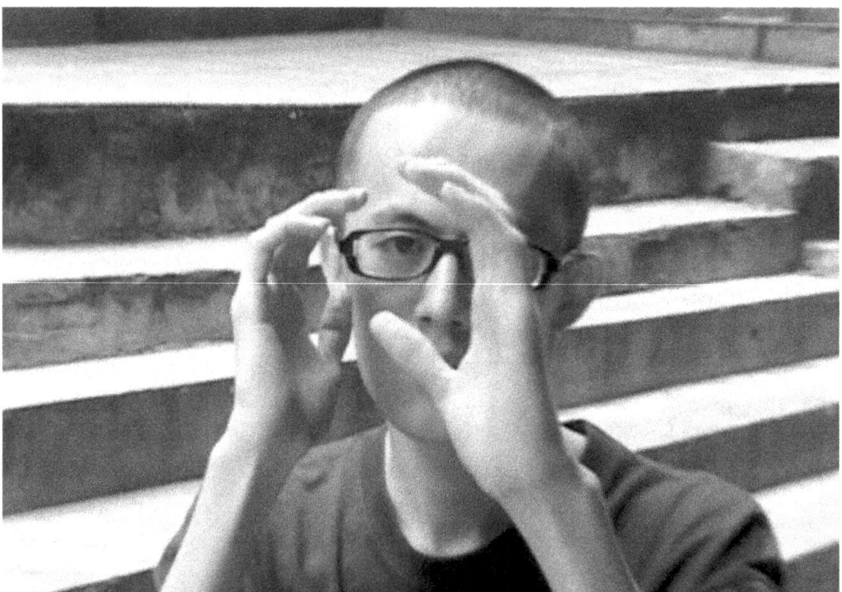

Figure 4.3 A man pretends to hold a camera and observe 'us' who look through the real camera in *Kun 1: Action* (2008)

'Love', Wu presents a close-up of a girl giving him oral sex in long take, then it cuts to Wu's face showing sexual pleasure, bathed in sunshine, while he leans on the wall in a public space. In another scene, after presenting a close-up of a young woman's face, the camera gradually zooms out, presenting the full face of a pretty young woman, later introduced as Bingbing (see Figure 4.4). Wu's voice-over states, 'Women, I need them. I want to make love with women, so I film them.' Presenting Bingbing as a beautiful flawless specimen who he is desperate for, Wu explicitly presents his instinctive sexual desire. Wu's voice-over later states that he has entered Bingbing's body. The directness of his sexual obsession also indicates his position of seeing women as objects to gaze at and possess.

Referencing Andy Warhol's blow job, Wu's insertion of female faces and sexuality is also influenced by Hara Kazuo's explicit sexual depiction in *Extreme Private Eros: Love Song 1974* (1974) in which Hara extensively filmed intimate scenes and intercourse with his ex-lover Miyuki. Speaking of Hara, Wu tries to differentiate his practice from that of Hara, stating that Hara's films are very destructive, but he wants to express a belief in his film. Around 2008, Wu was

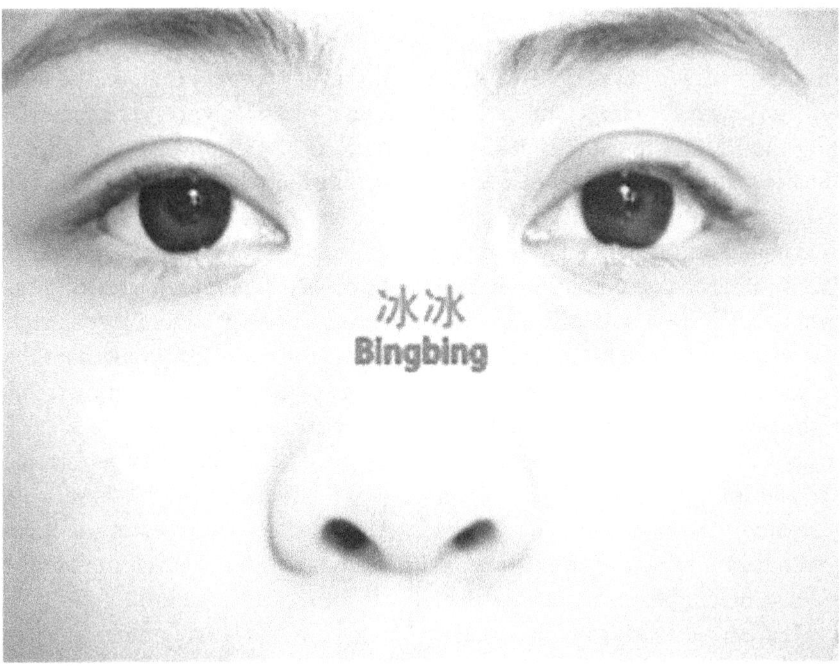

Figure 4.4 Wu's camera gazes at the young girl Bingbing as if observing a beautiful specimen in *Kun 1: Action* (2008)

eager to grab hold of something to pull himself out of the doldrums. He developed a strong interest in communism, which, for him, is not at all what China is like today (author's interview with Wu, 2010).

His monologue offers direct political comments, such as how young individuals feel confused about today's society and are nostalgic for Mao's era with its social welfare, even though it is a period they never lived in. The film inserts a scene of an underground rock band singing 'Long live Chairman Mao' in a club surrounded by many youngsters. The singer sings 'if Mao is still alive, we might not be able to play rock 'n' roll, but we would be able to live more like Chinese. If he still alive, we wouldn't see the corrupted leaders. If he still alive, we wouldn't have demolition.' Wu states: 'The young people take Mao as a symbol of idealism. They do not have passion for the current nation. They are confused. They refuse to see the reality, refuse politics, most of them just idling along.' Wu's commentary on his generation reveals his anxiety and longing for a reality in which he can have more direct involvement.

Following this, Wu starts his action of 'performing' his political ideas on camera. Wu and his friends produce a performance in Hongyan Park, a communist monumental park in Chongqing. The camera pans from the left to the right, showing Wu with longer hair, shouting 'Long live, the people! Long live, the people!' Then the camera quickly pans right, showing a man standing in front of the camera in a medium close-up. The man makes a bow to the camera. The camera tilts down, showing a gun on the floor, then it tilts up, showing the man putting on a KMT (Chinese Nationalist Party) uniform and picking the gun up from the floor. Pointing at the camera, the man shoots, then the camera immediately pans back to the left, as if the bullet travels through the camera, shooting Wu, who is standing at the wall. Wu pretends to fall down on the floor. We know that Wu is acting as the communist, being shot by a KMT soldier during the Chinese civil war. The KMT soldier comes to him, putting some red ink on Wu's shirt as if it were blood. Then he lies at the side of Wu and the two start to talk about the future. This scene is filmed in a single shot. The camera then pans away to the right, revealing that the surrounding passers-by are looking at them.

Wu and his friend try to imagine what the 'political' should be, by performing the political struggles that have contributed to the founding of China's socialist state and filming it. The music of the international song appears in the background, with some clips from old socialist realism cinema in which communist soldiers fight against the Japanese invasion to protect the homeland.

This part ends with Wu declaring the foundation of a New Communist Party group. In the highly commercialised culture in 2000s China, it is very rare for a young Chinese man to raise political issues and have a clear political position – not to mention that it is illegal to set up a new political party. As a demonstration, his friend walks around painting their logo in Chongqing's Cultural Revolution cemeteries. Wu filmed this performance and put it in fast forward. A playful act like this indicates the eagerness of some Chinese youth to make political gestures.

The last scene is a long shot of Tiananmen Square, and we see Wu in the distance standing at the bottom of the Chinese national flag, then running towards the camera. Wu arrives right in front of the camera, presents his face in extreme close-up, gives a loud shout, then stands still in front of the camera. Another close-up of him staring into the camera; however, this time Wu is no longer in his own private space. He and his camera have moved to a public space, and a place that is historically linked with various political events in China's recent past.

The Absence of Community and Problems of Interpersonal Communication in Xue Jianqiang's *Martian Syndrome*

The state of solitude and the desire for communication expressed in Wu Haohao's *Kun 1: Action* is also manifested in Xue's *Martian Syndrome.* Xue's personal camera records a one-night encounter with a homeless young man with neurasthenia who calls himself 'Martian', when Xue visits his artist friend in Caochangdi, a suburban artist's community in Beijing. The eighty-three-minute long film consists of only five long takes. Shot on a dark night, it is difficult to see what the physical space looks like. Xue's first person camera depicts this space as full of insecurity, coldness and deception. The lack of trust is explicitly illustrated through Xue's own problematic behaviour, as we hear him openly lie to his subject and beat him up.

Xue himself does not physically appear on camera, but he constantly speaks from behind the camera, asking questions, chatting with the subjects. Throughout the film, Xue holds the camera as an extension of his own eyes. Given the lack of light, Xue uses the night mode and puts the camera extremely close to the subjects' faces, capturing them in their most unprotected, fragile and vulnerable moments The night mode creates a greenish look that makes people's faces look very pale and emotionless, and their eyes lack focus. This visual style enhances what is depicted in the film: the problem of communication.

The film begins with a long take, tracing a young girl wandering in an empty, open, night-time street, slowly moving forward. The young girl leads the camera forward into the darkness. Switching to night mode, Xue's camera traces a long dark alleyway, looking for the way to his friend Xiaodong's place. The first voice that comes to him is from a stranger, asking Xue whether he is a painter or filmmaker. Another man, later known to be Xue's friend who accompanies him, reveals that the filmmaker Xue does not know anything about filmmaking but is only an amateur. Moving forwards, the stranger comes to talk to them, asking in a low but aggressive voice 'Has Xiaodong come back? I'm Wang Xi'

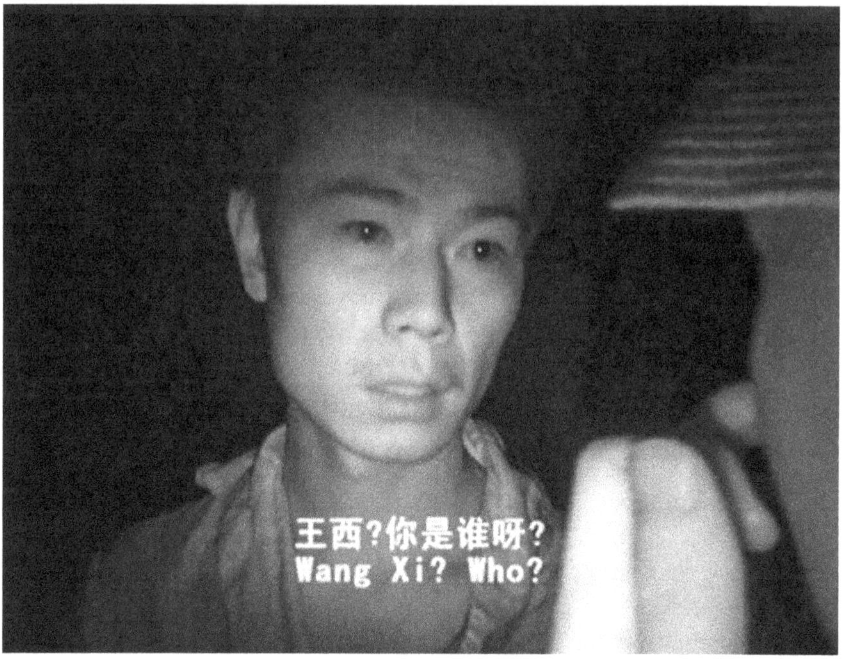

Figure 4.5 Wang Xi's pale, anxious face in *Martian Syndrome* (2010)

(see Figure 4.5). Xue and his friend start to talk to Wang Xi, while Xue's camera traces Wang's face in extreme close-up.

From their conversations, we know that Wang Xi was born in 1986 and comes from a region in the middle of China. He has been in Beijing for several months with a dream to become an artist, but finds it difficult to make a living. As he reveals, he does not have a place to live nor has he any food or money. He has been waiting here for a few hours hoping to talk to Xiaodong and get some food. Wang regards himself as 'Martian', coming from a totally different world. In this vast metropolitan city, where new sets of interpersonal relations have formed, 'Martian' finds it difficult to communicate with others, as he says: 'People do not express their feelings directly, pretending to speak in a civilised language that is in fact very cold.'

While the conversation builds up the audience's emotional engagement with 'Martian', Xue's camera enters Xiaodong's room outside which 'Martian' has been waiting. In the darkness, the image finally comes into focus and we see a half-naked man. This is Xiaodong. Seeing Xue's friend arrive, Xiaodong hugs him from behind and starts to cry like a baby (see Figure 4.6). Xue's camera forcibly captures the embarrassing moments of the subjects who do not even notice it being there. The masculinity that is usually shown in the mainstream media has

Figure 4.6 Xiaodong hugs his friend from behind, while his friend tries to comfort him. Then he starts to cry: 'It scares me,' in *Martian Syndrome* (2010)

totally collapsed. Xiaodong is being captured at his weakest and most vulnerable moment. Xue's friend tries to console him and accompanies him to the bedroom in the dark. Xiaodong is continuously crying while hysterically muttering that the way 'Martian' has been knocking at the door is so aggressive that he feels very scared and hopeless, and almost driven to neurasthenia.

The aimless chatting between Xiaodong, Xue's friend and Xue himself from behind the camera lasts almost uncut for more than twenty minutes. Throughout the film it is never revealed explicitly whether Xiaodong is homosexual, but in several places the subjects openly talk about homosexuality. Xiaodong mentions that he does not mind 'playing' with 'Martian' for a day as long as he does not bother him again (see Figure 4.7). To confirm this, Xue cuts back to an earlier shot and marks it in revised colour, showing that Wang Xi says Xiaodong wanted to have sex with him the night before (see Figure 4.8). The film does not reveal whether Xiaodong's neurasthenia is due to hiding a sexual identity that is not openly accepted in China. Apparently in contradiction to his homosexual identity is the fact that he has a wife – he says that he has been saving money with his wife, hoping to buy their own place to live. Without making judgement himself, Xue just presents these contradictions to the audience.

Figure 4.7 Xiaodong sits in the dark saying to his friend that he can have sex with Wang but he must leave on the second day

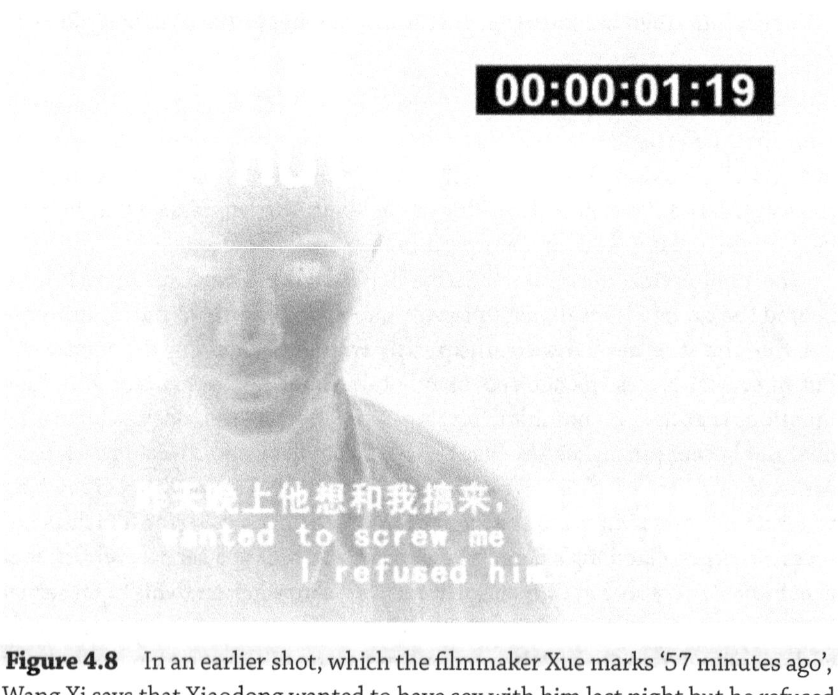

Figure 4.8 In an earlier shot, which the filmmaker Xue marks '57 minutes ago', Wang Xi says that Xiaodong wanted to have sex with him last night but he refused

Xue's handheld camera captures such extremely personal moments, which he experiences in his daily encounters. Even though he does not appear on camera, his presence is strongly felt: through his off-screen voice, aesthetic style and also, later, his off-screen fight with 'Martian', which we can hear from the recorded soundtrack. In the middle of their chat inside the room, Xue goes out talking to 'Martian', as 'Martian' asks him for the tape that he has just filmed. Xue lies to him, saying that he did not film him, and tells 'Martian' to go away otherwise he will call the police. As 'Martian' refuses to go, Xue puts the camera down on the floor and fights him in the dark. The camera captures the sound of Xue beating 'Martian' up.

When Xue's friend comments on his fight, Xue jokes that this is the new concept – action documentary, a new style in which the director should directly engage with the event he is filming (see Figure 4.9). It is possible that Xue is deliberately performing the fight for the camera so to experiment with the new concept he has just learnt from Hara Kazuo or Wu Haohao. The character Xiaodong is emotionless, asking whether Xue can still film as it is too dark. It seems that Xiaodong does not really know what Xue has filmed and what it is for. Though in Xue's later film, *Beat the Tiger*, he openly criticises older documentary filmmakers' problematic strategies, it seems Xue himself also

Figure 4.9 Xue's voice comes from behind the camera, saying to his friend and Xiaodong that his method of participating in the filmed event is based on a new concept

falls into the trap of using his subjects for his own filmmaking purposes. Xue's camera captures Xiaodong and 'Martian' in their unprotected moments, desperately searching for emotional support, while hysterically expressing themselves, finding it difficult to communicate.

After the one-night event, it cuts to a scene shot a week later, the only scene in the film that takes place in the daytime. It is a screening event where people are talking about a film; the camera then zooms in, focusing on 'Martian' sitting at the back. This is the moment Xue rediscovers 'Martian', again in a self-contained, independent art and film community. The openness of the ending and the roughness of the image indicate that what is being recorded in the film is part of the daily filming practice – of a young migrant individual who wanders around in the capital, Beijing.

Conclusion

In this chapter, I have discussed the notion of action documentary and how it is interpreted by two young generation filmmakers, Wu Haohao and Xue Jianqiang. Both filmmakers' practices challenge the conventional way of 'fly-on-the-wall' observation. This is quite similar to how Hara differentiated his practice from the older generation filmmaker Ogawa Shinsuke's naturalistic documentary (Hara 2009). Both *Kun 1: Action* and *Martian Syndrome* capture the sense of alienation and frustration among young individuals. They desperately use cameras to communicate with others, breaking social boundaries of the private and the public. *Kun 1: Action* demonstrates Wu's self-performance in front of the camera, and his idea of using the camera to engage with people and criticise the current social conditions. *Martian Syndrome* starts with an impulsive video-diary practice that captures Xue's encounters with individuals in his community at their most vulnerable moments. Xue's aggressive fighting with the 'Martian' in *Martian Syndrome* also seems to be a deliberate realisation of what he understands as 'action documentary'.

There are also explicit sexual references in these films. Wu is unsatisfied with being isolated in his own space, and is desperately looking for communication and resonance. Having sex or oral sex on camera offers him certain pleasure and satisfaction, in contrast to his lonely masturbation mentioned in the earlier part of the film. In Xue's *Martian Syndrome*, the sexual reference is a casual mentioning of homosexuality and of sex among men becoming a commodity. 'Martian' returns to knocking on Xiaodong's door to offer sex in order to get food and a place to stay, while Xiaodong wants peace after the exchange.

The parallel between women's individualised writing and women's first person filmmaking can also be found between the younger generation filmmaker's practice and the so-called post-80s generation writers such as Han Han. In the early 2000s, Han Han quit high school, openly criticised Chinese education and became a popular novelist. He explicitly demonstrated his political subjectivities by his rejection of the dominant education system and criticism of absurd social issues and conventions. Through the years, Han Han has become a well-known cultural celebrity, an opinion-leader, speaking for social justice and for the rights of public citizens, which normal scholars do not dare to speak about. Unlike Han Han, Wu and Xue started by documenting their own personal lives and the small circle of people around them. Their films are only shown in the independent documentary network and have not achieved the same popularity as Han Han's writing.[5]

Nevertheless, Wu and Xue's practice indicates the rise of individual political subjectivity among a much larger group. They take first person action documentary practice as a way of interaction, of raising their personal voice, hoping to understand the changing society and to be understood. The alienation described in both their films indicates the communication problems of younger generation individuals, or what we call the iGeneration. Action documentary practice foregrounds the filmmaker as the central subject/participator, forcefully breaking down conventional social structures and institutional forces. The ethics of *encountering* during this practice are also worth exploring, being further complicated when the encountering is also expanded to the audience. This will be discussed in the next chapter.

Notes

1. In my interviews, Wu Haohao thinks Xue takes this idea from him. Xue agrees that Wu influenced him, but his filmmaking is somehow different from that of Wu's.
2. This is not entirely true. Back in 1999 the filmmaker Ju An'qi made a documentary using an interactive approach, by asking people in the street, 'Do you think Beijing's wind is strong?' The film is called *There is a Strong Wind in Beijing* (1999).
3. There have been some heated debates on fanhall.com (现象网, *xianxiang wang*), the independent filmmakers' online forum founded by the film programmer and film festival director Zhu Rikun. However, the website was permanently closed in March 2011, which might be because of its explicit rebellion and opposition to the official media policy and ideology. In addition, such debates have also been discussed on the social media platform Douban, and through email exchanges in the Caochangdi email group, which is by invitation only.
4. David E. James regards film diary merely as 'a private event, where consumption, especially consumption by others, is illicit' (James 1992: 147).
5. To know more about Han Han, see http://www.hanhandigest.com and http://chinadigitaltimes.net/china/han-han/.

Chapter 5

The Problematic Public Self: Ethics, Camera and Language in Contestable *Minjian* Public Spaces

Whereas Wu Haohao's *Kun1: Action* and Xue Jianqiang's *Martian Syndrome* present the individuals in lonely personal spaces, desperately desiring a more politicised public community where they can find emotional security and guidance for value and trust building, in another two films made by these two filmmakers, Wu Haohao's *Criticizing China* and Xue Jianqiang's *I Beat the Tiger When I Was Young*, the two filmmakers are themselves proactively participating in *minjian* public spaces. *Minjian* literally means 'among the people' and represents a non-governmental organised grassroots public space. With a personal camera as a 'weapon', the 'public self' filmmakers, as agents, try to disrupt the established social structure and negotiate with changing forces and relations within the public spaces, including social relations among individuals, and between individuals and the state. These films also expose the problematic 'public self' in interpersonal communication, highlighting the ethical dilemmas.

Presenting the self as a key subject, all the first person filmmakers studied in this book reveal how they interact with other subjects. The camera as a force generates the interaction as well as documents the interactive process. Therefore, their first person 'action documentary' filmmaking is also a practice to explore and to experiment with how to act as an individual in multiple dynamic public spaces in contemporary China, and provides valuable material for analysing the changing sense of self in public spaces. These films demonstrate that the traditional moral norms influenced by family ethical relations are still playing an important role in defining interpersonal interaction even in *minjian* public spaces, and especially in the relationships between the old and the young.

New Sociality in Public Spaces: the Problematic Public Self

In mentioning 'public spaces', I do not simply refer to the 'public sphere' or 'civil society',[1] being aware of the danger of accepting these terms as a standard against which to measure the Chinese context. As shown in these films, the kinds of power relations and the nature of forces in current public spaces in contemporary China are not the same as in the idealised public sphere in the West. In current scholarship, three main positions exist simultaneously among scholars examining these two terms: 'Some believe that China is moving in the direction of these various models, others disagree, and a third group argue that China is too different for the application of these foreign ideas' (Berry 2010: 104–5). Berry argues that

> subscribing to such an idealized and ideological model as the public sphere blinds us to the complexity and range of publics and public spaces in general – in the Western just as much as in the Chinese context. Furthermore, it also binds us into an Orientalist posture where China's efforts to 'catch up' confirm the West – where it is assumed there is such a thing as the 'public sphere' – as a model for all to follow. (Berry 2010: 97)

Taking none of these positions, Berry draws from Foucault's idea of productive power and theorises an operable new term, 'public space', to describe the Chinese case. For Berry, 'public spaces' 'are not only multiple and varied but also positively produced and shaped externally and internally by configurations of power' (ibid.).[2] My understanding of 'public spaces' is grounded in Chris Berry's theorisation. In 'public spaces', individual self as a power, an agency, is negotiating with different internal and external forces and is situated in varying social relations. Hence, I term this self the 'public self'. These films are produced by the 'public self' as well as the representation of the problematic 'public self', in what Yan Yunxian regards as new types of sociality, 'social interactions among individuals as individuals (instead of as representatives of the family or other social groups)' (Yan 2009: 284).

In the de-traditionalisation and dis-embedment process, individuals have been brought together from previous social categories, breaking away from previous state-controlled institutions. This has enabled unrelated individuals to gather together based on their shared interests, and has seen the rise of *minjian* public spaces. Wu Haohao's *Criticizing China* (2008) illustrates one such space – the discussion corner in a public park where elder local residents gather together to discuss politics. His own filmmaking practice is a way of interacting with the locals in this park.

The retreat of the party-state from its previous control over public life and the replacement of the dominant communist ideology by neo-liberalism left a huge vacuum in public spaces (Yan 2009), especially in the pre-Xi era before 2012. The new forms of social space are highly commercialised, lacking political implications. The younger generation growing up in China during the 1990s and the beginning of the twenty-first century have therefore experienced a loss of values and a lack of orientation. This could be seen in the previous chapter, where the two filmmakers and their subjects return to the innermost, deepest and most intimate parts of life. They explicitly express sexual desire, such as Wu's own sexual exposure in *Kun 1: Action*, and display psychological conflict, as in *Martian Syndrome*. These young filmmakers are eager to understand the self and search for a new spiritual belief. In *Kun 1: Action*, Wu Haohao connects himself to the former communist movement and tries to understand communism. In *Criticizing China*, he reaches out in a public park to connect with public discussions among the local residents. More aggressively, Xue searches for self-understanding through 'attacking' the elder filmmakers in *I Beat the Tiger*, in the hope that they would take him seriously and engage in conversation.

Wu's and Xue's filmmaking practice also reveals the lack of social trust in such public spaces. Writing in 2009, Yan observes that the new kinds of sociality see the decline of social trust in an increasingly mobilised and open society, yet non-governmental independent social spaces are not ready to host these individual selves (Yan 2009). The newly emerged *minjian* social spaces, such as the independent filmmaker community in *I Beat the Tiger* and the public discussion corner in Wu's *Criticizing China*, still have a hierarchical structure that mirrors the traditional and socialist organisational structures, and interpersonal relations outside the domestic space still mimic family relations.

Much scholarship believes that individuals experience themselves – and forge an awareness of self – through social moral norms that explicitly refer to the family (Trauzettel 1990: 25; Feng 1934). Fei Xiaotong (1992) invented the notion of '*chaxugeju*', a 'differential mode of association' to describe how each individual in Chinese society has a different web of social relationships, and each network appears differently depending on which person is the focus of the web (Stockman 2000: 73). Although traditional moral ethics were attacked several times in the course of China's modernisation process in the early twentieth century, such moral ethics still play an important role in interpersonal relations. After the Communist Party came into power, a radical transformation took place to reshape the consciousness of the individual, creating 'new socialist men and women' (Inkeles *et al.* 1997: 31), even though in reality Confucian morality still determined interpersonal relations in some circumstances (Stockman 2000; Gold 1996).

In public spaces where different kinds of forces and quasi-family relations are merging together, how to act in these new societies that lack social trust also becomes a problem. Dan Edwards (2015) discusses the ethics of encounter in observational or participatory documentaries, such as Zhou Hao's *Using* (2008) and Zhao Liang's *Petition* (2010), which reflexively present moments of the filmmakers' interaction with the subjects, exposing the filmmakers' ethical dilemma. In the first person films discussed here, the interactions between the filmmakers and other individuals are deliberately accentuated. These filmmakers do not just document the *minjian* public space through their own personal vision, but also further provoke existing social relations in these spaces. Through close inspection of these films, I notice that even in *minjian* spaces, the traditional moral norms influenced by family ethical relations still play an important role in defining how individuals interact with each other, especially in the relationship between the old and the young outside of familial relations. The filmmakers' actions reveal the ethically problematic and unbalanced individuals who refer to a mix of moral norms to act as the 'public self'. In addition, these films also demonstrate the changing relationship between individuals and the state. Wu's *Criticizing China* illustrates the fact that many people still think individual rights are very limited, but there is also a sense of a new citizenship arising, requesting equal opportunities and individual rights. Furthermore, their use of language still mirrors the former ideology. This is especially obvious in *I Beat the Tiger When I Was Young*: when the filmmaker Xue tries to challenge his elders, the language he uses still shows a violent dictatorial and non-negotiable logic that aims to entirely demolish the old. In the following sections, I will examine these two films in detail.

The Camera as a Disturbing Power – Contestable *Minjian* Public Space in *Criticizing China*

In *Criticizing China*, the *minjian* space captured through Wu's camera is one of the urban communal leisure parks that typically exist in China's urban scenery. Such a public space brings people from local residential areas together to relax, to do exercise, to 'walk' caged birds, or for activities such as chorus singing or playing card games. The physicality of the space as a public park contributes to the formation of a community, re-emphasising the notion of collectiveness that was previously associated with socialist work units and state-subsidised residential areas (as depicted in Hu Xinyu's *Family Phobia*), which have been gradually transformed into private enterprises and private residential estates. The park in this film is a site where local residents spontaneously gather together for political debates. Many of the old people who talk to Wu in the film have been coming here nearly every day for a number of years. Everyone knows each other's political position and taste. They have no intention of forming a group with a political agenda, but just want to share their personal concerns about the nation and its socio-political situation.

The title of the film, *Criticizing China*, can be understood from different perspectives. It can refer to the activity of the local people criticising Chinese politics, as Wu documents in the film. Alternatively, it can also refer to Wu's action of criticising the local people who do not dare to face the camera. Lastly, from the audience's point of view, it can also refer to the criticism of the problematic social ethics practised by individuals, exemplified by the interaction of Wu with the local residents in the film.

Wu Haohao's initial idea was to record this group of retired old people gathering in a local park for public debates. Wu revealed that he had been observing the local public debates for a couple of weeks. He then decided to film them, thinking this was a very good phenomenon that reflected public speech in *minjian* spaces (author's interview with Wu, 2010). Entering this community, Wu does not introduce himself through traditional hierarchical relations, in which he is positioned as the youngster and has to listen and respect the elders' speech. Instead, Wu presents himself as an equal individual with social responsibilities by bringing a cameraman with him to film the elders' public debates.

Criticizing China presents Wu's self, the close-up of his face in the opening shots highlighting the performative nature of the film. As he stares at the camera – and by extension the audience – with anger, his first person narration sharply and concisely makes a statement about the aim of this practice:

> I need to intervene into people's lives any day. In fact, I am nervous of going into the crowd, to communicate, to fight with people, and record it. This personality of mine is cultivated in the environment that I've grown up, and those lousy Chinese people in this environment. But I am eager to do so, I need to rescue, and express my love. This is my struggle. (see Figure 5.1)

This indicates that his main aim is to provoke people, to join their discussion and to disrupt an established social order cultivated in people's minds. The film then cuts to an interior shot, where Wu sits in front of a computer where he does his editing. He looks back to speak to the camera, 'For this action, I need a comrade, a cameraman. I hope we can strive together. But I also understand a comrade is but temporary. I will try to avoid it . . .'

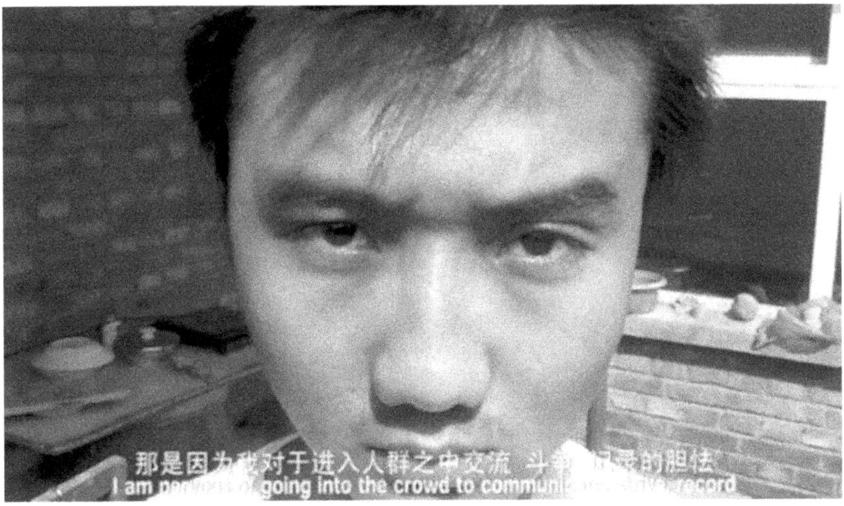

Figure 5.1 Wu stares at the camera in the beginning of *Criticizing China* (2008)

Then the film cuts back to the action of filming. Wu uses the camera as his own eyes, presenting a man's face in extreme close-up:

> When you shoot, I want the camera this close to the person . . . I want a feeling that you have entered their field. Not the older way of doing it, hiding someplace and shooting at a distance . . . I will talk to them and you can shoot me as well . . . Don't switch off the camera, keep it on.

This conversation reveals that the man he is talking to is the cameraman; Wu is outlining his requirements for the style of film and the agenda behind his action.

The camera is then in the hand of the cameraman, following Wu from behind as he walks towards people in the park. His voice-over expresses his worry and excitement: 'I have been waiting for this day for so long'. When he walks into the crowd, the camera captures people's reaction to him and the camera: people start to spread out, suddenly becoming very conscious of the camera. They express strong suspicion and, assuming that the camera is from a controlling power, which they try to avoid.

As soon as the camera enters the space, Wu's filmmaking raises new tensions about the role of the camera and the power of the individual. The film reveals that this *minjian* public space is still shadowed by the official public space. Most people in the park still regard a camera as a form of state power, the eyes from 'above', rather than the power of the individual to raise their voice.

Figure 5.2 (above and opposite) When Wu and his cameraman enter the crowd, people start to be very suspicious of his camera. All from one long take from *Criticizing China* (2008)

The camera documents how Wu delivers his idea of filmmaking to these people. Wu stands in the middle of the crowd, trying to explain his agenda. The camera follows their discussion in a long take, illustrating people's insecure feelings toward the camera, a kind of invisible power surrounding them. When the camera films a middle-aged man in a white shirt criticising Chinese politics, a man in brown walks up to him and suggests that he moves away from the camera. The

camera watches from behind, while Wu walks towards them and says: 'Don't be afraid really, we are just shooting a documentary.' The man in brown asks: 'What do you do?' Wu answers: 'We make documentary, independent documentary.' Another man asks: 'Where will you show it?' Wu answers: 'We want to reflect real people's lives.' The man in brown says: 'How can you reflect real people's lives?' Wu answers: 'We will try our best.' Facing away from the camera, the man in white says: 'They are from the state TV station.' Wu responds: 'We are not from the TV station, we are different from them. We are independent.'

The local people have a strong suspicion of the camera. They do not know where the camera comes from: police, journalists or foreign media? One man asks them: 'Who do you represent?' Wu replies: 'We are independent, representing ourselves.' 'Yourselves? Then you shouldn't film. If you are from state media, then you can interview us, but if you just do it for yourself, then you do not have the right. You intervene in our privacy.'

Such an eagerness to protect their privacy may not be linked to the capitalist idea of private and public, but more to the shared political experience in the Mao era. If the camera belongs to a peer or a private individual, it could lead to political persecution. This fear and suspicion is a long lasting after-effect of the Hundred Flowers Movement, the Anti-rightist Movement and the Cultural Revolution, when peers keeping 'watch' on each other was common, and often led to political persecution. There were only 'friends' and 'enemies', even among familial relations (Stockman 2000: 83).

Wu compares people's attitude to the camera with how people responded to the camera in Italian filmmaker Michelangelo Antonioni's documentary *China* (1972). Inserting some clips from *China*, Wu's voice-over comments: 'Look at these Chinese, they look alike. Times have changed, but their facial expressions haven't changed.' Wu explicitly criticises how individuals understand themselves in China, and the fact that people are still very much afraid of expressing themselves on camera.

The fear of the camera is, however, doubled by another power relation. Though these people see the camera representing the power from 'above', which is watching them, they, however, regard themselves as older and therefore senior to the filmmakers. For them, the filming of Wu and his cameraman, as the younger generation, lacks respect for the old.

'I really hate this kind of behaviour . . . Go away! We are all senior and you are even younger than my children. Who do you think you are! You are so disgusting, dressing like a woman.' A man wearing sunglasses shouts loudly at them (see Figure 5.3). People start to walk away. Then a woman talks to Wu in anger:

> You don't have permission to film them, so you are wrong. Child, if you shoot me again I will break your camera. You children! You need to respect, as an individual you need to respect them (the old) . . . See all of them are older than your father. They are all senior workers. You are weird.

Wu tries to communicate with them, stating loudly that 'The media in China needs transparency'.

The arguments raised by the personal camera indicate that the traditional social relations between the old and the young still constrain how many older generation people interact with younger generation individuals. People in the park reject his filming by positioning Wu as the junior, the youngster, in relation to them, the senior or elder.

Figure 5.3 The man in sunglasses refuses to be filmed in *Criticizing China* (2008)

People in the park even explicitly attack the masculinity of Wu and his cameraman, as they both have long hair tied in a ponytail. The man in sunglasses shouts at them 'You shameless people. You should go! Child, you should go off to earn money and not be doing this . . . You (long hair) like women, are you men or women?' The comments show that these people still have very conventional ideas of how modern men should look. Men with long hair are not ethically and aesthetically accepted, even though men in Chinese history have always been associated with long hair and cutting off a man's ponytail was once a political act to enter modernity. It is debatable whether the filmmakers have the right to film the public discussion of these people in a public park. People's rejection of the camera, through the use of such autocratic cursing and aggressive language and the excuse of invading their privacy, still indicates a fear of what the camera represents.

Even though some people allow them to film, they still question an individuals' ability to make any change outside of a collective group, especially when they are still so young. An old man comes to Wu, first asking whether he has a journalist's permission card. Finding out they are not journalists, the old man asks again 'If you film these discussions, either for and against the official line, will you show it on TV?' Wu answers: 'No, we cannot.' Then the old man says: 'Then it would not have any effect.' In another shot, a man says 'You are still very young. How much can you reflect the reality?' Another one says, 'You do not need to reflect our reality. Even if you do, you cannot change anything . . . You are still children . . . Children don't understand the society.'

The criticism does not stop Wu from filming nor discourage him from delivering his own agenda. Wu's idea of democracy seems to be influenced by so-called American values. Facing rejection, he loudly states that 'When the American people see the camera they all speak bravely in front of the camera, express themselves and address their problems. But look at us, seeing the camera like we have seen a gun.' Later in the film, he also says that 'The American President once said, "You always complain that the nation hasn't provided you with anything. But as individuals, what have you people brought to the nation?"[3] I have a digital video recorder now, so that's what I do.' While some reply that 'Our nation does not have the same soil as America', Wu replies 'Our Chinese always think we individuals are very small . . . What I care about is democracy in China. I need my camera to intervene in public events . . . If everyone thinks like you, then nothing can be changed.'

Throughout Wu's intervention in the debating corner in the park, he leads the whole event as a 'saviour' of the people he talks to. Wu says to the elders that he wants to do something different; as he mentions, most young people of his age do not care about this. He wants to use his action to change people's attitudes towards the camera and encourage public speech. Wu's 'public self' demonstrates a strong awareness of citizenship. As a younger generation individual, Wu interacts with people older than him as equals, and openly manifests his understanding of the camera, democracy and individual relations. By doing so, he has stimulated people in the film and the audiences to think how to interact with each other as individuals in public space. His brave intervention into this space occupied by the elders has gradually made some accept him. As is shown in the second half of the film, people gradually become more relaxed with his camera and re-start their public discussions again.

Challenging the Old and the Problematic Rhetoric of Language: *I Beat the Tiger When I Was Young*

The title *I Beat the Tiger When I Was Young* is an old Chinese saying that indicates the action of a younger generation criticising and denying the older generation in order to establish their own position. The film presents Xue's attacks on several filmmakers at different independent film festivals and screening events, including on Wu Wenguang, Guo Xizhi and Xu Tong.

The film begins with a scene of an award ceremony at the Beijing Independent Film Festival. It starts with a long shot of the stage filmed by Xue from among the audience, then the camera is passed on to the person next to Xue when he is announced as the winner of 'Young Promising Filmmaker' for his previous film *Martian Syndrome*. Xue walks onto the stage to receive the award and make a speech. Beyond the expectation of the audience in the ceremony, and the audience of this film, his speech is rather an aggressive statement:

> My next film will criticise you – documentary filmmakers. You take yourself as a flaw in your film . . . While you ask the society to open up, your subjects to open up, you hide your selves behind the camera. You cut off all the footage that shows you. This is dictatorship. This is violence.

This is the first time Xue presents himself on camera and he establishes himself as a highly provocative figure, epitomising the young individuals who have a desire for self-recognition and equal dialogue. While in *Criticizing China* the attention on the camera is raised when Wu enters the park, in *I Beat the Tiger* Xue deliberately creates and raises attention to a conflict through his provocative language and aggressive manner of filmmaking.

The *minjian* public space in *I Beat the Tiger* is the independent filmmaking community that has been established on the basis of a shared interest in independent filmmaking practice. There is no solid or concrete physical space to this community. Here *minjian* is more like an idea of independent screening spaces, which include many independent film festivals and screening venues spread out in different places in China. Marginality and mobility are the main characters of this space in physical form, which mirrors the themes of independent films that usually focus on socially and geographically marginal identities or places. As an insider, Xue turns the camera inward to explore the community he is part of. Travelling around different film festivals for screenings, Xue talks to filmmakers during their informal gatherings, 'attacks' elder filmmakers, provokes generational conflicts, and probes the older independent filmmakers to reflect on the idea of independence.

The film reveals the ethically problematic filmmaker Xue Jianqiang, who uses his camera and his language to provoke the older filmmakers of the independent filmmaking community. Although it shows that the traditional social relationship between the old and the young also exists in this so-called independent community, Xue does not receive the same kind of criticism as Wu encounters in *Criticizing China*. Instead, after his 'attack', the older filmmakers share their thoughts on documentary filmmaking with him and allow him to express his thoughts. However, his challenge is expressed in an aggressive autocratic manner that is historically inherited. His filmmaking practice challenges the traditional social and moral norms of interpersonal communication, which makes himself a problematic character for the audience to relate to.

After the opening scene, the film cuts to a black-and-white long take filmed by Xue himself while he is walking into Wu Wenguang's studio – then based at Caochangdi, an artists' cluster in the northeast suburbs of Beijing. Walking through the yard, Xue captures the environment of Wu's studio, surrounded by big walls and doors, and some people sitting in the yard. Xue enters the room and the camera captures Wu, who is about to leave the shot. Xue asks from behind the camera: 'Could I talk to you? Do you have time?' Wu does not even look at him and continues walking out, while saying 'I do not have time'. Xue does not give up and asks if he can talk to Wu later. Wu continues doing his own thing and does not reply. Xue keeps asking: 'How about when you finish your work? . . . Can you give me a reply?' Wu walks away, and replies 'No time!' Xue insists 'Can I make an appointment with you?' Wu walks away from the camera, impatiently saying 'No time. I have things to do.' Xue turns around, leaving Wu's studio, while saying to himself, 'Such a busy man.'

Shortly afterwards, Xue accompanies another director, Ying Liang, to Wu Wenguang's studio. This time, in the presence of other people, Wu does not refuse Xue, but jokes that Xue might want to curse him and put it online. While the camera points directly at Wu's face, Xue speaks from behind that camera: 'I want to know what you think of me? . . . Have you seen my film?' While making fun of Xue's appearance, Wu says 'Not yet.'

Xue replies,

> You are degenerate now as you don't watch new filmmakers' films . . . I watched your films so I want to have a talk with you. However, you said you didn't have time . . . Right? I want to learn from the elders, but the elders do not want to learn from the younger ones anymore . . . This is what I think personally.

Wu tries to justify himself but Xue does not give him a chance, saying, 'Can I express my feelings about your films?' Even though Wu tries to avoid Xue, Xue insists that he will keep it brief. Finally, Wu allows Xue to speak. Xue puts the camera in Wu's face and states firmly: 'You do not have talent in documentary filmmaking anymore and should not make films anymore. But your China Villagers documentary project is very good . . . I want to learn from you, so I watched all of your films . . .' Looking shocked, Wu is unprepared for such criticism. However, Wu does not give any response and keeps calm and silent.

In the first encounter between Xue and Wu, Xue's polite request for a dialogue has been impolitely refused by Wu (see Figure 5.4). However, we should also mention that Xue does not ask Wu for permission to film him. In their second encounter, Xue first asks Wu what he thinks of him. Having received in return a joke and a cold reply, Xue asks permission to express his opinion to the older man. Finally given a chance to speak, Xue does not do what a youngster is expected to do with ethical correctness, which is to show humbleness and modesty. Instead, he puts the camera in Wu's face and attacks him through the use of aggressive language, which provokes discomfort (see Figure 5.5). In my interview with Wu Wenguang a few months after Xue's visit, Wu states

Figure 5.4 In the first encounter, Wu Wenguang walks away, saying 'No time' in *I Beat the Tiger When I Was Young* (2010)

Figure 5.5 In the second encounter, Xue criticises Wu to his face: 'I think you do not have talent in documentary filmmaking anymore.'

> The younger generation wants power [*quanli*, 权力] so much. They [Wu Haohao and Xue Jianqiang] have been repressed for too long and they want their own authority, however, the way they do it is to beat all others . . . How does he ever have the authority to say that 'you should not make films anymore'? He does not have the authority to say so! (Author's interview with Wu, 2010)

From Xue's perspective, Wu's impoliteness and arrogant attitude to the younger filmmakers and his hierarchical position have prevented the younger people from having an equal opportunity to express themselves. Hence, with the power of the camera, Xue directly challenges Wu, which many young people in the field do not dare to do. From Wu Wenguang's point of view, Xue's directness and aggression seriously challenge the conventional social and moral norm, *xu* (the order), between the old and the young. Neither does Xue have the quality of a modern independent individual, as he does not show respect to others. In Wu's view, Xue's in-your-face camera style and aggressive language from behind the lens indicate Xue's misuse of the power given to him by the presence of the camera.

After attacking Wu Wenguang, the film cuts to a screening tour of independent films in Chengdu. On this occasion, Xue talks to several filmmakers during a casual gathering in between screenings. As filmmakers sit around in an open yard, Xue comes to talk to them and expresses his idea that filmmakers should reflect themselves. He puts his camera directly facing Ji Dan, an established female filmmaker, and comments that Ji Dan's film is just beautiful but she does not reflect herself enough.

Ji Dan, however, does not feel challenged at all. Instead she replies calmly that people have different personalities. Not every film should be the same. Another filmmaker, Guo Xizhi, sitting nearby, makes reference to how new literature in the 1980s criticised the old forms of writing to indicate that 'we also used to beat the tiger when we were young'. He mentions that

> It is not because something is new that it is always good . . . One style should not totally replace another. In those days everyone followed the 'on-the-spot' realism, now everyone follows the private personal documentary . . . One should think what one really wants and everyone has their own personalities.

Ji Dan points out the different kinds of rhetoric and language structure used by different generations. She states that

> For a long time we Chinese did not have confidence in our language . . . Since we were young we learnt about how to talk correctly and nicely. But this is not a language of our own. So a filmmaker friend of mine always says that I am making a (formal) speech . . . It's very sad that I cannot even remove it from myself. It becomes part of me . . . I am very afraid of writing. Whatever I write, it might be a word from any magazine or from any reading. Your generation do not have this problem. You are the sun. So you can criticise anyone and no one would hate you.

Ji Dan goes on to say that 'I don't think getting old is a good thing. At least I don't think so myself. We should be equal, so you do not need to discriminate against the elders . . . We are the mirror of your future.' Ji Dan's words crucially point out how the rhetoric of language has constructed people's way of thinking. She is self-critical about how her generation's use of language is constructed by a doctrinaire education. When she says to Xue, 'You are the sun', 'the sun' she uses is exactly Mao's phrase to depict the younger generation.

In the same way, Xue's autocratic language can also be seen as socially constructed. Xue uses the power of his camera to 'attack' his elders and to deliver his 'theory' of documentary. However, the way he speaks is still in a violent dictatorial manner that aims to entirely demolish the old without any space for negotiation. Towards the end of the film, Xue goes up on stage after his film is shown at the Chongqing screening tour. Standing on the stage for a question-and-answer session, he restates his agenda that documentary should explore and 'anatomise' the self. 'The best function of documentary is to discover the weakness of the self, and reflect self, rather than entertaining.' While disseminating his own understanding of documentary, Xue is, however, speaking like an arbiter, telling others what the best function of documentary should be – as a new way to replace the old, rather than as an alternative. The same kind of logic of language and rhetoric is also shown in Xue's film *Martian Syndrome*, in which 'Martian', Xiaodong and even Xue himself speak in a violent and self-contradictory way, telling others what to do and then violently denying what they have said.

I argue that this kind of dictatorial language or formula is historically inherited and influenced by the traditional patriarchal structures in which one authority, such as the father of the family or the state, can make rules for all others to follow (Feng 1934; Fei 1992; Liang 1990; Stockman 2000). This kind of patriarchal structure was transformed into new forms in Mao's socialist era. Formulae, as important 'cultural and linguistic artifacts' (Yuan *et al.* 1990: 61), play a crucial role in constructing and constraining how individuals think and express themselves, such as in the revolutionary and destructive language spoken during the Cultural Revolution.

Conclusion

Among the growing number of first person filmmakers, Wu Haohao and Xue Jianqiang turn the camera outwards to create a place within public spaces for the self to sit in. While the 'public spaces' in Berry's understanding are multiple and shaped by configurations of different powers, the 'public self' can be seen as an agency, a power that is shaped by – and, in turn, shapes – public spaces. Through first person filmmaking practice, the 'public self' filmmakers try to disrupt established social relations. Their films illustrate the changing sense of self in one's own space, and how the varying sense of self has an impact on how one relates to other individuals and the state in contemporary China.

At the turn of the twentieth century, Liang Qichao mentioned 'public morality' in his famous volume (written 1899–1903) *Renewal of the Role of the Citizen* (*Xinmin Shuo*). Liang states that 'modern society required that the allegiance of individuals be widened from an overriding commitment to kinship obligations, the sphere of private morality, to a concern for civic virtue and public morality' (quoted in Stockman 2000: 79). Wu's and Xue's practices reflect their eagerness to construct more politicised public spaces and to further understand the self in order to achieve 'public morality'. However, as I observe, while regarding themselves as heroes or saviours within their communities, aiming for revolution, some of the practices revealed in their films challenge the audience to think seriously about the ethics of encountering.

Unlike most Chinese independent filmmakers, Wu openly distributes his own films on DVD at an unusually high price in China, a critique of the reality that most Chinese independent documentaries do not have DVD distribution. Both Wu's and Xue's films have been shown domestically on the independent film festival circuit. Wu Haohao's *Criticizing China* was first shown at Yunfest 2009 and *Kun 1: Action* was first shown at the Beijing Documentary Film Festival 2009. Both films immediately received many positive responses from the judges and the audience.

Apart from being hyper-provocative, Wu is also highly productive. He made more than twenty documentaries in the following two years, which have all taken the form of criticising an institution, a person, or have been in the continuous series '*Kun x: Action*'. These films have been shown at several domestic screening events. Through these works, he has established his style of openly criticising his subjects on camera to see how they respond to him. His perspective on the self and the method of 'action documentary' challenge the conventional Chinese documentaries that usually take a third person viewpoint to observe the 'others'. The action of directly criticising others also challenges traditional social ethics in the Chinese context, where 'courtesy' and quasi-family ethics still play an important role in social practice among individuals.

Wu's provocative 'action documentary' filmmaking receives different responses. Some elder filmmakers are tolerant of his films, thinking it is good to have something different, though not encouraging this practice among a wider number of filmmakers. This may be because Wu's off-screen personality is also highly problematic.[4] When *Kun 1: Action* was selected for international film festivals, such as Vancouver, Turin and Rotterdam, Wu did not have the money to go. Some elder filmmakers lent him money and supported him so that he could attend the festivals and expand his vision. However, some observed that Wu became more arrogant because of the sudden attention he received. He tended to use aggressive language when approaching others. He also used provocative and sexual language talking to me when I first contacted him, refusing to be interviewed if I did not have sexual relations with him. However, in recent years, after receiving criticism from many individuals inside the community, Wu has been 'learning' how to behave himself and adapt to the environment. When I approached again him during my second round of fieldwork, he accepted my interview; I was careful to choose a public space in a university campus for the meeting. Wu, however, appeared to be not as aggressive in reality. When I commented on his behaviour to other filmmakers and to myself the previous time, he revealed his fragility and extreme loneliness, saying that he wants to change himself and make friends with people rather than enemies (author's interview, 2010).

Like Wu Haohao, Xue Jianqiang is also a challenging figure in the community. In *I Beat the Tiger When I Was Young*, Xue openly criticises the elder documentary filmmakers' problematic strategies of filming others for their own ends; however, in *Martian Syndrome*, Xue also aggressively turns his camera on marginalised others suffering from neurasthenia for his own filmmaking purposes. As I point out in the last chapter, when 'Martian' asks him for the tape, he lies that he was not filming, and even beats 'Martian' up. The other character in the film, Xiaodong, was also not sure whether Xue filmed him or not. But Xue does not cut himself out of the film. He presents his ethically problematic actions on camera and even shows how other filmmakers criticise him. In *I Beat the Tiger*, Guo Xizhi, a filmmaker and scholar, criticises Xue for exploiting his own subjects and Xue documents such criticism and presents it for the audience to judge.

In addition to Wu and Xue, other filmmakers have also made similar films that show the self in public social spaces, such as Li Ning – who's *Tape* was completed in 2011, Ai Weiwei – whose filming practice will be examined in the next chapter, and the amateur filmmakers in the 'China Villagers Documentary Project' – which will be explored in Chapter 7. It is interesting to note that most filmmakers who take a first person approach in engaging with subjects outside the familial space are men; few female filmmakers explore their selves in this way. Among them, is the middle-aged villager/amateur filmmaker Shao Yuzhen of the China Villagers Documentary Project. Shao explores her daily life in a village in the suburbs of Beijing and her confrontation with the journalists working in state-owned TV stations who come to interview her. Another is Zhu Yi, a student at Nanjing University at the time of making her first student film, called *Scrap* (2008). In her film, Zhu investigates the local public issue of the control of illegal street merchants in Nanjing. Taking a small DV camera, Zhu records the different perspectives of merchants and policemen, as well as her own experiences of trying to interview the local police. Regardless of aesthetic achievement, their films deserve special attention sociologically. It illustrates features of how individuals behave themselves in public spaces, how they use the camera as a mediator and a power to interact with other individuals and institutions.

The rise of the 'new sociality' and the problematic social ethics in interpersonal communications as discussed throughout this chapter have their roots in 1990s and 2000s Chinese society. This also laid the ground for the increasing state intervention into public life, and a re-emphasis of traditional Chinese ethics and moral education in the mainstream media discourse since Xi's leadership in 2012.

Notes

1. In the broader field of Chinese studies, the model of the public sphere and civil society, and their conceptualisation in the Chinese context have received enormous scholarly attention.
2. Berry believes that this approach 'avoids any assumption that its appearance must indicate Westernization'.
3. What Wu refers to is John F. Kennedy's speech at his inauguration on 20 January 1961: 'And so, my fellow Americans, ask not what your country can do for you; ask what you can do for your country.'
4. This is reviewed during my conversation with the filmmaker Zhou Hao, 2010.

Chapter 6

Camera Activism: Provocative Documentation, First Person Confrontation and Collective Force

> I used to believe in the classic understanding of documentary, which is how I as a filmmaker see a particular reality. But now, I think myself is a medium. The 'I' is only produced when the 'I' is expressing his or her self. The so-called 'I' is in this process, being deconstructed and reproduced. If there is no such process of self expression, there is no self.
>
> Ai Weiwei (interviewed by Zhu Rikun, 2010)

This self-portrait of Ai Weiwei (Figure 6.1), the most politically outspoken contemporary Chinese artist, was taken during an arrest on 12 August 2009, at the time of his investigation (along with many volunteers) into the substandard 'tofu construction' of school buildings during the aftermath of the 2008 Sichuan earthquake. Ai and his volunteers had travelled to Sichuan to testify in defence of Tan Zuoren, a Sichuan-based writer and environmentalist, who had also been independently investigating the school buildings scandal, but had been prosecuted for subversion of the state power. The night before the trial, the local police forced their way into the hotel room where Ai's group were staying, beat Ai, and arrested one of the volunteers. This is the moment when Ai was accompanied by the police into a lift after being beaten. Ai raised his left hand holding a mobile phone above his head. The flash of the phone-camera sparkles, documenting this moment as visual evidence, as if he were using a gun to fight back against state authority. Immediately after the incident, this image, together with a sound recording, were posted onto social networks and then reposted by thousands of international viewers, creating a strong sense of immediacy and urgency.

In addition to the self-portrait and the sound recording, Ai's volunteer Zhao Zhao also recorded the whole journey with a digital video camera. The footage was

Figure 6.1 Ai takes a picture of himself surrounded by policemen with a mobile phone

soon edited into a documentary entitled *Lao Ma Ti Hua* (*Disturbing the Peace*). The film, documenting the journey of Ai and his group visiting local legal institutions asking for justification for the brutal illegal treatment, has become a monumental activist documentary, portraying investigation into an exceptional case in the history of Chinese independent documentary in a highly influential way. As a piece of visual evidence, it shows face-to-face first person confrontations between a group of rights-conscious individuals and the state authority. The direct challenge to authority and explicit advocacy for social change create a collective identity among the participants and the audience. The social media circulation of the film acts as a continuation of the activism, with the potential effect of mobilising awareness among viewer-followers and fellow filmmakers/artists, the international communities and even the decision-makers.

In the last two chapters, I have discussed what the young generation filmmakers Wu Haohao and Xue Jianqiang regard as 'action documentary' and the problematics of their practice of taking the camera to challenge conventional social ethics in public spaces. In this chapter, attention has been given to practices in which the camera is used as an activist tool to provoke political constraint, through a close examination of *Lao Ma Ti Hua*. I propose the term 'camera activism' to understand such camera-enabled individual participation in activism as a form of socio-political intervention. Acknowledging the power of the film in constructing a collective political subjectivity, and the discursive effect through screenings and discussions, this chapter focuses on the very action of first person confrontation and proactive documentation of one's witness, to engage with fellow-participants as well as viewer-followers to maximise the collective effort. In the following section, I first introduce Ai Weiwei's public-engaged art practices and the wider context of rising political activism in China in the past twenty years. Then I offer an exploration of what I regard as 'camera activism', with a detailed analysis of *Lao Ma Ti Hua*. Lastly, this chapter also highlights some of Ai's problematic actions as a charismatic celebrity, which sometimes have hindered his acceptance by Chinese individuals, overshadowing and obscuring the complexity of resistance by other individuals within China, and preventing full recognition of the complex collective forces which support Ai.

Political Activism and the Rise of Individual Rights in China

In addition to being an artist, cultural critic, architect and curator, Ai Weiwei is also recognised internationally as a political activist and celebrity dissident. Political activism has become a key theme in his art practice, and has gained much public awareness, especially since his 'Public Citizen Investigation Project' in 2008. This project, which involved many of Ai's followers and volunteers, has been developed into several public-engaged artworks. These explore and expose the cause-effect relationship between 'tofu construction' – the low quality, fragile school buildings which were not built to regulations because of local officials' corruption – and the death of a large number of school children in the devastating high-magnitude earthquakes in Wenchuan, Sichuan province. One example of these artworks is a visually astonishing installation called 'Straight' shown at the 2013 Venice Art Biennale. 'Straight' is a collation of 150 tonnes of steel support beams that Ai and his group collected from the collapsed school sites, which were painstakingly re-straightened. The work has been shown together with an installation of a wall of names of the dead children, with an audio accompaniment speaking the names through the voices of anonymous volunteers.

In many of Ai's political activist artworks, he encourages his participants to use digital video cameras as a weapon to document their investigations, his most well-known film being *Lao Ma Ti Hua*. Artists' political engagements such as this have been aligned with increasing activist movements in China in recent decades. In what Yan Yunxiang regards as the state-enforced decollectivisation process in post-socialist China, the state's retreat from public life has meant that individuals have gained more freedom (Yan 2009, 2010). Along with the desire for personal happiness is a growing concern for individual rights, not just for political rights, equal opportunities and the recognition of marginalised identities, but also the right to enjoy a better environment and safer food.

Speaking of individual rights, as I mentioned in the Introduction to this book, current studies share the view that in the history of struggle over the moral and political meaning of the self throughout the twentieth century, individual subjects have been encouraged to challenge Confucian constraints; however, it is still the conformity of the individual towards the state that has been emphasised, rather than the individual's rights against that of the state. Mulhahn notes that the concept of individual rights, which shield an individual from excesses of state power, has never existed in Chinese history (Mulhahn 2010: 145).

Fei Xiaotong, one of the best-known social scientists to have emerged from China in the early twentieth century, argues that the rise of individual rights has not been encouraged in, what he regards as, the Chinese pattern of social relations, *chaxugeju* (differential mode of association), which I have mentioned in the Introduction. It is order, in the form of *li* (propriety), one of the five constant virtues, as the 'publicly recognised behavioural norm', rather than *fa* (law, 法) that is in force (Fei 1992: 70).

> The concept of public was the ambiguous *tianxia* [all under heaven, 天下], whereas the state was seen as the emperor's family . . . The state and the public are but additional circles that spread out like the waves from the splash of each person's social influence. Therefore, people must cultivate themselves before they can extend outward. Accordingly, self-restraint has become the most important virtue in social life. The Chinese thus are unable to assert themselves against society to ensure that society does not infringe on their individual rights. In fact, the Chinese notion of a differential mode of association does not allow for individual rights to be an issue at all. (Fei 1992: 70)

Therefore, in Fei's understanding, in the Chinese pattern of social relations *chaxugeju*, the boundary between public and private has never been clear and does not encourage the rise of individual rights.

Even during the Late Qing and May Fourth periods at the turn of the twentieth century, the intellectual framework profoundly mirrored the state-focused intellectual tradition (Svarverud 2010: 195). Along with the introduction of the modern Western concept of the individual, ideas of citizenship, individual autonomy and individual rights became key terms openly discussed by early modern intellectuals. However, the interpretation of these words still mirrored the traditional relationship between the individual and the state – that the construction of individual identity involved a dual task of both self-cultivation and obligation towards the state (Zarrow 1998). Peter Zarrow states:

> Chinese intellectuals in the late Qing availed themselves of the symbolic and conceptual resources both of Confucianism and of Western history and thought. From Confucianism came such ideas as moral autonomy and from modern Western ideas the notion of individuals as rights-bearers. We cannot assume that *quan* [rights, 权] in its various guises and compounds was used in the same sense as 'rights' carried earlier in the West or possessed today. (1998: 210)

As an important reformist intellectual at the time, Liang Qichao's ideas of *zizhi* and morality published in *Xinminshuo* (1998) emphasised the restriction on individuals through self-discipline and moral achievement for the construction of a modern nation state, but he focused less on the individual's rights. Svarverud argues that though Liang's term of *zizhi* can be translated as 'autonomy', it is different from the Kantian notion of autonomy (2010: 207);[1] instead, it should be best translated as 'self-discipline', sharing some similarities with the traditional Confucian value of self-cultivation – a kind of self-legislation that man places upon himself (ibid.). In addition, scholars note that Liang's concept of morality is in fact based on a dichotomy between *gongde* (public morality, 公德) and *side* (private morality, 私德). While 'public morality' refers to 'one's ability to strengthen group cohesion', 'private morality' refers to 'the means of creating individuals of use to the group' (Zarrow 1998: 219). Therefore, he emphasises self-discipline and moral achievement of the individual for the national project of modern state-building, rather than focusing on the individual's rights.

During the May Fourth period, the intellectual Gao Yihan created the terms '*xiaoji*' ('lesser self') and '*daji*' ('greater self'). However, Lydia Liu argues that Gao's terminology does not disrupt the hierarchical order between the individual and the state (Liu 1993a: 179–80). Svarverud also states that 'to Gao Yinhan, true freedom of the self may only be obtained through self-restraint, echoing Liang's arguments from *Xinminshuo*, when the individual is able to sacrifice his smaller [lesser] self and strive for the larger [greater] self' (2010: 217). Following Gao's division of 'lesser self' and 'greater self', the contemporary Chinese scholar Xu Jilin concludes that individualism, as developed during the May Fourth period, was a combination of '*xiaowo*' ('lesser I', 小我) and '*dawo*' ('greater I', 大我). The ultimate goal of *xiaowo*, a self equipped with a sense of reason and social obligation, is to serve the *dawo*, embedded in the sense of public interest and the nation (Xu 2009).

After the Communist Party came into power a radical transformation of social structures took place, which was based on the complete submission of the self to the state. The socialist ideology requests the submission of all individuals as socialist workers to build the new socialist state. 'Every citizen was to be a fellow comrade, engaged in the common task of building a new social order, sharing the same "will" or "ambition" to combine their efforts in the common cause' (Stockman 2000: 81). Although 'the socialist new men' were empowered to fight against the traditional constraints, the new socialist state asked for a new kind of submission for the construction of a communist state.

However, in post-Mao China, individuals have been increasingly asserting their rights in relation to the state, especially through online activism and recent political volunteering/ participation. This marks a major difference in the individual–state relationship, compared to previous eras. The decline of socialist institutions and marketisation in the context of decollectivisation has resulted in social inequality and uneven distribution of wealth. Although the socialist workplace has not been entirely abolished, it provides social security and resources for individuals who are mainly urban, middle-level income earners (Thelle 2004). For the majority of the rural population and laid-off workers, the structural changes mean the loss of state protection in employment, medical care and housing benefit. Hu's *Family Phobia* illustrates how the cut in socialist social benefits affects the lives of Hu's family members, especially his aged parents, who are former socialist workers.

In the context of the lack of social security and protection, individuals through different means start to link the self with a set of rights and raise their voices to ask for legal protection, hence the rise of rights-assertion (Yan 2009: 280). What Wang Hui regards as China being in an era of depoliticised politics over the last four decades might be the case on the macro level, but there has been increasing micro political activism in the Peoples Republic of China. The most developed of this is the rise in consumer rights consciousness through consumer protection movements since the 1980s (Hooper 2005), which led to the establishment of the Consumer Protection Law in 1993 (Palmer 2006: 57).

Since the late 1990s there has been increasing voluntary social participation and political activism in cyberspace, which reflects the rise of a new citizenship asking for equal opportunities, the protection of human rights and the recognition of marginalised social identities (Damm and Thomas 2006; Lagerkvist 2006; Yang 2009). Yang Guobin regards this as 'online activism', which is a direct reflection of the new citizen activism and 'a response to the grievances, injustices, and anxieties caused by the structural transformation of Chinese society' (2009: 7). Such activism is visible in the constant environmental protests, migrant worker protests, anti-official corruption movements and fight for freedom of speech on Chinese social media such as Weibo (微博, literally meaning 'mini blog'). Individual self-expression has formed streams of political activism in the PRC, which continue to push boundaries. For example, in January 2013, when journalists of *Southern Weekly*, the most politically outspoken of Chinese newspapers, openly refused to participate in the censorship order enacted by the provincial propaganda bureau, individuals from all over the country showed enormous support through street demonstrations as well as via social media.

More activist movements have moved beyond the Internet, with the support and assistance of digital technologies, easily accessed digital cameras, mobile phones and social media. Among Chinese independent documentary – which has long had a reputation of representing a reality that is in opposition, or alternative, to state-controlled media production – there has been a growing number of politically engaged and activist-related independent documentary productions. For example, Zhao Liang's documentary *Petition* (2009) is a long-term documentation of a large group of marginalised petitioners/activists, who for many years travelled from rural areas to gather in the suburbs of the capital Beijing to appeal against various miscarriages of justice. While the petitioners fight for legal justice, the filmmaker Zhao has aligned his independent intentions to encourage free artistic expression with those of his characters, searching for fair treatment and human rights.

Compared to the *cinéma-vérité* style of politically engaged Chinese documentaries, Ai's documentaries could be seen as part of a small group of activist documentary cinema that explicitly urges social change (Qian 2014: 182). In addition to *Lao Ma Ti Hua*, Ai's studio has also produced some other non-first person narrative activist documentary, such as *A Lonely Person* (2010), investigating the cause and effect of an incident in which a young citizen, Yang Jia, broke into a local police station in Shanghai and killed a group of policemen. Other makers of activist documentaries include Hu Jie and Ai Xiaoming, who have been subversively conducting investigations into social injustice and human rights abuses (Zhang 2012). While Hu Jie investigates and exposes repressed historical issues or moments, such as in his films *Searching for Lin Zhao's Soul* (*Xunzhao Lin Zhao de Linghun*, 2004) and *Though I am Gone* (*Wo Sui Si Qu*, 2006), Ai Xiaoming focuses more on contemporary social issues, such as women's rights and inequality in her documentary *The Vagina Monologues: Stories Behind the Scenes* (*Yindao Dubai*, 2004), and village elections, land ownership and village-level anti-corruption in *Tai Shi Village* (*Tai Shi Cui*, 2006). Both filmmakers have also been engaging intensively in activism through camera and documentary, such as in their collaborative film *Our Children* (*Women de wawa*, Ai Xiaoming and Hu Jie, 2009). More recently, Nanfu Wang's award-winning activist documentary *Hooligan Sparrow* (2016) tells the story of her own journey with a group of feminist activists and 'the extraordinary revolutionary Sparrow'[2] who battle for girls' and women's human rights despite state surveillance. During the process of making this film, the female filmmaker Wang also becomes a target of the state, but she continues shooting, confronting the political constraints with hidden-camera glasses and secret recording devices, and eventually smuggling the footage out of the country. Such activist documentary practices provide crucial insights into the increasingly individualising and technologically mutable contemporary Chinese society.

Camera Activism as a Form of Critical Social Engagement

In the international field of documentary studies, recent works (Aguayo 2005; Whiteman 2004; Christensen 2009) provide significant insights on analysing the impact of activist documentary. Aguayo focuses on the finished production as a political object and points out the constitutive nature of activist documentary and its potential to generate a sense of shared subjectivities among the viewers. 'The activist genre has the potential to create a spectator, deliberative, consumer or viewer-citizen identity that has varying ramifications for the process of social change' (Aguayo 2005: 6). Likewise, *Lao Ma Ti Hua* has the potential to create 'collective audience identity' (ibid.) during the viewing process. However, the number of viewers it has had is still very limited, and it remains difficult to follow the audiences' identification process so as to measure the effectiveness of how such activist documentaries are received.

Lao Ma Ti Hua was made shortly after the beating incident discussed earlier and was first posted on international social media platforms such as Twitter and Facebook. This incident, along with the Xinjiang riots on 5 July 2009, raised intense online debates within and outside China during that period, which ultimately resulted in the ban on Twitter and Facebook in China in August 2009. Meanwhile, the film was also circulated through Chinese video-sharing sites, such as tudou.com, and online forums under its jovial non-sequitur '*Lao Ma Ti Hua*', which is the name of a local Sichuan dish of boiled trotters and also the name of the restaurant where the group gathered the evening before the incident – chosen as the film's title in an effort to avoid detection by the authorities. Nonetheless, the film was soon discovered by Chinese 'Internet police' and was subsequently blocked for users inside China. Ai Weiwei's studio produced a large number of DVDs[3] which were circulated freely, but mainly to sub-communities, when requested. Given the enormous population of China, the number of viewers who have accessed the film is still very limited. To focus only on the film as a political object would be to overlook the fact that official banning of Ai's work in China may create more desire for seeing the film. As Whiteman argues, focusing on the finished film text offers 'a very limited understanding of the complex and multifaceted ways in which film enters the political process' (2004: 54). For Ai's group, the dissemination of the film itself could also be seen as a crucial part of their activism.

Looking at the larger political context of the production, distribution and exhibition of activist documentary and the extended social movements that relate to it, Whiteman proposes a 'coalition model', to

> evaluate a film's potential effects on its producers and other participants involved in production, on activist groups that might contribute to or use the film, and on decision makers and other elites that might hear about the film. A political documentary has a more extensive range of effects beyond changes in individual understanding or attitude. (Whiteman 2004: 54)

For Whiteman, 'coalition' refers to a mutually beneficial 'feedback loop' between filmmakers, film subjects, grassroots screeners, audiences and political activists. This loop creates a coalition of organisations and individuals who use the documentary as a point of connection.

In the case of *Lao Ma Ti Hua*, in addition to its impact on the viewers (which is difficult to quantify, as previously mentioned), the film has become a point of connection that links the participants together. We should also not underestimate the importance of Ai's elite identity as a globally well-known artist and political advocate in attracting volunteers to participate in his activist network. The volunteer individuals collectively made this film possible. Concurrently, the worldwide circulation of the film through social media has also influenced fellow independent filmmakers and cultural elites in China, as well as some decision-makers, even though the official recognition of the impact was through a ban on Ai Weiwei and his subsequent house arrest in 2011. The leading Chinese independent filmmaker Wu Wenguang has great respect for Ai's filming practice, regarding it as 'complete action' (author's interview with Wu, 2010), a medium to create social contact and civic engagement. The 'coalition model' provides great insight into understanding the discursive impact of *Lao Ma Ti Hua* at different stages of the film, and from varying perspectives. However, it is not the aim of this chapter to over-emphasise its political nature in the context of production and circulation. By looking at the beneficial 'feedback loop', Ai himself might be the biggest beneficiary of his own activist public-engagement. The international recognition of this film, together with Ai's previous public artworks, have further enhanced Ai's position in the art world and as one of the few critical voices on contemporary Chinese society from within China recognised by the West.

This chapter explores the very action of first person provocative documentation, or what I regard as 'camera activism', a camera-empowered individual gesture of critical socio-political engagement. It is especially crucial to have an understanding of activist films made outside Western democratic political systems, particularly in politically repressed states. Camera activism highlights individuals' utilisation of digital cameras like a shield to document one's witness as evidence for self-protection, and like a gun to directly confront the opposition and engage with fellow activists as well as potential viewer-followers. The action of confrontational filming by the participants, most of whom are amateur filmmakers, demonstrates the very act of engaging and enraging, and also generates affective and critical responses among the viewers, potential followers. In *Our Children* (2009), multiple witnesses, parents who lost their children in the 2008 Sichuan earthquake, took amateur footage with their mobile phones and digital cameras to document the collapse of school buildings as visual testimony. In *Meishi Street* (2006), the director Ou Ning handed the DV camera to his protagonist Zhang, a local resident in Da Zhanlan, Beijing, which was facing state-enforced demolition. Zhang then used the camera to protect his rights and to confront local officials as he fought for his personal familial space.

Such a phenomenon taking place in the contemporary PRC in the twenty-first century mirrors what Henry Jenkins calls 'participatory culture', which emphasises the human participation rather than interactive media as a technological advance (2006: 137). The key features of this concept include low barriers to artistic expression and civic engagement, strong social connections among members to make and share creative endeavours via informal mentoring, and a belief in collective effort (ibid.). Though initially Jenkins discusses 'participatory culture' in contrast with mass commercial culture and corporate media in the national context of America, it seems relevant to understanding the grassroots or *minjian* cultural political participation, in contrast to the official and commercial media production in the contemporary PRC. By paying attention to who is making the documentary and who is speaking, we notice that the once consumers or receivers also become active producers and deliverers of their own creations and agenda. Camera activism also echoes the recent rise of 'citizen journalism', 'the spontaneous actions of ordinary people, caught up in extraordinary events, who felt compelled to adopt the role of a news reporter' (Allan and Thorsen 2009).

In such a provocative and confrontational act of documenting, camera activism demonstrates subjective, first person perspectives. It is the moment of 'I' being there, eye-witnessing what is happening, often together with many other like-minded, camera-enabled individuals, that is foregrounded. Such subjective visions edited together form a force of the first person plural. The emphasis on individual self-expression by the use of personal and digital technologies precisely locates camera activism as being an important part of China's iGeneration moving image culture.

In addition to its confrontational documenting activities and subjective visions, camera activism has another dimension, which is the collective force of all the participants. *Lao Ma Ti Hua* is made through the collective effort of all the participants. Digital technologies have lowered the barrier for like-minded anonymous individuals to take part in Ai's political art projects. The footage was taken by multiple cameras by different members in the group, including Ai Weiwei himself and the main cameraman Zhao Zhao. Using amateur footage, sound recording and photos of all the participants in the end sequence, Ai and his volunteers construct a first person plural of a group of rights-conscious selves drawn together by their shared concern for individual rights. In the next section, I will examine how the making of *Lao Ma Ti Hua* becomes camera activism.

Lao Ma Ti Hua: Provocative Documentation, First Person Confrontation and Collective Force

Lao Ma Ti Hua begins with Ai sitting under a spotlight, directly addressing the camera in a medium close-up (see Figure 6.2). Subsequent to the beating incident, Ai is explaining the purpose of their trip to Chengdu, which is to support an independent investigator, Tan Zuoren. As the leader of the project, he addresses

Figure 6.2 Ai directly addressing the camera in a medium close-up in *Lao Ma Ti Hua*

the message of the film: 'We are doing what any citizen should for fairness and justice in our society.' Emphasising '*we*' (*women*, 我们) and '*our*' (*womende*, 我们的), rather than an individual '*I*' (*wo*, 我), Ai represents the collective voice of himself and his volunteers. By addressing the audience directly, he creates a connection between the participants and the audience. This opening establishes the political gesture of Ai's group, presented by Ai, of seeking social justice for the children who were victims of the Sichuan earthquake, as well as human rights for all Chinese individuals in the PRC.

The majority of the film is shot by Zhao Zhao, who is also an artist, one of Ai's closest followers, and is involved in many of Ai's investigations. The closeness to the '"raw visibility" of the political' (Corner 2009: 115), documented through personal vision, creates an intimate experience whereby the audience is able to immerse themselves in what is happening to the character-participants as events unfold.

It is important to notice the changing role of the camera before and after the arrest incident. Ai reveals in an interview that, before the incident, the camera served simply as a recorder for archival purposes, documenting their journey without an intention to craft the footage into a film (Weishi 2011). The hand-held image is shaky and in low resolution. Zhao does not seem to care whether it is too dark or too noisy to film, and neither does he intentionally capture anything dramatic. After the incident, Zhao seems to be more conscious of the power of the camera to record what they have experienced as evidence, as well as to disturb the local authorities.

In one sequence, where one of the participants, Liu, is released from custody, Zhao takes the camera to look for her in the police station to interview her. Zhao does not try to hide his identity when he talks to Liu from behind the camera. Their conversations are not only informative but also expose the audience to more voices, which together construct a rights-conscious collective.

Zhao exercises the power of the camera to investigate and also as a weapon to engage and provoke the state authorities. His fearless and forceful filmmaking demonstrates his persistence in the fight for individual rights. Mostly using long takes, the images are very rough. However, this roughness and the imperfect framing indicate the difficulty in filming, and give a sense of being there on the spot. In one scene, when the group forces themselves into a local police station, Zhao holds the camera facing up from a low angle, pretending it is not switched on. As a witness, it captures the arguments between the police and the group. At the most heated point of the dispute, when it is difficult to film, Zhao puts the camera facing the floor, using it as a secret sound recorder, capturing the evidence of the awkward behaviour and procedures of the police. Ironically, when Ai uses his mobile phone to take a picture of the police, several policemen also hold up small DV cameras and start to film the protestors. At this moment, Zhao openly turns his camera towards the faces of the policemen. The two groups are in an irreconcilable confrontation, not only through their dialogue, but also through using cameras as weapons and an extension of power. While Zhao's and Ai's cameras are a demonstration of exercising their right to film, the police's cameras, on the other hand, are shown as an authoritarian eye keeping the citizens under control (see Figure 6.3).

Figure 6.3 A police officer in a local police station also films them with a small DV camera

Figure 6.4 When they ask Ai not to film, Ai insists on seeing the police officers' identity cards in the ending sequence of *Lao Ma Ti Hua* (2009)

In the last scene of the film, when Ai's group comes out of the police station, Ai uses his camera to take a picture of the building. Immediately a guard comes to him, asks him to switch off his camera and forces him to leave. Ai insists that he is in a public space and should have the freedom to film. Zhao's camera records this absurd moment when the policemen try to aggressively force them to turn off the camera. Because Zhao's camera is still on, the policemen do not dare do anything more violent. When Ai insists on seeing their police IDs, they can do nothing but present their IDs to Ai (see Figure 6.4).

While Zhao's recording takes up the majority of the film, there are two important moments that are of Ai Weiwei's own first person documentation. One is the self-portrait photo mentioned in the beginning of this chapter, and the other is a sound recording made by Ai's audio recorder. In the first part of the film, after the group goes back to their individual rooms, the screen suddenly turns black. At the upper left corner, the time is shown as '3 am, 12 August, 2009'. In the darkness, we hear the sound of fierce knocking on the door. Ai's determined voice asks firmly: 'Who is it?' A voice says: 'Police!' Ai asks: 'What police?' No one answers. Ai asks again, and the voice says 'Police from the local police-station.' Ai insists: 'Why are local cops knocking at my door at this hour?' 'Inspection!' 'Inspect what?' 'Inspect ID!' Ai does not yield: 'Who allows you to check ID at this time? . . .'

Having had dealings with the police for a long time, Ai is very conscious of the importance of keeping a record with any means possible. At this point,

Ai switches on the sound recorder to document this moment of violence. Ai refuses to open the door, demanding a response to the question 'How can you prove you are the police?', which is answered by them breaking in and beating him. Admittedly, there are elements of performance by Ai at this point. While Ai knows that the event is being recorded, the police do not. Though Ai is the victim, he clearly has control over how the event will be interpreted. Facing illegal treatment by the so-called police, Ai does not show any compromise, but keeps asking in the dark: 'Is this how police behave?', which invites the audience to question their heavy-handed approach.

Tension between the Collective Effort and Ai's Individual Public Image

While camera activism focuses on the actual action of provocative documentation, Leshu Torchin argues that to have a camera is not enough, because images need an ideological framework to reinforce the messages that images are meant to convey (2012). In Ai's camera activism, his celebrity image, just like that of the American documentary-maker Michael Moore, is used to deliver messages and attitudes. While Ai's public persona of a subversive power has become increasingly well-known internationally, he has also accumulated authority among his followers. Ai knows well how to use the collective power of his volunteers to construct an activist message, and is highly aware of the kind of media attention he can attract. He successfully articulates the power of art, camera, the Internet and the media to engage with the public and to achieve an interactive effect on society.

In *Lao Ma Ti Hua*, some of Ai's actions are conscious performances of his public image. Given Ai's image as a symbol of resistance to Chinese authority, starting the film with his image and voice clearly marks the nature of the film. After the police break in, there is a shot taken in the hotel corridor in which Ai stands in front of the camera wearing a white T-shirt with a big face printed on it. It is difficult to recognise the face – whether it is the face of Tan Zuoren, the independent investigator they seek to defend, or Ai's own. No matter whose face it is on Ai's T-shirt, Ai standing in front of the camera is clearly a political gesture speaking to the international audience.

However, Ai increasingly presents himself as a highly individualistic and sometimes ostentatious political figure. When Ai comments on the 2013 contemporary Chinese art exhibition at the Hayward Gallery London as being misrepresented, Paul Gladston criticises Ai's reductive view of the criticality of Chinese contemporary art. Gladston (2013) points out that Ai's assertive confrontational approach towards authority is more easily accepted in the Western democratic context, hence it is easy to gain support from the international media: however, it somehow simplifies the specific and complicated conditions of political struggle within China. Raising Ai's personal voice does not seem to do much good for the voices he is trying to represent. Behind his individualistic and sceptical voice, there are many different voices, which do not surrender to the state authorities, but are not all identical. How Ai Weiwei destabilises and decentralises his own authority has become an important question.

In *Lao Ma Ti Hua*, the individual activists who work with Ai are less well known. One of the major reasons for the making of this film was the personal incident of Ai being beaten by the police, even though other volunteers experienced similarly aggressive treatment. The struggle for justice for the collective victims has become a story about the persecution of the celebrity Ai Weiwei. After the beating, Ai and some other participants visit several local legal authorities searching for an explanation. As a power of his own, Ai speaks in a language that is highly aggressive and domineering. While the camera is used as the power to confront the authorities, it nevertheless also records Ai's own speech, which is delivered in a violent dictatorial manner with little space for negotiation. As Ai challenges the authoritarian state, he mirrors exactly the authoritarian features of the system they seek to resist. Following *Lao Ma Ti Hua*, Ai has uploaded another documentary, *So Sorry* (2012), named after his exhibition in Munich in 2009. It is a continuous documentation of his period of hospitalisation following the life-threatening injuries he received from the authorities. While his role as an artist attracts more individuals to participate in his activism, these collective efforts in return also further promote his artwork.

Beyond the tension between the collective efforts of Ai's activist group and Ai's individual public image are the changes in the larger political landscape in the PRC. The positive aspect of Ai's celebrity image has the potential to encourage more political participation among young Chinese individuals. As for the state authority, it is hard to say whether the large amount of camera activism circulated on Chinese social media, as well as the series of offline activist movements in the past few years have had any impact on the recent change of policy. Since the change in the PRC's leadership, centred on Xi Jinping coming into power in 2012, the anti-corruption movement and restructuring of the Chinese civil service have led to a series of arrests of corrupt officials in central and regional government, as well as in state-owned enterprises. Whilst Ai himself was under house arrest for a while from 2012 to 2015, he has undeniably increased the debate about the possibility of activism in China. Camera activism, as demonstrated in the political art practice of Ai and many others, provides a channel for individuals to act as watchdog for social problems.

Acknowledgement

An earlier version of this chapter was published in *Studies in Documentary Film*, 9: 1 (2015).

Notes

1. Svarverud states that 'autonomy in the Kantian sense points to man's innate disposition and freedom of moral self-legislation based on his pure reason, only limited by the purposiveness of nature directing human morality' (Svarverud 2010: 207).
2. From the documentary's official website: http://hooligansparrow.com/.
3. In the year following the incident, 100,000 copies of the film were given out to people. Ai reveals this in his public dialogue with Dr Katie Hill at the Tate Modern, 2010.

Chapter 7

Whose Self on Camera? Motives, Mistrust, Disputed Authenticities

> The significance of this project is not about whether they can make a film with a camera in their hands, but when we are given the freedom to speak for ourselves, how do we understand such freedom, and how to use it. When we all use this freedom and walk along, why do we backbite each other and pull each other out? It examines the idea of citizenship.
>
> Wu Wenguang, author's interview 2010

In this book, I have discussed first person films made by women at the turn of a new century, films made about the transition of filmmaker's '*laojia*' ('old home'), young generation filmmakers' first person action documentary and the celebrity Ai Weiwei's camera activism. This chapter focuses on a group of individuals who I have not yet discussed elsewhere – socially less empowered, subaltern villagers – through a case study of the 'China Villagers Documentary Project'.[1] This project, started as a one-off in 2005, was originally part of an EU–China village governance training programme. Led by Chinese independent filmmaker Wu Wenguang and project co-ordinator Jian Yi, ten villagers across China were selected to each make a ten-minute short documentary on their own village with a portable amateur DV camera. After the first year, the project continued, financed by Wu's studio. Four of the village filmmakers, Wang Wei, Shao Yuzhen, Jia Zhitan and Zhang Huancai, continued their first person filmmaking and made documentaries annually from 2006 to 2009. Their films are titled 'My Village 2006/2007/2008/2009'.

Since the completion of the first year of the project, the villagers' films have been toured around festivals, universities and art centres in the USA, Europe and Hong Kong,[2] and have attracted much scholarly attention. Most current studies emphasise how this project empowers the villagers to express themselves, and provides an authentic perspective on grassroots China through the villagers' own lens that could not be obtained by professional filmmakers (Wang 2005; Huang 2016). Among them, Huang Xuelei studies the peasant Jia Zhidan's documentaries in this project from the angle of everyday life (2016). She provides a nuanced analysis of how Jia's documentaries provide an insiders angle on 'everydayness', such as the passage of time demonstrated through the growth of crops, festivals, food, 'leftover kids' (children who remain in the villages while their parents find work elsewhere). However, like other scholars, Huang's primary focuses is still on the film text itself, and she does not explore the complexity of the relationship between the filmmaker Wu and the villagers. Taking the production context into consideration, Matthew D. Johnson offers a distinctive sociological perspective and discusses usually overlooked aspects: the transnational influence of this project; how it came into being; and the power relations behind what he calls the 'NGO aesthetic', 'a specific form or mode of staging which characterises documentaries produced within the space of international organisations and related projects' (2014: 259). Johnson traces the earliest practice of this participatory mode in China back to the early 1990s.[3] However, he does not offer much detailed analysis of what this specific NGO aesthetic is, apart from identifying a reliance on 'the participation of villagers' (Johnson 2014: 266).

The attention given to the vernacular narrative in China by international NGOs and Chinese intellectuals mirrors the shifting paradigm from the metanarrative of a Western worldview to a decentralised, localised micro-narrative investigation, even though it is not triggered by the same reasons. In the West, the delegitimisation of cultural imperialism and the rise of cultural relativism called for a more self-reflexive view to work with indigenous communities, with local participation. In China, it is argued that the idea of socially engaged projects was first brought up by international NGOs such as the Ford Foundation, to understand ethnic minorities widely spread out in southwest China. It was then adapted and further developed by urban independent filmmakers and intellectuals, with the intention of uniting the local and rural to produce a vernacular narrative to balance the official narrative and political discourse. It is this perspective that has attracted so much scholarly attention.

Acknowledging the importance of the transnational influence on this project and how it was initially designed as an empowerment exercise for the villagers, this chapter, however, explores the production context, the interaction and power relations between Wu Wenguang as the project's 'creative instructor' and the villager amateur filmmakers within this socially and community engaged art project. Claire Bishop points out that projects like this aim at diffusing single authorship into collaborative work, and are perceived to transform the symbolic capital of the artwork into a constructive social force (2012: 12–13). As Tom Finkelpearl argues, social practice is 'art that's socially engaged, where the social interaction is at some level the art' (Finkelpearl 2013).

Existing literature usually focuses on the idealistic wish of this project to turn the passive villagers into active makers, participants in a seemingly harmonious collaboration between the urban filmmaker Wu and the villagers. However, this only shows the façade of this project. Distrust and conflicts between the villagers and the urban filmmakers, and the villagers' resistance to being manipulated by intellectuals have been largely overlooked in the current scholarship. Therefore, this chapter provides a corrective intervention to explore this largely ignored aspect of the power relations between Wu as 'creative instructor' and the villagers. The subaltern villagers were invited to 'speak for themselves'. When their films were shown to domestic urban and international audiences, they were labelled as 'authentic' in terms of the material and 'original' in viewpoint, as they provided an alternative vision of the local by the locals themselves. However, I argue that the pure 'authentic' and 'original' appearance of these films does not exist. The seemingly authentic views of village China in the first ten films are in fact the result of manipulation by the urban-intellectual filmmakers who project their ideal vision of peasants through the very hands of the peasants.

Nevertheless, I am also aware of the criticism of only looking at such a project sociologically through an ethical lens, which regards the participators as still 'inferior to those who are able to look, to contemplate ideas, and have critical distance on the world' as it 'serves only as an allegory of inequality' (Bishop 2012: 38). Instead, this chapter explores how all participants – Wu and the villagers – have come to understand themselves more clearly through the processes of participation and interaction. This project problematises how all the participants perceive themselves and their action of filmmaking.

In the first stage of this project, when the chosen ten villagers first participated, the villager filmmakers remained quiet when they were taught how to film. The conflicts accumulated during the production and editing process of their first ten 10-minute short films. The villagers were not very happy with their films, saying they were not being made according to their own will, but to satisfy what Wu thought should be the right portrayal of Chinese rural life through the lens of the villagers. The afternoon before their first screening at Wu's studio, the villagers gathered together in their hotel and discussed whether they were happy with the films. They all showed some level of dissatisfaction towards Wu and the other editors' supervision. Their discussion was recorded by one of the villagers, Wang Wei, and the tape was later given to Wu. Wu screened their discussion with the other editors and volunteers. While Wu felt betrayed by the peasant filmmakers, he also started to reflect on his relationship with the villagers. The second stage, when four of the villagers continued to participate and made feature-length documentaries, was an important stage when the filmmaker Wu Wenguang and the villagers all got to know each other, and themselves, better. At this stage, the villagers had more space to discuss and negotiate with Wu on an acceptable self-representation of their own villages.

In the following section, I first introduce how this participatory documentary project started, and then analyse the villagers' response to and dissatisfaction with Wu's motives and suggestions. Attention is then given to Wu, examining from his position as an intellectual, his own distrust towards the villagers and his interpretation of the villagers' resistance. Taking both perspectives into consideration and looking at their communication via group email exchanges[4] and by examining the villagers' documentary films, I aim to unpick the power relations between the urban-intellectual filmmakers and the peasant villagers. Behind the collaboration are how the villager amateur filmmakers unconsciously and consciously deconstruct and resist their 'given' social identity as subaltern selves, and how they negotiate a presentation of their own subjectivities through the documentary filmmaking practice. Their understanding of their own selves influences their choices of aesthetic strategies, subject matter, ethical relations and their audience. Their actions of rebelling against their given roles, challenging the idealised image given by intellectuals, and questioning the established social relations within the filmmaker communities reflect their effort to reconstruct their identities through filmmaking. This project affects how the urban filmmaker Wu understands himself as much as how the villagers understand themselves. Ultimately, the value of this socially engaged project, in my opinion, is not to see what the villagers' self-portraits are like, but to examine the negotiation process through which both the villagers and Wu came to understand themselves and each other, and to construct an acceptable self-representation.

Inviting the Villagers to 'Speak for Themselves': Mutual Distrust between the Peasant Selves and Cultural Elites

The China Villagers Documentary Project was initially a project commissioned by the EU – the China Training Programme on Village Self Governance, a collaboration between the EU and China's Ministry of Civil Affairs. In 2005, when the training programme had run for five years, its public communication manager Jian Yi approached Wu Wenguang to do a documentary on China's village self-governance. Initially having no intention of taking this commission, Wu revealed that he later came up with the idea of a participatory mode by inviting villagers to film their own villages with amateur DV cameras (Wu 2009).

This participatory mode, as pointed out by several scholars (Un 2009; Zhang 2010; Johnson 2014), was first used by the Ford Foundation's NGO projects in China in 1991. It was used in the Yunnan Women's Reproductive Health and Development Programme where fifty-three rural Chinese women took photos of their own daily lives with the goal of educating and promoting awareness of women's reproductive health. In 2002 the Ford Foundation launched another participatory project called 'Learn Our Own Traditions', run by Guo

Jing and Zhaxi Nima, which recruited villagers from Yunnan to document their distinctive local cultural practices. Given this background, the China Villagers Documentary Project was not the first in China to put cameras in the hands of villagers – but for most villagers selected for this project, it was their first experience of working with a DV camera and making a film.[5]

After the China Villagers Documentary Project was approved by the EU–China Training programme committee, Wu and Jian started to place adverts in several newspapers, which soon attracted applications from forty-eight peasants from eighteen provinces. Wu and Jian selected ten, of different age groups, areas of origin, gender, and so on. The chosen villager filmmakers' ages ranged from twenty-four to fifty-nine; there were two from ethnic minorities: one from the ethnic Zhuang minority in Guangxi and the other a young girl of Tibetan ethnicity from Yunnan Province. There were two women among the ten: one the Tibetan girl, the other a fifty-year-old housewife from a suburban village near Beijing. The villagers were provided with free tickets to travel to Wu Wenguang's studio in the grassroots artist's district Caochangdi in Beijing, to learn how to film. Then they went back to their villages to film for a few weeks, before returning to Beijing to each work with a professionally trained editor to edit their film.

Along with recruiting villagers, the project also recruited ten young filmmakers and university students to make a short film at the same time. The final project comprised ten short films made by the villagers, ten short films made by university students or young filmmaker volunteers, 100 photos, and a fifty-five-minute documentary called *Seen and Heard* made by Jian Yi, documenting how the project got started and the process of recruiting and training the villagers. As shown in *Seen and Heard*, and as seen by outsiders, intellectuals and professional filmmakers inside and outside China, this was a successful public or community engaged, multi-authorship project. However, behind the glamorous label there was mistrust between the two classes in this autoethnographic project.

In the beginning, the chosen villagers could not quite believe this project was real, saying 'It is too good to be true' or 'It might be a scam'. Some villagers recall:

> I called my brother that day and my brother said, 'Are you being fooled? It is too good to be true, to give you a camera and pay for your trip.' I told him it was even the night sleeping seat. He said, 'It is too good to be true, don't go, don't go.' I said, 'Why would they fool me? I don't have money; even if they don't pay for my trip eventually, it'd be a visit for me to Beijing.' (Zhang Huancai, from Shaan'xi Province)[6]
>
> I told some people in the village, those who I thought have seen the world. They all worried I was being tricked. Almost everyone thinks that way, asking 'Is it a pyramid selling organisation?' (Wang Wei, from Shandong Province)[7]

> My son said, 'It must be a conman . . . You are so old and have experienced some scams like this before, how could you think it is a good thing? Don't be so naive.' I said, 'It is in the newspaper, *Southern Weekly*.' He said, 'They put it in the newspaper, but when you go, they'd ask you to pay all kinds of fees, thousands; they want you to give all your money to them, you won't even know that you have been cheated.' (Nong Ke, from Guizhou Province)[8]

The villagers' suspicion of this project indicated a long term distrust between the rural and the urban in China, which also reflected the low social trust discussed by sociologist Yan Yuanxiang and as shown in the films discussed in Chapters 4 and 5 of this book. For rural residents, the urban seems to be very distant and cold, whereas urban residents also have stereotyped views of rural people, which were reflected through Wu's attitude towards the villagers. As Wu revealed after proposing this idea, even he did not quite believe that the villagers would be able to make films. He even suggested buying second-hand DV cameras for the villagers, but out of respect, the team eventually bought new cameras. Wu and his team taught the villagers how to use the cameras in Wu's studio, but they also recruited ten professionally trained young filmmakers to make ten short documentaries, just in case nothing came of the villagers' efforts (Wu 2009).

Still speaking from the position of an intellectual, and regarding himself as an educated person, Wu reveals:

> In fact, I didn't trust them either. Even in the beginning, it was mainly to fulfil my wish to do something different, as if I cannot continue doing what I was doing then I can do something else. Many art projects were like that. Have a try, get a taste of it, then give up. I was also one of those urban intellectuals, a bit frivolous with capricious passions. (Author's interview, 2010)

For Wu, it was out of curiosity and as an artistic experiment that he started this project. Being among the first group of independent filmmakers that emerged in the early 1990s, Wu had reached a time when he started to seriously question the meaning of documentary in the form of direct cinema. He did not want to repeat what he had done before, which was filming the marginalised others. He confessed that the most obvious result of this kind of independent documentary was the accumulation of the filmmakers' own international reputation. He was excited to see 'what could be turned out if we put cameras in *their* [author's emphasis] hands. Of course they would film something, but whether they could film with their own style, whether they could compete with professional and institutionalised filmmakers at the same level, I couldn't quite believe' (author's interview, 2010).

In early November 2005, still with their suspicions, the ten chosen villagers went to Wu's studio, Caochangdi Workstation in Beijing. The encounter between the villagers and Wu in his *minjian* art space was an encounter between two grassroots marginal groups – the peasants as the subaltern, and the independent non-official filmmakers as the alternative to, and often repressed in, the mainstream media discourse. These two groups were both seen as subordinate to the party-state in different ways; very often the sense of marginality posits independent filmmakers in the same position as the peasants and workers. Even so, inevitably, there was also a power relationship between them, which became more obvious as the project progressed.

At Caochangdi, the villagers were given a one-week intensive workshop arranged by Wu. They learnt the basic technical skills of video shooting and discussed their proposed topics. At the end of the workshop, each villager was given a Panasonic NV GS28 camera, a tripod and ten blank video tapes, before travelling back to their home village to film. The villagers spent the month of November shooting in their own villages.

During the production, Wu paid a visit to five of the villagers, watching their material and teaching them, on location, about what to film and how to film. This was the time when the tensions between Wu and the villagers started to emerge. Wu recalled his visit to Wang Wei, a young villager from Shandong province, who was only twenty-seven years old at the time,

> Wang was very quiet (when I visited him), but I was only there for three days. I needed to know what had been filmed, and gave him my important and key instructions. When I realised he was very concise when he speaks, I immediately told him that 'your style would be like this: when you film, you also comment with your off or on screen voice in this very concise manor. It could give a very meaningful style and very effective.' I walked around in his village with him, told him what to film, and how to film. I didn't notice he was unhappy at the time. (Wu 2009)

Even though the camera had been given to Wang, the hands from the city were still trying to control it, and took this role for granted. Wu's instruction was not only given to Wang, but also to other villagers. When Wu visited Jia Zhitan, an older villager who was in his mid-fifties, he found that Jia was very keen on intervening in contemporary village issues. Jia used the DV camera to confront village officials, but he was rejected when he tried to interview the village secretary, who scorned him as taking part in a nameless grassroots project. Wu was very angry when he realised that Jia was producing an investigative journalism-style documentary, just like the CCTV programme called 'Focus' (*Jiaodian fangtan*, 焦点访谈). Wu looked down on this conventional media reporting method which he regarded as the mouthpiece of the government. He tried to persuade Jia to document everyday life in the village, to adopt a grassroots position and express his own voice independently, rather than pretending to be a village TV reporter. Wu believed that his intervention in Jia's filming was necessary, 'because what he knows about film comes from television, programmes such as 'Focus', but we are not doing an investigative TV programme to expose something' (author's interview, 2010).

The villagers were inevitably influenced by the investigative TV documentary programmes they usually watched, a style they were exposed to and also a style that, in their eyes, represented power and influence. Wu overlooked the fact that even though they mimicked mainstream TV style, they were investigators in their own right, aiming to get their own voice heard so as to make an impact. They would probably have believed that only by using this 'powerful' style would people listen to their message. As an 'insider' in his own village, Jia did not want to do what Wu told him to do – to document everyday life like an 'outsider' urban filmmaker. Living with the social problems that concerned him, Jia was desperate to expose the problems to a higher power, hoping to get the problems solved and the situation changed. This was very different from Wu's purpose: to document, so as to preserve, a village perspective and rural everyday life, as analysed by Huang (2016). Wu states that 'The camera does not mean power for him [Jia], but freedom and self-emancipation' (quoted by Huang 2016: 166). But in my understanding, it was exactly for the power that Jia was filming; not the power to control, but the power he aimed to gain for himself, so he could resist being spoken of and speak for himself. In her study, Huang acknowledges that she chose to study Jia because his work was more influential and had been shown more in and outside China. This hints at Wu's role as the gatekeeper; villagers such as Jia did not have the power and connections to get their own work known to the outside world. Indeed, Jia attracted the attention of a *New York Times* journalist who was willing to screen his film, but this was rejected by Wu.

In the editing stage, all the villagers went back to Wu's studio and each of them started to edit their footage into a ten-minute film with the help of a volunteer editor. There were occasional arguments between the villagers and Wu in the editing suites, but the largest outpouring of the villagers' dissatisfaction was at a meeting when nine villagers[9] gathered together in one of their hotel rooms and expressed their feelings on the project. This valuable meeting was spontaneously organised by the villagers themselves to air their own views.

Some believed that the films did not show their personal viewpoints at all, as from beginning to end, it was Wu who taught them how to film, what to film, and the editors (most of the time) who controlled the editing and constructed the representation of their villages. The meeting lasted over an hour and was documented by Wang Wei with his DV camera. The villagers then voted on whether they should show their discussion to Wu. As most of them agreed they should, they eventually gave the tape to Wu before they left Caochangdi on the second day.

Resisting the Given Identities: the Villagers' Response

The tape recording of the villagers' own dissatisfaction and anger with this project had a huge impact on Wu in the following years. A few years later, the discussion on the tape was transcribed, proofread by Wang Wei himself, and published in Wu's email group to everyone involved. The discussion reveals their resistance to constructions of their own representation formed through the hands of urban intellectuals, and also the differing views of the older and younger peasants.

In this recorded meeting, Wang Wei revealed that it was his interest in the issue of self-governance that had led him to participate in this project, not the idea of filmmaking itself, but what he wanted to express was not there in his film anymore:

> Every time Wu came, there would be something cut off. In the end, I feel the film was not as sharp as I intended it to be. I wanted the film to be called 'Nonsense', as no matter what, the village officials, the county government, they all speak nonsense; so do ordinary villagers who do not really fight for what they want, but only wrangle. But what I wanted to express was not there [in the film] anymore. Wu gave it a new title, called 'Subdivision of the land'. It is too general and not really what I want to express . . . When I talked about my feeling to some other villager-filmmakers, I found I was not alone. If they only want to open the cover of the vat and have a look inside, they should not have us here. We are people who are actually living in that vat; if they want us to participate, they should let us show what it is really like in the vat. Only opening the vat cover to have a look would not have any effect.

Wang's experience clearly highlights one of the key issues of this participatory documentary project: the conflicting motivations and purposes of the project initiator – the outsider, and the villager participants – the insiders.

What was more urgent for the insider, in this case, was to make the problems visible and to try to solve them; for the initiator, it was to inform the outsiders about the local lifestyle in general. Wang was not alone in experiencing contradictory purposes to Wu; Jia also showed similar dissatisfaction. For Jia, the divergence in purpose was reflected not only through the content he wanted to film, but also the aesthetic style. Jia expressed his anger at being 'told off' by Wu for making a TV-format investigative journalism report:

> I filmed five tapes in my village. When Wu came, he watched all my footage and seemed to be very bored by it. After watching it all, he said, 'Old Jia, you didn't film well. We are not doing investigative journalism, but you made it look like a 'Focus' TV investigative programme. If you continue filming [like this], would you get any result? Would they [village officials] let you film? Would the police let you film? Would the leader of the village government let you film? Are you influenced by your son or your daughter? Because your daughter is working for a TV station?' I was extremely angry, but I wasn't as young as Wang any more, so I controlled my anger. I said: 'Wu, were my application materials not about village self-governance? Wasn't what I said in our first meeting in Beijing also about this conflict, which may lead to litigation? But whether or not it could lead to court, this is the war between the villagers and the village master, our own conflict, completely belonging to the issue of self-governance. How could you say that I was influenced by my daughter? How could you say that this is not what you want? I said that I would continue with my position, which is a standard village self-governance issue, a very interesting, complicated and sharp self-governance issue. I said this is a very representative issue, truly revealing the real situation of our peasants and it is what I want to film.

Like Wang, Jia's purpose in joining this project was to show the problems of the state-initiated village self-governance – but that was not the aim of the documentary project. Jia wanted to expose these problems to the view of outsiders and the higher authorities. On another occasion, Jia revealed that the reason he took up the camera was to resist the power that interfered with 'vulnerable social groups' like himself and his fellow villagers, and 'to record evidence about the infringement of their rights and interests. In doing so, we can petition to higher level officials in the hope of getting justice' (Jia, quoted by Huang 2016: 174).[10]

To this end, Jia used a style that he was familiar with – investigative journalism; but Wu was prejudiced against this TV programme style and believed that Jia could not change anything by using it. Wu believed that the villagers should just document their rural lives, rather than using the camera as an activist tool. From the position of urban filmmaker, Wu patronised the elder Jia by accusing him of being influenced by his children. Wu ignored the fact that even though the peasants might have been influenced by a TV style, they still wanted to express their own concerns from a local perspective, not the intellectual's perspective. In her analysis of Jia's later documentaries, Huang examined how the growth of crops, agricultural festivals, home-produced food (*Larou*), spoke of peasant identity and presented an 'intimate look' at the everyday life of villagers. This might have been what Wu wanted them to express, but it was not Jia's initial idea of what he wanted to show most.

Apart from the conflicts on what to film, in which style and what to include in the editing, there were also conflicts concerning the different portrayals of ethnic minorities. The twenty-four year-old Tibetan female filmmaker Zhuo Ma complained that there were different views on Tibet:

> For example, the shot of a pig being killed, they didn't want to include this shot, believing that outsiders regard Tibetan people as harmonious, peaceful, kind people, who would be nice to all kinds of animals. It feels like the film has to be beautified so to please them. If it were for myself, I would not want to do this. What should be should be. That is real life.

Having participated in a Yunnan-based community filming project before, Zhuo Ma was given more freedom to film and edit on her own, and the conflict she encountered was regarding the issue of representation – whose self and what kind of self should be seen on camera.

The oldest villagers, such as Nong Ke (fifty-nine years old) and Shao Yuzhen (fifty-five years old), held a very different view. Having been born and grown up in Mao's China, they believed that they were only peasants who did not have any power and that individuals like them did not have the right to speak for themselves. Nong Ke stated:

> To be honest, I am not like you. I have a different view on this issue. Who am I? Just a normal peasant, who is given this opportunity to film. What could you say? What could you do? From my perspective, it is only a game that they'd like us to participate in. Don't be too serious. Even if you can film what you want, would it represent Chinese peasants at large? What impact would it have? I don't think there would be much [impact]!

Nong believed that peasants should not interfere in political issues. 'Issues regarding regime and the nation's system, such as village election and self governance, should not be discussed by villagers.' Instead, he believed that they should be grateful to have the opportunity to go to Beijing and participate in the project. Even if the money was from the EU, it was still Wu who had chosen them. Nong's perspective was very different from the younger villagers like Wang Wei, who believed that they carried a responsibility to represent the peasants in China at large.

This self-organised discussion revealed the villagers' true feelings; there was little self-censorship as they had not intended to show it to any outsider. Later, they voted among themselves and the majority decided to show their recorded discussion to Wu, and even to an audience, to let 'them' pass judgement. The image of these villagers and how they actually felt about the project is very different from what we see in *Seen and Heard*, where the villagers are shown to be excited as they are being trained in the workshop, are shown taking on the privilege and responsibility to speak for themselves, and accepting it as a good chance to develop themselves. While independent filmmakers like Wu criticise the mainstream media's portrayal of the ordinary, their representation of the rural, from an urban intellectual filmmakers' perspective, was also stereotyped in their own way.

Wu's Self-criticism and Reflection

Started as an idealistic experiment, the project had as much impact on Wu as on the villagers. As discussed in the last section, many peasants who participated in this project were primarily interested in the idea of self-governance. They were eager to use the camera to expose wrong doings, so as to raise public attention and try to bring about change. To the contrary, Wu was more interested in the act of documenting and preserving, rather than using documentary to interfere in the situation. This seems to be no different from what Wu was doing before, filming the marginalised and screening the films abroad to increase his status as a filmmaker. The project itself worked to raise Wu's profile as an humanist independent filmmaker, accepted by Western intellectual and domestic urban viewers.

As an intellectual, Wu had his ideal image of peasants and hoped the project could help them raise their voice. As an independent filmmaker, he also had an idea of how the peasants' films should look, to present an authentic image constructed by the peasants themselves. The format of a ten-minute short documentary film had to be very selective in order to be what Wu thought of as a 'good' film. However, the seemingly 'authentic' image of villager selves was not fully accepted by the peasants themselves, as revealed in the last section. The villagers felt that they were just puppets of the urban filmmakers, who held their hands to construct an imagined image of peasants for the cultural elites.

In 2009, Wu wrote the manuscript 'Me and these peasants that I know' (2009, unpublished), which retrospectively reflected on this project from 2005 to 2009, through his first person narrative. Wu revealed all the distrust and his feelings when he first watched the tape after the villagers left. In his writing, Wu criticises himself,

> Wang Wei thinks that the essence of life is to criticise reality until it is changed. Doesn't it indicate that my intention was only to let the peasants 'have a play with a DV camera'? Doesn't it criticise my stubborn belief in art rather than life itself? . . . What does he [Wang Wei] mean by 'opening the cover of the vat only to have a look at the inside'? Does it point to the Achilles heel of this project? Revealing that the project I was so passionate about was only a 'guise'? 'Only to have a look inside' – Doesn't it mean to play art in the name of 'village governance'? Use the idea of 'peasants playing with DV' to build my own stage? And the fact that after ten films were made, ten villagers went back home with a DV camera, and it's none of their business anymore. I take their films, am interviewed, and people remember the name 'Wu Wenguang', and 'those villagers'?

Later, in 2010, Wu Wenguang made a first person documentary entitled *Bare Your Stuff* (*Liang Chu*, 2010), constructed out of video archives filmed over several years by Wu's assistants and the footage of the villagers' own discussions filmed by Wang Wei. As a self-criticism, this film revealed Wu's involvement in the project from 2005 and how communication with these 'subaltern' villager filmmakers had helped him to understand his own social position as a self-claimed intellectual superior. Wu's self-questioning indicated a prominent impact of this project – a more thorough self-understanding and better insights into others. Wu confesses later that he takes the villagers' criticism as a gift offered to him that has touched his most vulnerable part. He must chew it slowly to fully savour it (2009).

Negotiating the Sense of Self for Both Villagers and Elite Filmmakers

After completion of the first ten villager short films as part of the EU–China village governance training programme, Wu proposed to keep the project running with the villagers continuing to document their own village lives, but the theme would no longer be limited to village self-governance issues. Caochangdi Workstation provided tapes, technical support, editing space and equipment for the villager filmmakers to return and edit their films. This marked the beginning of the second stage of the project. Four of the ten original villagers actually continued filming and came back to Caochangdi to edit their own films. As suggested by Wu, these later films were named as a series: 'My Village 2006, 2007, 2008, 2009'.

If the first stage was only an experiment, in the second stage, the villagers gained more freedom to present what they wanted. Through email exchanges and face-to-face discussion during the editing stage, the villagers went through a negotiation process with Wu.

Gaining more freedom, the villagers had to face decisions on self positioning, what to present and to whom. During a few screenings at domestic universities and independent spaces, they had been given the label 'auteur' by urban filmmakers and intellectuals, even though they may not have regarded themselves as auteurs yet. This made the question of 'Whose self on camera?' more complicated. The image of the self that one constructs on camera depends heavily on how one wants to be seen and by what kind of audience. In other words, they have to decide who they want to present their films, and thus the issue of taste arises.

In regards to the subject matter of the films, Wu had suggested not limiting the topic to self-governance issues. The villagers could film whatever they wanted, such as village life, their own family, neighbours, or festivals and rituals. They could of course continue filming public issues, such as local elections, or any conflicts regarding self-governance. The four villagers who continued to film had different preferences: Jia continued to use his camera to provoke and get involved in social problems; Shao documented everyday life in her village; Wang wanted to interview the old villagers and document his village history; Zhang had a love of the literary and wanted to use the camera for his own artistic expression. Their different focuses also indicated diverse aesthetic choices and expectations of the audience. Vice versa, the choice of audience also explained how the villagers chose their subject matters and styles.

In terms of aesthetic style, what was favoured by both Wu and the villagers was an amateurish 'authentic' look through the villagers' own lens. The villager's presences are strongly felt in the films. They either speak from behind the camera, introducing the audience to people or issues in their village and conversing with other villagers, or directly present themselves on camera and use their first person narration to thread the film together. Wu described how they use the 'camera as an organ of their body' (2009), to give a direct '*xianchang*' on-the-spot aesthetic.

Figure 7.1 Shao Yuzhen filming her villagers

Of the four, Shao wanted to make her films for her fellow villagers, 'for themselves'. Before the project, she was only a peasant housewife: now she also had a hobby, which was to make films. She still worked on the farm, but filming was her hobby when it was less busy or when she had finished the farm work (see Figure 7.1). As she primarily wanted to do this for her villagers, she focused on the public spaces in the village, shooting the laughter, jokes and lightness of everyday life, and occasionally some sorrow. With a camera in her hand, she walked around the village filming anything that interested her: casual gatherings of the men, festival performances or villagers doing their farm work. Sometimes her off-camera voice would comment on what she saw and encountered. The openness in her films carried a special 'aura' of authenticity, just like *nongjia fan* – peasant food, or food with a special countryside flavour – that could not be obtained by urban-trained filmmakers. In *My Village 2007*, when Shao was interviewed by a professional TV crew, Shao's small amateur DV camera even openly criticised how the TV journalists set them up for the camera (see Figures 7.2 and 7.3).

Wang wanted to reveal the history of his village; even when it was very sensitive and difficult to show, he still wanted to do it, even if it was only for himself. Like Shao, he also regarded it as a hobby, not to make money. In Wang's film, he

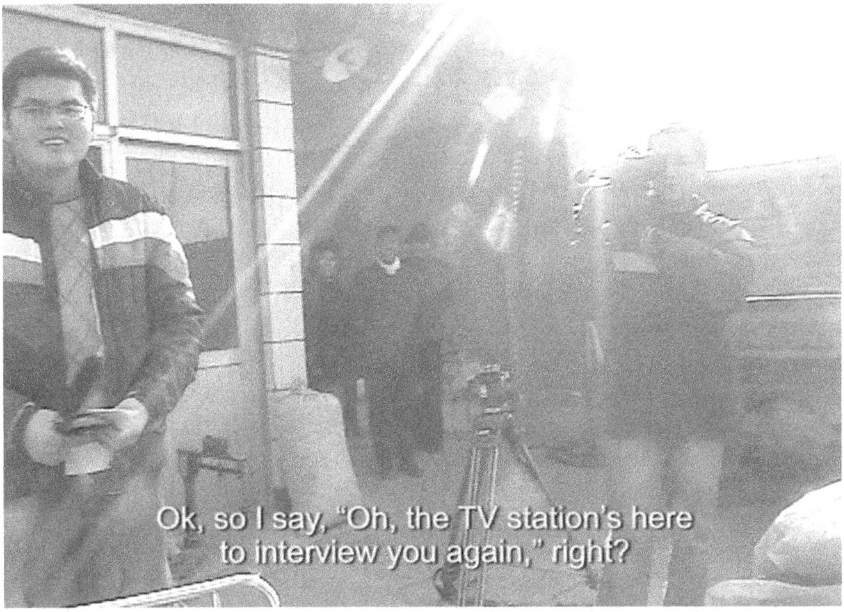

Figure 7.2 Local TV journalists come to interview Shao Yuzhen, as her being a peasant woman making films has caught their attention

Figure 7.3 Shao openly states that she does not want to be set up by the TV journalists

sometimes presented himself directly facing the camera, speaking to the audience about the problems. He used this style in his first short film, which starts with a long shot of Wang squatting in front of a camera on a hill with his village in the background. There is a motorway in between him and his village. Wang speaks directly to the camera, introducing himself and the problems around self-governance in his village. However, the sound of traffic in the background is so loud that it overshadows his voice. During the first screening of his film, the audience laughed at this point, which made Wang feel humiliated; he left during the screening, and cried loudly when Wu went outside to see him. However, this did not make him change his style. In his later films, he still presented himself on camera, such as when he watched TV or had a meal after feeding the hens. He also spoke from behind the camera to his villagers or gave his own comments. However, differing from Jia, Wang did not or could not really intervene in the social issues of his village.

Zhang took himself very seriously as an artistic auteur. He wanted to make something 'earthshaking' to change his fate as a peasant. He wanted to be a writer when he was young and filmmaking fulfilled his artistic ambition. Zhang even regarded Caochangdi as a utopian place where he could be away from real life and pursue his art and creative thoughts. Zhang's filming was more personal than the other three villagers. His films were more about his own personal life in his personal space, rather than the public life of the village. Not only did he present himself directly on camera, he even put the camera in his bedroom and recorded his morning and evening conversations with his wife. Narcissistic as it might appear, his films showed the conflicting life of an artistic peasant, who could not fulfil his ambition through education, yet the dullness and pettiness of everyday life had not worn down his passion (see Figure 7.4). Filmmaking had become a new hope for his life.

These three villagers' choices of subject matter and aesthetic style were supported by Wu, who believed the way to be a film auteur was to film the everyday life of the villages, to observe it rather than directly intervening. Jia's idea of filmmaking was, however, very different from that of Wu. Jia still primarily focused on political issues in the village, such as self-governance, democracy or village politics. Apart from describing village life, Jia's films presented himself in the middle of village politics and conflicts. He actively engaged with social issues and problems in the village, using his camera like a gun, with which he gained the power to fight against the injustice in the village.

Jia wanted his critical messages to be delivered to a wider public, so as to have an immediate social impact and improve the situation. If there was the chance, he wanted his films to be shown on television, either at the request of CCTV journalists or international journalists. Broadcasting his films on public media would

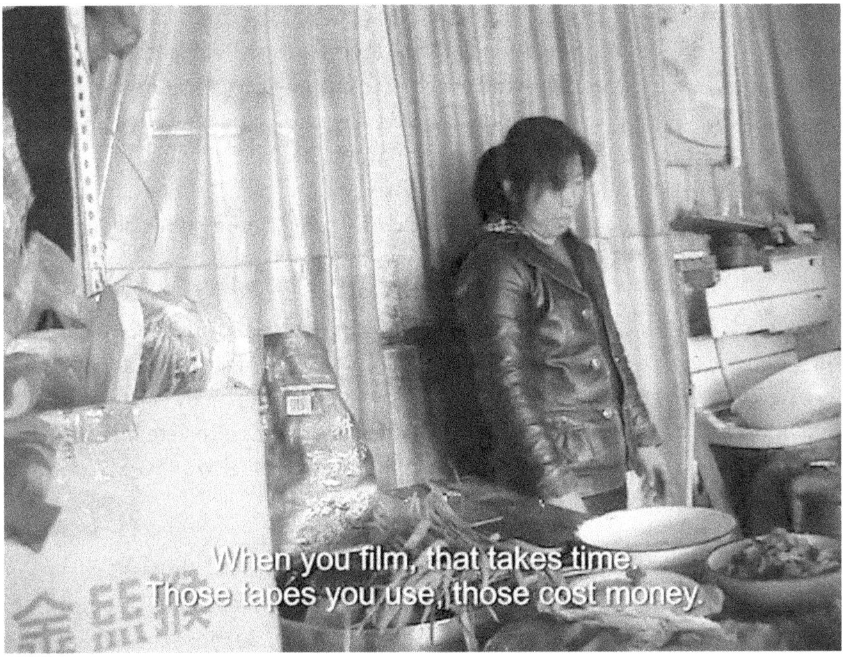

Figure 7.4 Zhang's wife criticises him for taking too much time filming, an expensive hobby

give him more power to confront local officials. When he first got involved in village politics with his camera, local officials regarded him as being from a nameless grassroots organisation. Therefore, Jia desperately wanted to gain power from outside his village to legitimise his filming activities in the village.

However, in Wu's opinion, Jia should not have tried to please TV programme editors, as they were not making films for the television. 'Jai cannot get what he filmed broadcast anyway. He wanted to use it for a direct impact, but I know it (CCTV programmes) is only a bubble' (author's interview, 2010).

What Wu said again indicated that his motives for the project were different from those of the villagers. In addition, Wu did not believe that the media could have an impact to solve problems. When I asked Wu why he did not give time to the villagers to film what they wanted in their own style, such as using this so-called 'Focus' TV style, Wu replied:

> I didn't have much time, nor the experience of filming 'Focus' TV programme-style material. I only believe in documentary, and believe documentary has the deepest meaning. What can peasants film? We needed a (coherent) form

> for this project . . . To document contemporary life and what happens in everyday life – now, that is good. To use investigative TV documentary style, to interview, to investigate and make a ten-minute investigative news piece? That's not quite possible. Local officials have already shouted at him [Jia] about his filming. They shut the door when he tried to film. But they do not dare to refuse someone from the television. He [Jia] doesn't have the media power, so he cannot make a Focus TV programme-style documentary. (Author's interview with Wu, 2010)

Wu believed that the media carried a certain power, but in the Chinese context, individuals like Jia did not have the power that the state media did to interfere in village issues and politics. This indicated how Wu perceived the power of individual self on the one hand, and Wu's intention to disassociate himself from the mass media on the other. Commenting on Jia's desire to show his work on television, Wu stated:

> television is . . . not reliable, neither CCTV nor BBC. All rubbish; all media work for their own interest. For ordinary people, maybe they need some news, that's fine. But for an independent auteur, we have to ignore the media . . . If one wants to use their media power to solve problems, that's to rely on them (media). Then where is your independent thinking? And the ultimate aim of this project is not to solve an urgent problem like a house on fire or a polluted river. These kind of problems are always there. But the aim is to build the independent consciousness of the villager auteurs. (Author's interview, 2010)

Even when Jia's footage was requested by state and international media, Wu believed that the media just wanted to use Jia and his footage for their own agenda and it would not really bring any benefit to the villagers. When a journalist from the *New York Times* asked to use Jia's footage, Wu did not allow Jia to give it away:

> My first reaction is, Why should he give the footage to you? Where have you been when Jia was filming? My second thought is, If they really want to use it, can it solve problems? Can you trust them? A TV journalist wanted to do a programme on Jia's village, but it didn't get past the internal approval stage for television . . . A *New York Times* journalist told Jia that they were the biggest media in the West, and they can protect him. How can they protect him? But Jia needs them, needs television to solve his problem and to show off 'see, even NYT comes to report it'. (Author's interview with Wu, 2010)

At first, Wu believed that Jia did not have the ability to make an investigative TV programme, and later, when Jia attracted media attention, he showed his scepticism of the mass media and his belief that they had their own agenda and could not help to solve Jai's problems either. Such disjunction in Wu's responses indicated his intention to maintain the power in this project. It also suggested what kind of perception Wu wanted associated with this project. For Wu, the main purpose was to make a documentary film as a piece of work. Wu believed that independent authors should have independent thought, and the essence of this project was to build the villagers' independent awareness, to construct them as rights-conscious citizens, rather than to directly solve actual problems. For villagers like Jia, however, what was important was to solve problems in their social reality. This was not to say that the villagers did not have independent awareness. Their involvement in this project, and the way they actively recorded and revealed the problems, have already shown their political awareness.

Audiences, Politicality, Disputed Authenticities and Changing Perceptions of the Self

Nevertheless, the desire of the villagers to show their films to their fellow villagers, the general public and 'decision makers' was still filtered by the intellectual gatekeeper Wu, whose ideal audiences sit in museums, art centres or universities, and have high cultural capital. In Wu's reflective writing in 2009, he showed satisfaction that their films had been shown at art centres over the years and that the project had received the attention of urban intellectuals and international scholars.

Differing choices of audience indicates different expectation of this project. Wu objected to the villagers showing their films on television, which is associated with the masses and has lower cultural capital. Instead, he opted for elitist cultural spaces, and tried to legitimise the works he was associated with by choosing to present these films in art centres and universities, for cultural elites to recognise the aesthetic value of the peasants' films and the very act of peasants making films. The cultural capital of the exhibition space gave status to the films, which may or may not bring long-term engagement with the villagers. Wu himself also relied on Western cultural critics to build his own reputation as an intellectual humanist filmmaker. Wu's choice itself is also an elitist act – to prefer exclusivity.

However, the audience with the higher cultural capital may not have the immediate impact required for problems of great urgency, such as the polluted river in Jia's village. The divergence between Wu and the participant villagers on their different choices of audience, for different perceptions, sheds light to the core of the issue of public-engaged art – whether it is to engage the public for the sake of making an artwork or to use a participatory mode of art practice, in this case filming, for effective public intervention. In other words, if we say all documentaries are political, in terms of them having a political engagement, as John Corner (2009, 2011) argues, then should the implication of the politicality be a political intervention through art or simply be using public engagement as a new form of aesthetics, for the sake of making an artwork?

Such a dilemma still deserves investigation. The key subject of this book, the individual selves, in this case both intellectual initiators and invited villagers, have gone through a complicated process of *encountering* each other, the audience, and more so, their own selves. As a series of works,[11] the villagers might not have realised who their audiences were in the beginning. By attending some screenings in art centres, universities and institutions, they have gradually got to know the kind of audience who watch their films. Such a process of knowing their audience is also a process of knowing themselves, so the question of what kind of self to construct becomes more complicated, as the self itself becomes more multidimensional. They are no longer purely villagers, as they were before participating in this project, but now have an awareness of being a film auteur, a label they gradually learn to associate themselves with. The camera connects them to wider society, through filming and screening. They are becoming aware of the power they carry in representing their village. Their films have also gradually obtained an 'independent' documentary 'look' that has been influenced by Wu and the other independent films they have watched over the years.

With a small camera in their hands, three other villagers, in addition to Jia, have inevitably got caught up in political issues, and the politicality of their filmmaking practice has also become more obvious. For example, Shao used her small camera to document how television journalists interviewed her husband and herself with a professional camera, deconstructing the way TV journalists manipulate the truth. Shao also went to court with her cousin to support her on a case. However, as she filmed the court she was discovered by the police, who beat her up and accused her of being a spy, forbidding her to film. She felt extremely hurt by such unjust treatment, as she had imagined that the police would protect her. Similarly, Wang Wei took his DV camera to court to support a relative, and the camera was taken by the police, only to be returned through '*guanxi*' ('networks of influence'). Even the more artistic villager filmmaker Zhang has been asked by a school teacher to reveal the unequal treatment he has received.

As for the initiator Wu Wenguang, it has also been a process of learning more about his self and the villagers' needs. In my interview with him in 2010, Wu reflected on his own criticism of Jia and confessed his lack of understanding of the urgent needs of the villagers like Jia. He also revealed his scepticism about Jai's documentary filming in general:

> I didn't know enough about Jia's enthusiasm for 'Focus' TV-style investigative programmes. I only regarded it as a TV style, but didn't know that he relied on this and needed it so much. It feels like when fire is going to burn down a house, someone is in front of it, someone is thousands of miles away. His feeling is like wanting to extinguish the fire when it's happening in front of him. Even though I still think he shouldn't do 'Focus'-style programmes, I've now understood his feeling of being swallowed by the fire . . . Jia's film last year was mostly about the pollution of their river. I rejected it initially and didn't want him to make a film about pollution. I thought, his village did not just have a polluted river. There were other things too, throughout a year of four seasons. But it was a misunderstanding. I couldn't understand his anxiety about the pollution. But if there was some depth [in his investigation], why not let him do it? I was changed by him. He could certainly do a film like this, as it was what he thought was the most important thing at that moment. He couldn't think of anything else. Then he could do it. (Author's interview with Wu, 2010)

What this project offers is not just the portraits of the villagers made by the villagers themselves. Exploring the unbalanced and changing power relations behind their practice is to understand how the participants, including the initiator Wu, have come to understand themselves, and each other, during this process of negotiating whose self is shown on camera.

> If one cannot bravely face oneself, then any kind of project cannot make any change. To change the country, one has to change one's own village, one's own reality. Even to change what one cannot stand, one should change oneself first. But people are too lazy, that's our reality. We cannot face ourself, just like it's so difficult for us to face our history. I know that I have many problems, I have always been reflecting and this is what I think a powerful thing. (Author's interview with Wu, 2010)

The value of first person documentary is not just in examining what the self looks like on camera, how authentic it is for a particular audience. The process of constructing an 'authentic' self-representation is a complex, socially engaged act. The problem lies in when one has the freedom to speak what one wants and access to the power of the camera, how does one execute such power in relation to family, self, community, strangers in society? This problem is sharpened by the current digital participatory culture and in the 'post-truth' climax, where the individual can even present and perform the self through a smartphone camera on live web broadcasts to an imagined audience which will be discussed in the final chapter.

Notes

1. Also called 'China Village Documentary Project', 'Village Documentary Project', or the 'Villager Documentary Project'. It is also called the 'Chinese Villagers' DV Documentaries on Village-Level Democracy'.
2. The first ten short films were shown at the International Conference on Village Governance in Beijing in 2006. They were then toured around New York University, Yale University, Columbia University and the University of Notre Dame in the same year. The audience were mainly scholars, students and artists. The films were also shown at film festivals including the Hong Kong International Film Festival, Singapore International Film Festival and International Documentary Film Festival Amsterdam.
3. This overarching participatory form can be viewed as a product of the Ford Foundation's activities in China, dating back to the early 1990s, and especially the importation of Ford Foundation developed and funded Photovoice (*yingxiang fasheng*) public health strategies intended to give aid recipients an opportunity to communicate their concerns and coping strategies to policymakers and service providers (Johnson 2014: 166).
4. To communicate with the villagers, Wu created an email group so the villagers could connect together and share their thoughts. They could write and send to everyone in this group, and the reply would also be seen by everyone. As they did not have computers, in the early days they had to go to a public Internet bar to check their emails. Wu received messages almost every day, which he then sent on to all the villagers.
5. Apart from the youngest participant, a Tibetan female villager Zuo Ma, who had participated in the 'Learn Our Own Traditions' project.
6. From the Caochangdi group email exchange.
7. Ibid.
8. Ibid.
9. All except Yi Chujian, who was asked to help with the post-production and prepare for the screening that evening.
10. In the same interview, Jia later says 'Even if we fail, these materials can serve its historical purpose for posterity' – indicating his historical sensitivity.
11. They continued to make films in 2007, 2008 and 2009.

Chapter 8

From Fragile First Person Documentary Practice to Popular Online First Person Live Streaming Broadcast – *Zhibo*: Changing Intentions, Changing Individual Selves

> I may not be an online celebrity; may not sing well, may not be self-disciplined, may not be brave, may not win, but on Inke, I am definitely myself. Get on Inke, broadcast (*zhibo*) myself.[1]
>
> Advertising slogan of *Inke Zhibo*, a live-streaming broadcast platform

When I began researching first person narrative documentary practice in China, there were not so many films of this kind around and there was a general suspicion of this practice within the independent documentary community, of it being too private or too narcissistic. Little attention had been given to the *politicality* of this practice: how individual makers communicate through a personal camera with their family, surroundings or society as a social engagement. Focusing on how filmmakers turn the camera inwards on their own selves, this book explores a twofold research question. Firstly, how is the self represented on camera in a contemporary Chinese context and what does the filmic self-representation explore? Secondly, during the process of filmmaking, how does the first person filmmaker position his or her self within complex relations with others, society and the state? Responding to this, I took the *film text* as an aesthetic and cultural object, and examined how the self is constructed for one's own camera. I also examined first person *filmmaking* as a practice, through which individual filmmakers as agents experience a process of deconstructing and reconstructing their subjectivities. In addition to the eleven films by nine filmmakers examined in this book, and the China Villagers Documentary Project involving Wu Wenguang and ten village filmmakers, more first person documentary films have emerged in the 2010s during the writing of this book.

From the First Person on Camera to the First Person Online in the 2010s

Since 2010, or even earlier, when Wu Wenguang started to reflect on his own practice in the making of *Fucking Cinema*, there has been a general move to explore the personal at Caochanghdi Workstation Beijing, which was mentioned in the last chapter, a studio of documentary filmmaking and theatre dancing initiated by Wu Wenguang and Wen Hui, Wu's then long term-partner since the early 1980s, a dancer and filmmaker who was mentioned in the Introduction.[2] Wu Wenguang, Wen Hui and younger filmmakers-in-residence, including Zou Xueping, Zhang Mengqi and Wang Hai'an, have practised first person documentary under the banner of the 'Folk Memory Project' from 2010. Around 2009, some villagers of the China Villagers Documentary Project, such as Jia Zhitan, started to use their small DV cameras to document oral histories of the old villagers in their villages, particularly their personal memories of Mao's era. This act of exploring the past through a personal camera was encouraged by Wu, and later inspired Wu to start the Folk Memory Project. Some young filmmakers and students joined this project, and went back to their own villages to film and interview the older generation, especially about their memories of the period of the Three-Year Famine (1958–61). Most of these films take a reflective, first person approach; that is, the filmmakers start from their own positions, document their journeys, their return home and the search for oral histories. Their practice explores the relationship between the personal and the collective in historiography and one's origin. Wu Wenguang himself made a first person documentary entitled *Treatment* (2010), a personal, nostalgic memoir about his mother who had passed away. Wen Hui also made two documentaries related to her home village in Yunnan, *Listen to Third Grandma* (2012), an oral history of her third grandma, who she had neither met nor even heard of before she went back, and *Dancing with Third Grandma* (2015), an experimental short documentary made on the same trip, with scenes of Wen and her third grandma dancing together. More recently, Wu Wenguang completed *Investigating the Father* (2016), in which Wu investigates the history of his father during the 1960s and 1970s in China.

Among the young filmmakers-in-residence at Caochangdi are Zou Xueping and Zhang Mengqi, two productive female filmmakers, both of whom participated in the Folk Memory Project. Zou Xueping has so far made five films about her village – *The Starving Village* (2010), *The Satiated Village* (2011), *Children's Village* (2012), *Trashy Village* (2013) and *Fools' Village* (2015) – which are all narrated from a first person perspective, either through her off-screen voice commenting or speaking to the villagers, or by presenting herself on camera. *The*

Starving Village documents her first return to her village in Shandong province, when she visited elder members in the village and asked them about their memories of the Great Famine during 1958–61. On her second visit, Zou Xueping showed her first documentary to the villagers and explored the villagers' reactions to this film, which she then documented in her second film, *The Satiated Village* (2011). *Children's Village* (2012) documents her third visit. While she continued to interview old people about their memories, she gained help from the local children who also engaged in this memory project by collecting names and donations to erect a memorial for famine victims. In *Trashy Village* (2013), children continued to work with the filmmaker Zou. The camera becomes a social tool with which Zou and the children respond to a massive garbage problem in the village. Zou reveals that 'this film again, is my act of against the high wall of reality, a print of a difficult inner exploration of myself and how I reposition myself for the future' (Zou 2014, filmmaker's note). In *Fools' Village*, Zou reflects on her own position in the village as someone who has gone to the city for university and for work, and still remains single in her late twenties, which is seen as uncommon for women in rural China. By showing her interactions with and associating herself with those who are regarded as fools in her village, Zou questions her own identity in the eyes of other villagers as being a 'fool'. Zou's ongoing first person documentary practice demonstrates a young woman filmmaker's willingness to engage with her social reality and at the same time question what she has encountered during the process.

Similarly, Zhang Mengqi has also produced a series of first person documentaries, firstly about her relationship with her mother and grandmother, then, like Zou Xueping, about her village, and more precisely, her ancestor/grandfather's village. Trained as a dancer under Wen Hui, Zhang has been a regular participator in Wen Hui's documentary theatre projects, such as *Hunger* and *Birth Project*. Responding to Wu Wenguang's call to go back to one's home village, Zhang Mengqi takes her small DV camera to explore the familial side of her self, like the female filmmakers discussed in the first chapter. While Zou organises her film as a 'village' series, Zhang names the films about her village as the 'self portrait – 47 KM' series. So far she has made five personal documentaries: *Self-Portrait with Three Women* (2010), *Self-Portrait: At 47 KM* (2011), *Self-Portrait: Dancing at 47 KM* (2012), *Self-Portrait: Dreaming at 47 KM* (2013) and *Self-Portrait: Birth in 47 KM* (2016). In *Self-Portrait with Three Women*, Zhang explores the burning question of her relationship with her mother and grandmother, and how she wants to search for her own dreams and love carrying burdens from the previous two generations, a spontaneous quest about growing-up and constructing her self-identity. Her later films on the village are more like assignment films under Wu's umbrella project of 'Folk Memory', made during a period when she tries to establish herself as a recognisable filmmaker. To explore a cinematic language that combines documentary and dance on location, she returns to her grandfather's village to film her conversation with older family members, her performance, and her interactions with the village today.

The dancer, performance artist and filmmaker Li Ning's *Tape* (2010) is a self-portrait interweaving both the private and public aspects of the filmmaker's own life through a first person lens since 2005. The film portrays Li Ning as a highly conflicted figure, dedicating himself to creating art while being stuck in an environment where ordinary 'normal' people only care for social conventions and moral responsibilities, job, marriage and family. It directly stages Li Ning's personal familial conflicts with his mother and wife, and his private sexual life with his mistress, on camera. It also includes the documentation of Li Ning's solo art performances, and performances with the students of his dance troupe in public spaces such as on streets, in an empty building or in residential areas. This film violates ethical norms, by presenting his problematic relationship with his family members. In some places he lies to his mother about his filming, or keeps recording when his wife or his mother objects to being filmed. His unfiltered representation of his own privacy and sexuality reveal the complexities of being a modern man and a contemporary artist in a provincial city. It also places the audience in an uncomfortable and upsetting position. From this perspective, the film deserves further exploration both textually and contextually, on the aesthetic and ethical level.

Among the male filmmakers, and in addition to Li Ning, Wei Xiaobo has made three first person films, entitled *Days I* (2011), *Days II* (2012) and *Days III* (2017), in which he turns his camera inward to film his personal life with his girlfriend, who later becomes his wife, and exposes their private life to the audience. Wei films his domestic life as almost from a third-person perspective, as the camera very often sits on a tripod and observes his everyday mundane life. He acknowledges the influence of Hu Xinyu, whose work is explored in the second chapter of this book. In 2011, Wei Xiaobo made *Days I*, which documents the everyday life of himself and his girlfriend as young graduates trying to survive in a big city, their personal concerns and questions about marriage. One year later, he made *Days II*, documenting the everyday mundane events of his now married life with his wife (his girlfriend of *Days I*), either holding the camera in his hand while talking to his wife, putting it in a corner to film himself doing things or filming them being together. In 2017, he finished the third film in this series, *Days III*, which covers his married life from 2013 to 2017, and the new problems they face in life – having a baby. Wei reveals that filming his own life has become part of his everyday activity. But when he edits his film, he looks at it as if it were someone else's life. Issues such as marriage, buying a flat, trying to conceive a baby, miscarriage and dealing with new roles as parents are familiar to many young couples in urban China today.

The first person films that have emerged since 2010, as mentioned above, continue to explore the familial or the private through either revisiting history or foregrounding tensions between the individual and the familial. Whereas these films reflect a growing trend for documentary filmmaking in China today, they also continue to explore the themes that appear in the earlier first person documentaries discussed in this book, especially the relational sense of self, the gendered expectations, the tensions between individual desire and collective family obligations, and how individuals act as individuals in their own right. However, the filmmaker's outward engagement with other individuals in public spaces is rarely seen. Both Zou Xueping's *Village* series and Zhang Mengqi's *Self Portrait* series reflect some dimensions of interactions with the villagers, but works showing a filmmaker's first person confrontation with state authority are very few and such films are still very much repressed in mainland China. The camera's role as provoker of discussion about social problems had a short period of visibility in 2000s China, at a time when, internationally, social media had become a crucial tool to assist and encourage activist movements and to spread shared interests among fan communities.

However, after a series of activist events in China were escalated by social media coverage, such as the Xinjiang Riots on 5 July 2009, Western social media such as Twitter and Facebook were banned in August 2009, and China's own social media sites such as Weibo were also closely monitored. Where socially engaged art practices elsewhere have been criticised for over-emphasising the ethics involved, given the inclusion of viewers as equal participants still results in an unavoidable hierarchy on creativity (Bishop 2012), critical socially engaged art practice in China is still rather out of favour in the hegemonic cultural discourse.

In *Hooligan Sparrow* (2016), an activist documentary which records the feminist Ye Haiyan and her fight for victims of sexual abuse, the filmmaker Wang Nanfu uses her own voice-over to narrate the difficulties she encountered in the production of this film in China, making the film strong evidence of Wang's first person political participation. Knowing it would be very difficult to get such a film shown within mainland China, Wang chooses to speak in English, to an international audience, of her experiences and the feminist activist fights of her subjects, rather than speak in Mandarin to the domestic audience. Since voice-over is an important performative element in first person documentaries, Wang's approach of linking to the international for support and recognition reveals a recurring feature when addressing the tension between the individual and the state in China – the involvement of international forces in balancing this relationship.

Ideological control has intensified since the new leadership of Xi in 2012, the year when I completed the initial research for this project. The continuous depoliticised atmosphere and state control makes critical individual socio-political participation very difficult, if not totally impossible. In recent years under the new leadership, however, the emergence of a kind of constructive socially engaged documentary practice for socialist nation-building has been seen. For example, a first person documentary, *The Last Bang-Bang* (2016), was made by a former Liberation Army soldier He Ku on his experiences as a 'bang-bang man', one who carries heavy luggage for passengers in the 'mountain city' of Chongqing. It documents how he learns his trade, his experiences and the other 'bang-bangs' he encounters. The voice of a migrant worker is heard on big screens and personalised small screens through a first person narration. *The Last Bang-Bang* won the best short documentary at the Golden Tree International Documentary Festival, an international film festival organised by a Chinese company and supported by cultural minsters, but held overseas – in Germany. The film also has a series of thirteen episodes available to watch on China's own copyrighted video streaming site, IQIYI.com.

The 2010s is also the decade when the so-called post-90s generation has come of age – the cohort labelled as being the more self-concerned, more economically affluent, single-child generation. In summer 2013, I returned to China to work. The close contact with young Chinese students born in the 1990s offered me a great opportunity to understand their mentality and the sense of self of this iGeneration, even though the number of students I was in touch with was still quite small. In a course assignment in which I asked them to write a documentary proposal, a large number of students chose to focus on themselves, their relationship with their parents or to explore their family history, wanting to understand how they became who they are today. One male student questioned his love for his father and planned to make a documentary to criticise his father and to understand fatherhood, as he wanted to become a better father in his own lifetime. One girl described her problematic relationship with her single mother who had too much expectation of her and often criticised her. She wanted to use the documentary film as a way to confess her feelings and to communicate with her mother so as to improve their relationship. A Han Chinese girl, born and raised in Xinjiang Uyghur Autonomous Region, felt confused about her cultural identity and wanted to know why and how her grandparents, as skilled workers in a state-owned factory, migrated there with the whole family in the 1960s. A personal family history like this reveals the family separation, relocation and dislocation caused by the national project of constructing western China in the 1950s and 1960s. Such a personal story would be a favourite subject in fictional independent cinema or auteur cinema of the fifth or sixth generation, but was, however, told through the first person narration of a young Chinese girl in a non-fiction format.

One should not ignore the technological context, which has also changed dramatically. Like elsewhere, booming digital technologies and new media in China have pushed through a post-cinematic era, with ubiquitous screens and miscellaneous content. Personal videos, which are produced with DV cameras, webcams and smart phones, are streamed on domestic video-sharing sites and watched on personalised portable digital devices. In *China on Video* (2010), Paola Voci provides an in-depth examination of the then more edgy and diverse video content on these non-conventional online screening platforms. She explores how the 'smaller screens' create new kinds of public spaces 'where collectivity and individuality are negotiated and where the boundaries between elite and popular culture are effectively blurred and dissolved' (2010: xx–xxi). Social media also facilitate mediated first person self-expression on a much larger scale. Sharing one's personal life through texts, photos and live recorded moving images, such as on WeChat (微信, *Weixin*), has become common practice for some individuals, and a necessary part of everyday communication. However, these alternative public spaces are regularly redefined by constant modifications in the state regulations that monitor them.

The self is constantly on camera, in personal photos and instant recorded personal videos shared on WeChat, Weibo, and so on. The online first person visual expression requests us to rethink the construction of the self. Social media not only provides platforms for celebrities to directly broadcast their lives to fans through amateurish-looking home videos and snapshots, and to interact with their fans, but also gives rise to micro-celebrities from grassroots beginnings, or in Chinese '*wanghong*' (网红), literally meaning 'net red' or 'Internet celebrity'. The construction of the self, as read by Cover through a Butler perspective, is 'a never-ending process of "always becoming"' in a digital media context (Cover 2014: 57).

Performing the Self to an Interactive Audience: Audio-visual Self Construction on *Zhibo*

The post-cinematic era has also given rise to online *zhibo*, the Chinese name for live web streaming broadcasts,[3] through which individuals can instantly express and perform the self for an interactive audience. *Zhibo* apps/platforms offer a space for individuals to commodify their own self-expression, where the desire

Figure 8.1 *Zhibo*: performing the self to an interactive audience

for self-expression is tangled with corporate and commercial imperatives. In China, *zhibo* has experienced a rapid expansion since 2012, with huge business investment in this new online playground. In the USA, it is reported that live web streaming was initially launched in spring 2015, with Meerkat and Periscope, and has become a platform for sharing breaking news (Tang *et al.* 2017: 124). The wild growth of *zhibo* in China was most obvious in 2015 and 2016. In 2015, there were around 200 live web-broadcast platforms with more than 200 million users. By the end of 2016, there were around 300 *zhibo* platforms. The number of people who have watched *zhibo* reached 344 million in 2016, which is nearly half of China's Internet users.[4]

Internationally, personal web broadcast could be seen as early as 1996. On jennicam.com, Jenny Ringley, the first 'lifecaster', broadcasted her mundanity through a webcam on top of her computer. Then it was the world watching a nineteen-year-old college girl exhibit herself, now on *zhibo* platforms, it is millions of eyes watching thousands of self performers. *Zhibo* can be practised by anyone who registers an account on a live web-broadcast platform, being either a website or a mobile application. It celebrates the staging and performance of subjectivity.

There are different categories of *zhibo* platforms for various purposes and different groups of audiences, including live gaming, fashion-show broadcasting, sport watching, art shows, or as social media with first person performances for entertainment, such as talent shows, talk shows, product direct sell, for the new rich, for geeky males, for regional small town youngsters, and so on. However, like many other industries in China, the ecosystem of the *zhibo* platform is still developing. Many *zhibo* platforms still rely on angel investment for human and equipment costs and cannot fully finance themselves.[5]

Responding to the large amount of vulgar, violent and erotic content on *zhibo* (Wang 2016) since late 2016 more policies and regulations have been introduced by the national cultural bureau to regulate this rising human interactive virtual public space. Around thirty *zhibo* platforms were taken down by the regulators in July 2017, including the *zhibo* service on Weibo, China's largest social media site. Some *zhibo* platforms have been forced out of the market, or are under investigation. As much as to regulate sexual and vulgar content, this also shows the state's paranoia toward the *zhibo* medium itself. The state believes airing videos online through *zhibo* platforms can cause harm and instabilities within society that are difficult to control during live streaming.[6]

From September 2016 to August 2017, for around one hour every day, I observed *zhibo* performances on a few different platforms, such as Kwei, Inke zhibo, Panda zhibo, YY zhibo, Blued zhibo and Taobao zhibo. Some of the presenter-performers I watched over this period of time have gradually gained more fans, and turned celebrity into commercial value. In first person documentaries I saw digital personal cameras being used for self-recovery, self-analysis, to heal broken family relations, to record evidence of everyday life through a view from below, or to provoke other individuals in public spaces. *Zhibo* also embeds the complexity of the self: it is for self-expression, for the self as performer to play an alternative online identity, to become a micro-celebrity, with certain identities becoming a selling point; for self-performance or self-revealing as a new kind of entrepreneurship, to entertain the audience and share information with monetary motives; or for the self to be the self, for social interaction, for recognition, or to search for a sense of existence (see Figure 8.1). In the following sections, I will explore the aesthetics and forms of self as performer-presenter, the temporality of the self-in-making, the role of the audience in making the self of the performer-presenter, and the surrounding ethics of expressing and performing the self for recognition and profit.

Aesthetics of self as performer/presenter

Among the different kinds of *zhibo* show, the one that highlights and exhibits the self as the *performer-presenter* is the kind I call a 'one man *zhibo* show', where the *zhubo* (leading presenter) is solely on camera, sometimes with another guest presenter. The body of the presenter is centralised on a personal screen, reaching to the audiences on their personal screens. In this form, *zhibo* can be seen as one of the 'identity technologies' (Poletti and Rak 2014), not just a platform, but a space where the self is constantly in the process of construction, and where interactions with the audience are also directly displayed. The self as performer/presenter either stays in a room set as a private space or carries a mobile device on a selfie stick, with selfie-tailored lights surrounding the small screen. The screen of a smart phone or a tablet device becomes the frame of the camera or a live window that connects the performer/presenter's own space to the spaces of many others.

One typical and highly recognisable presenter-performer type is the usually pretty, innocent young woman with make-up, dressed in a cute or sexy outfit, sitting or standing in front of the mobile phone camera set in a corner of a bedroom or a living room (see Figure 8.2). The background is usually filled with cute cuddly toys, a bed or a sofa. Such a setting indicates the performer being in her private space, fetishised for the viewer, as she performs and exhibits her 'self', inviting the anonymous and imagined stranger-audience to watch her. In a way, such cute female faces become popular self portraits or moving-image selfies of the twenty-first century, which are a process of communicating or interacting with others.

The presenter-performer performs audience requests, which can be sent through instant messages appearing live over the screen, as 'bullet-curtain' (*danmu*, 弹幕)[7] conversations. Requests include to sing a song, to dance, to show certain products for sale, to be somewhere, to perform certain gestures.

Figure 8.2 A typical *zhibo* presenter-performer

For example, there are direct displays of highly sexual gestures, such as a female presenter showing off her body, taking off her clothes by audience request. There were even live broadcasts of sexual intercourse, which resulted in a ban on broadcasting provocative sexual gestures, such as the erotic banana-eating gesture (Phillips 2016). The self as presenter-performer can also be asked to share a personal experience, to offer emotional support, or to give advice on certain issues, such as on relationships, love, sex, business, travel, and so on. The audience can send virtual flowers or virtual currency to the presenter-performer as rewards, which can be turned into actual money.

It is important to note that many of the young women portraying such cute young girl images have been trained to do so by agents, as this image has more 'celebrity' potential. It is also what they choose to portray as their alternative selves. The alternativeness of online identities goes beyond the physical appearance. There are also migrant workers who work on assembly lines during the day but play a much more creative and characteristic role on *zhibo* during their own time. There are even foreigners, such as one African-American, who presents himself on *zhibo* to tell his stories and experiences of being in China, so that the Chinese get to know more about BAME (black, Asian and ethnic minorities) identities.

For entertaining purpose, there are also sensational performances to attract attention, hence a higher click rate and more income. Male presenters/performers are usually young men singing or giving relationship-related advice, or doing abnormal or comedic things as entertainment. In fact, live-broadcasting

Figure 8.3 Weird behaviour on *zhibo*, such as eating chillies

outrageous or extravagant behaviour has become a new lucrative income source for the provincial population – behaviour like eating insects, light bulbs, or large amounts of chillies or any kind of food (see Figure 8.3). Some *zhibo* apps, such as Kwai, are famous for broadcasting such vulgar extravagant performances, which can be reposted on other social media sites such as Weibo. The vulgarity of such behaviour invites discussions on the ethics of broadcasting, which is difficult to censor or classify. In contrast to broadcasting the extravagant there is the *zhibo* of the dullness and mundanity of everyday life. Migrant workers such as urban security guards, waitresses, shop-keepers and real-estate agents broadcast and communicate the drabness of their own existence, or middle-aged women express their boredom and look for interaction and conversation.

The temporality in the self-in-making and the role of interactive audience in zhibo

Whereas first person documentary practice could be seen as a communicative practice between the filmmaker as self and the subjects they encounter, *zhibo* is the communication between the self as presenter and a crowd of imagined interactive audiences. *Zhibo* challenges how we think of communication, human interaction and performance, and invites us to further investigate such notions together with how they affect the ways we think of the self in the contemporary post-cinematic virtual environment. In *zhibo*, the non-fiction live performative act of presenting the self questions the binary opposition of staged and non-staged, performing and non-performing, real and unreal; the self is live, presenting and performing the self, as well as the process of becoming what she/he wants to or is asked to be.

Staging one's performance and interaction with the audience becomes part of the self-construction. The audience's live interaction also contributes to the process of self-making of the presenter-performer, as well as to the making of the audience's self. The audience interacts with the presenter/performer through watching them, asking questions, having conversation with them, or giving certain requests. Improvisation is a strong feature of *zhibo*, as even though the self as presenter/performer prepares what to present, the audience can interact with them at any time. The audience is also often in their own space, staring at their own personal screen, gazing at the intimate first person performance of the presenter. They interact with the performer out of curiosity, for voyeuristic pleasure, or to find a sense of existence, a connectedness in a highly atomised world.

In other words, *Zhibo* is a process of *celebrification* contributed to by both the presenter and the audience. In analysing micro-celebrity, Marwick sees celebrity as a verb or

> a set of practices and self-presentation techniques that spread across social networks as they are learned from other individuals. In these contexts, celebrity becomes something a person does, rather than something a person is, and exists as a continuum rather than a binary quality. (Marwick 2015)

Zhibo, as a way of producing micro-celebrity, has created a set of techniques and strategies that are used as training tools and are practised by individual presenter-performers when they interact with the audience. The presenter-performer takes into consideration the kinds of interactions that receive a higher response or generate more 'followers', and develops them into strategies to use again.

The performer/presenter in *zhibo* experiences *for* the audience, and is constantly advised by their requirements and manipulated by the audience's imagination. I encountered a beautiful *zhibo* girl in the street on a summer Shanghai night. She was sitting on a small stool at the crossroads of Nanjing West Road and Changde Road, one of the most prosperous streets in Shanghai with modern skyscrapers and luxury brand flagship shops in the background. Using a small stand to hold her phone in front of her, she was chatting with her followers about her experience of being there. Through the small screen, the *zhibo* girl brings Shanghai to her fans who may be in smaller towns and cities, dreaming of being able to experience the international and cosmopolitan. *Zhibo* girl becomes the person the fans want to be, as they imagine what it would be like to be there.

Ethics of interactive communication and commercialisation of the self

The new ways of *zhibo* interaction challenge the traditional ethics of interpersonal communication and raise the ethical question of live interaction among strangers. Social media have increased the amount of interactive interpersonal communication among strangers, and communication between strangers has never been so personal. In *zhibo* live streaming broadcasts, such communication has been centralised and exploited. The audience is anonymous, and perceived to be in a superior position because they can decide which performance to watch and for how long. An anonymous online comment states watching a 'one man *zhibo* show' is like wandering around in a bordello; one can choose which one to consume. This echoes what Polette and Rak states: 'the proliferation of self-representation in digital media has the effect of making anyone into a celebrity, a cultural construction where the representations of one's person becomes a commodity' (2014: 11). Watching and interacting are a form of voyeurism, for curiosity or emotional connection. The one being looked at, the self as performer/presenter, also gains profit through getting virtual currency, digital flowers or simply by the number of people watching, which pushes one to investigate further the intention of broadcasting the self.

Live-streaming web broadcast has indeed generated a new kind of economy, through commercialising one's online self-performance, similar to Instagram micro-celebrities. The political economy of *zhibo* self-expression deserves further exploration in future research, in terms of how *zhibo* is organised and the different agencies involved in this practice, including *zhibo* platforms, *zhibo* agents that recruit and manage the presenters, the presenters themselves and the audience.

It is reported that this new economy is geographically specific in China. For example, in the northeast, where the transition from industrial to post-industrial economy has not been a success, the high unemployment rate among the younger generation has urged the young to look for alternative income. The rise in the digital media economy, such as live web broadcast, has provided a self-administering alternative route. It is noted that among the most popular live web-broadcast sites, more than half of the mostly visited 'presenters' are from the northeast. The monthly profit for a 'presenter' can be from a few thousand up to tens of thousands RMB. For an individual living in a tier two or tier three city, it is indeed an affluent wage. Nevertheless, it is important to note that what a presenter earns is only one portion of the profit: *zhibo* agents, who manage presenters, and *zhibo* platforms as gatekeepers hosting *zhibo* activities, gain a split of the profit from each presenter. The commercial imperatives undermine or empower the intension of self-expression and performance. The tangled relationship between the two reflects the complexity of the construction of self in the age of social media.

Zhibo is also used by new media journalists and editors to create events that call for participation from the public. For example, *Xin Shi Xiang*, a new media content outlet on WeChat created an event called '*Why don't you want to go back home for the Mid-autumn Day?*' It recruited ten ordinary participants to go back to their home and chat with their parents about their most private concerns, such as being so-called 'leftover women',[8] 'coming out' as gay or other identities that are still not well accepted in China, or psychological problems such as depression, which are common among the urban youth today. These conversations and confrontations between parents and children were broadcast live. Even though the intention of the participators might not have been to 'get more likes', the platforms that broadcast it were aiming for higher viewing rates and popularity. This reminds me of the female filmmakers Tang Danhong, Yang Lina and Wang Fen who took cameras to challenge their parents in 2000 and 2001, which I have analysed in the first chapter. In these women's first person documentaries, some of the private content raised many debates and some of them have faced personal persecution in a society that still does not quite accept females challenging the patriarchy, or the young challenging the hierarchy. But in the age of reality TV and social media individual privacy and how to deal with private controversies can be selling points for an entertainment show, to evoke audience emotion to gain more social capital and increase viewing rates.

At the turn of this century, reality TV programmes as first person media have been criticised for the inversion of public and private under neoliberalism, where the individual experience as the consuming subject has replaced the collective experiences of identity formation (Dovey 2000: 176). The over-exposure of the private and the intimate, according to Dovey, has made the distance between the inner and outer world collapse (2000: 88–9). Today, an increasing amount of intimate self-made first person content has filled virtual public space globally. Not only is our sense of existence increasingly associated with our presence on social media, but the over-exposure of self-expression and personal images on the Internet encourage public voyeurism. *Zhibo*, as a way to directly present and perform the self and as a process of self-construction, also invites the audience into the process of self-making – both of the presenter and the audience.

Conclusion

I hope this book offers some insights into first person documentary practice in twenty-first-century China. Combining textual analysis and contextual studies, I have argued that this practice can be seen as a form of provocative social participation that stimulates important individual critical thinking and helps to form new kinds of subjectivities, to reconstruct political values and contribute to the transformation of social ethics. These films, as camera-mediated self-representations, illustrate individual selves as multi-layered and conflicted, situated in complex social relationships. The filmmakers do not just actively deconstruct their selves for self-understanding and self-analysis, but also further probe current problematic social relations. Their films reflect some aspects of how individuals conceive their selves, in relation to the changing role of the family, as a traditionally formed collective institution, and in relation to China's modern state as a powerful authority in individuals' lives.

While these films and the filmmaking practice reflect the changing notion of individual self in contemporary China, they have also further contributed to the construction and constitution of individual subjects. This book examines the complex characteristics of the changing relations between the public (*gonggong*) and the private (*siren*), between the collective (*jiti*) and the personal (*geren*), between the individual (*geti*) and the party-state (*dangguo*) in twenty-first-century China, questioning their binary relationships. By doing so, this book also demonstrates the mutability of the notion of the self in China, with interesting similarities and differences compared to discussions of 'self' in first person film and media from other parts of the world.

I hope this study contributes to the current debates in the international field of first person documentary practice and first person media, in Chinese cinema and cultural studies, and also offers some new directions for further exploration. The approach of taking the individual self as a focus for exploration can and should be expanded to other fields of study. In China, the autobiographical has also been an important dimension of art and cultural production, including literature, visual art, contemporary moving image and new media art. Looking beyond the practice in contemporary China, we can also examine first person documentary practice as a form of socio-political participation in other regions and cultural contexts. And in the current era of social media and identity technologies, to compare the ethics involved in first person documentary practice and online self-expression can reveal further how the sense of self is changing. In addition to examining the socio-political, cultural and technological conditions that have cultivated the practice of exploring the self, we can also explore, from the filmmaker's point of view, how he or she has further expanded or challenged social and ethical relations through the act of filmmaking.

Notes

1. The original Chinese of the slogan of Inke live-streaming broadcast platform 映客直播: '我，不一定网红，不一定会唱，不一定自律，不一定勇敢，不一定会赢。但，在映客，我一定是我。上映客，直播我'.
2. Caochanghdi Workstation was, however, wound-up in 2015 after Wu Wenguang and Wen Hui separated in 2014.
3. In conventional media, *zhibo* is used to refer to television or radio live broadcasts. The word was then used to describe online live broadcasts in the computer game community for their 'live' competitions. Gradually, more online live broadcast social media platforms have been developed for entertaining and communication, and *zhibo* has become a general term to describe this new form of live streaming on web-broadcast platforms. It can also be used as a verb, meaning the action of live streaming web-broadcast information.
4. As reported on http://www.latimes.com/world/asia/la-fg-china-live-streaming-crackdown-20170624-story.html.
5. As a business, the digital infrastructure of a *zhibo* platform is easy to set up, but it has high operational and promotional costs, so many small to medium platforms

have been taken over by larger ones, and industry forecasts suggest that there will be only a few *zhibo* platforms belonging to the large social media companies in the future, i.e. *Zhibo* will become a commonly used communication tool, as part of larger social media platforms, similar to the live web-broadcast platform within Facebook.

6. Tightening control of *zhibo* through closing down some live-streaming platforms was a way of demonstrating that Xi's leadership was in control, before China's nineteenth National Party Congress in November 2017.
7. 'Bullet curtain' or 'barrage' is the literal English translation of '*danmu*' in Chinese. It means displaying live chat messages over the streaming screen on the top or at the bottom of the screen, or even completely over the screen. It originally comes from the Japanese word '*danmaku*'.
8. A Chinese word in the official discourse to describe highly educated and high-income single women, who are in their late twenties or older. For more, please see Leta Hong Fincher (2014), *Leftover Women: The Resurgence of Gender Inequality in China*, London: Zed Books.

Filmography

Chinese Language Titles

Bare Your Stuff (亮出), dir. Wu Wenguang, 2010.
Criticizing China (批判中国), dir. Wu Haohao, 2008.
Days I (生活而已1), dir. Wei Xiaobo, 2011.
Days II (生活而已2), dir. Wei Xiaobo, 2012.
Days III (生活而已3), dir. Wei Xiaobo, 2017.
Dancing with Third Grandma (与三奶跳舞), dir. Wen Hui, 2015
Family Phobia (家庭恐怖), dir. Hu Xinyu, 2010.
Fuck Cinema (操电影), dir. Wu Wenguang, 2005.
Home Video (家庭录像), dir. Yang Lina, 2001.
Hooligan Sparrow (流氓燕), dir. Wang Nanfu, 2016.
I Beat the Tiger When I Was Young (年轻时也打老虎), dir. Xue Jianqiang, 2010.
Investigating the Father (调查父亲), dir. Wu Wenguang, 2016.
Kun 1: Action (Kun 1: 行动), dir. Wu Haohao, 2008.
Lao Ma Ti Hua (*Disturbing the Peace*, 老妈提花), dir. Ai Weiwei, 2009.
Laotou (老头), dir. Yang Lina, 1999.
The Last Bang Bang (最后的棒棒), dir. He Hu, 2016.
Listen to Third Grandma (听三奶奶讲过去的事情), dir. Wen Hui, 2012.
A Lonely Person (一个孤僻的人), Ai Weiwei Studio, 2010.
The Men (男人), dir. Hu Xinyu, 2003.
Martian Syndrome (火星综合症), dir. Xue Jianqiang, 2010.
Meishi Street (煤市街), dirs Ou Ning and Cao Fei, 2006.
Memories Look at Me (记忆看着我), dir. Song Fang, 2012.
Memory of Home (关于家的记忆), dir. Yu Tianqi, 2009.
My Family Tree (家谱), dir. Yang Pingdao, 2008.
My Name is Fenfen (我叫芬芬), dir. Guo Lifan, 2008.
My Private Album (我的私人相册), artist Feng Mengbo, 1996.
My Sister (我的姐姐), dir. Hu Xinyu, 2006.
Nightingale, Not the Only Voice (夜莺不是唯一的歌喉), dir. Tang Danhong, 2000.
Nostalgia (乡愁), dir. Shu Haolun, 2009.
Our Children (我们的娃娃), dirs Ai Xiaoming and Hu Jie, 2009.

Oxhide I (牛皮 I), dir. Liu Jiayin, 2005.
Oxhide II (牛皮 II), dir. Liu Jiayin, 2009.
Petition (上访), dir. Zhao Liang, 2010.
The River of Life (生命的河流), dir. Yang Pingdao, 2012.
Scrap (饭碗), dir. Zhu Yi, 2008.
Searching for Lin Zhao's Soul (寻找林昭的灵魂), dir. Hu Jie, 2004.
Seen and Heard, dir. Jian Yi & Villagers, 2006.
So Sorry (深表歉意), Ai Weiwei Studio, 2012.
Tape (胶带), dir. Li Ning, 2009.
There is a Strong Wind in Beijing (北京的风很大), dir. Ju An'qi, 1999.
They Are Not the Only Unhappy Couple (不快乐的不止一个), dir. Wang Fen, 2000.
Though I am Gone (我虽死去), dir. Hu Jie, 2006.
Treatment (治疗), *dir.* Wu Wenguang, 2009.
Unknown Pleasures (任逍遥), dir. Jia Zhangke, 2003.
Using (龙哥), dir. Zhou Hao, 2008.
The Vagina Monologue: Backstage Stores (阴道独白), dir. Ai Xiaoming, 2004.

China Villagers Documentary Project 村民影像计划:
My Village 2006 series (我的村子2006)
My Village 2007 series (我的村子2007)
My Village 2008 series (我的村子2008)
dirs Shao Yuzhen, Wang Wei, Zhang Huancai and Jia Zhidan.

Wen Hui's Documentary Theatre Performance:
100 Verbs (100个动词), choreographer Wen Hui, 1994.
The Toilet (马桶), choreographer Wen Hui, 1995.
Birth Report (生育报告), choreographer Wen Hui, 1995.
Memory (回忆), choreographer Wen Hui, 2008.
Memory 2: Hunger (回忆2: 饥饿), choreographer Wen Hui, 2011.

Zhang Mengqi's *Self Portrait* Series:
Self Portrait with Three Women (自画像: 三个女人), dir. Zhang Mengqi, 2010.
Self-Portrait: at 47 KM (自画像: 在47公里), dir. Zhang Mengqi, 2011.
Self-Portrait: Dancing at 47 KM (自画像: 47公里跳舞), dir. Zhang Mengqi, 2012.
Self-Portrait: Dreaming at 47 KM (自画像: 47公里做梦), dir. Zhang Mengqi, 2013.
Self-Portrait: Birth in 47 KM (自画像: 生于 47公里), dir. Zhang Mengqi, 2016.

Zou Xueping's *Village* Series:
The Starving Village (饥饿的村子), dir. Zou Xueping, 2010.
The Satiated Village (吃饱的村子), dir. Zou Xueping, 2011.
Children's Village (孩子的村子), dir. Zou Xueping, 2012.
Trashy Village (垃圾的村子), dir. Zou Xueping, 2013.
Fools' Village (傻子的村子), dir. Zou Xueping, 2015.

Non-Chinese Language Titles

The Alcohol Years, dir. Carol Morley, 2000, UK.
Birth/Mother, dir. Naomi Kawase, 2006, Japan.
Capturing the Friedmans, dir. Andrew Jarecki, 2003, USA.
China's Capitalist Revolution, dir. Robert Coldstream, 2010, Brook Lapping Productions, UK.
Dear Pyongyang, dir. Yong-hi Yang, 2005, Japan.
Daughter Rite, dir. Michelle Citron, 1980, USA.
Extreme Private Eros: Love Song 1974 (Kyokushiteki erosu: Renka 1974), dir. Hara Kazuo, 1974, Japan.
I for India, dir. Sandhya Suri, 2005, UK/India.
Intimate Strangers, dir. Alan Berliner, 1991, USA.
Impressions of a Sunset, dir. Suzuki Shiroyasu, 1975, Japan.
Katatsumori, dir. Naomi Kawase, 1994, Japan.
The Maelstrom, dir. Péter Forgács, 1997, Netherlands/Hungary.
Man with a Movie Camera, dir. Dziga Vertov, 1929, Soviet Union.
News From Home, dir. Chantal Akerman, 1977, Belgium/France.
Nobody's Business, dir. Alan Berliner, 1996, USA.
Reassemblage, dir. Trinh-T. Minh-Ha, 1982, USA.
Reminiscences of a Journey to Lithuania, dir. Jonas Mekas, 1973, USA.
Sans Soleil, dir. Chris Marker, 1989, France.
See the Heaven, dir. Naomi Kawase, 1995, Japan.
Sherman's March, dir. Ross McElwee, 1986, USA.
Six O'Clock News, dir. Ross McElwee, 1996, USA.
Sun on the Horizon, dir. Naomi Kawase, 1996, Japan.
Sunday in Beijing, dir. Chris Marker, 1956, France.
Time Indefinite, dir. Ross McElwee, 1994, USA.
Tongues Untied, dir. Marlon Rigg, 1989, USA.
Treyf, dirs Alisa Lebow and Cynthia Madansky, 1998, USA.

Bibliography

Author's Own Interviews with:

Hu Xinyu, 14 July 2010.
Shu Haolun, 2 August 2010.
Wang Fen, 19 July 2010.
Wu Haohao, 16 July 2010.
Wu Haohao, 28 October 2010.
Wu Wenguang, 21 July 2010.
Xue Jianqiang, 11 November 2010.
Yang Lina, 15 July 2010.
Yang Pingdao, 13 July 2010.
Zhang Yaxuan, 16 July 2010.

English/European Publications

Aguayo, Angela J. (2005), 'Documentary film/video and social change: a rhetorical investigation of dissent', Doctoral dissertation, University of Texas at Austin.

Allan, S., and E. Thorsen (eds) (2009), *Citizen Journalism: Global Perspectives*, New York: Peter Lang.

Anderson, Benedict (1983), *Imagined Communities: Reflections on the Origin and Spread of Nationalism*, London: Verso.

Astruc, Alexandre (1948), 'Du stylo à la caméra et de la caméra au stylo', *L'Écran française*, 30 March.

Austin, Thomas, and Wilma De Jong (eds) (2008), *Rethinking Documentary, New Perspectives, New Practices*, Maidenhead: Open University Press.

Barthes, Roland (1999), *Camera Lucida: Reflections on Photography*, trans. Richard Howard, New York: Farrar, Straus & Giroux.

Bauman, Zygmunt (2000), *Liquid Modernity*, Cambridge: Polity Press.

Bauman, Zygmunt (2001), *The Individualised Society*, Cambridge: Polity Press.

Beattie, John (1964), *Other Cultures – Aims, Methods and Achievements in Social Anthropology*, London: Cohen & West.

Beck, Ulrich (1992), *Risk Society: Towards a New Modernity*, trans. Mark Ritter, London: Sage.

Beck, Ulrich (2000), 'The cosmopolitan perspective: sociology for the second age of modernity', *British Journal of Sociology*, 51, pp. 79–106.

Beck, Ulrich, and Elisabeth Beck-Gernsheim (2002), *Individualization: Institutionalized Individualism and its Social and Political Consequences*, London: Sage.

Beck, Ulrich, and Elisabeth Beck-Gernsheim (2010), 'Varieties of individualisation', in M. Halskov Hansen and Rune Svarverud (eds), *iChina: The Rise of the Individual in Modern Chinese Society*, Copenhagen: Nias Press, pp. 1–38.

Beck, Ulrich, and Johannes Willms (2004), *Conversations with Ulrich Beck*, Cambridge: Polity Press.

Beck, Ulrich, Anthony Giddens and Scott Lash (1994), *Reflexive Modernization: Politics, Tradition and Aesthetics in the Modern Social Order*, Stanford: Stanford University Press.

Bennett, W. L. (2003), 'Media power: the internet and global activism', in N. Couldry and J. Curran (eds), *Contesting Media Power*, Lanham: Rowman and Littlefield, pp. 17–39.

Berry, Chris (2006), 'Independently Chinese: Duan Jinchuan, Jiang Yue, and Chinese documentary', in Paul Pickowicz and Zhang Yingjin (eds), *From Underground to Independent: Alternative Film Culture in Contemporary China* Lanham: Rowman and Littlefield, pp. 109–22.

Berry, Chris (2007), 'Getting real: Chinese documentaries, Chinese postsocialism', in Zhang Zhen (ed.), *China's Urban Generation*, Durham: Duke University Press, pp. 115–34.

Berry, Chris (2010), 'New documentary in China: public space, public television', in Chris Berry, Lynn Spigel and Soyoung Kim (eds), *Electronic Elsewheres*, Minneapolis: University of Minnesota Press, pp. 95–116.

Berry, Chris, and Mary Farquhar (2006), *China on Screen – China and Nation*, New York: Columbia University Press.

Berry, Chris, and Lisa Rofel (2010a), 'Introduction', in Chris Berry, Xinyu Lu and Lisa Rofel (eds), *The New Chinese Documentary Film Movement: For the Public Record*, Hong Kong: Hong Kong University Press, pp. 3–14.

Berry, Chris, and Lisa Rofel (2010b), 'Alternative archive: China's independent documentary culture', in Chris Berry, Xinyu Lu and Lisa Rofel (eds), *The New Chinese Documentary Film Movement: For the Public Record*, Hong Kong: Hong Kong University Press, pp. 135–54.

Bishop, Claire (2012), *Participatory Art and the Politics of Spectatorship*, London: Verso.

Blumler, J. G., and M. Gurevitch (2001), 'The new media and our political communication discontents: democratizing cyberspace', *Information, Communication & Society*, 4: 1, pp. 1–13.

Boym, Svetlana (2001), *The Future of Nostalgia*, New York: Basic Books.

Braester, Yomi (2010), 'Excuse me, your camera is in my face: auteurial intervention in PRC new documentary', in Chris Berry, Xinyu Lu and Lisa Rofel (eds), *The New Chinese Documentary Film Movement: For the Public Record*, Hong Kong: Hong Kong University Press, pp. 3–14.

Bruzzi, Stella (2013), '"The performance documentary": the performing film-maker, the acting subject', in B. Winston (ed.), *The Documentary Film Book*, London: BFI.

Butler, Judith (1990), *Gender Trouble: Feminism and the Subversion of Identity*, Oxford: Psychology Press.

Butler, Judith (1993), *Bodies That Matter: On the Discursive Limits of 'Sex'*, New York: Routledge.

Chen, Eyi (2009), '*Shanghai Baby* as a Chinese chick-lit: female empowerment and neoliberal consumerist agency', *Asian Journal of Women's Studies*, 15: 1, pp. 54–93.

Christensen, Christian (2009), 'Political documentary, online organization and activist synergies', *Studies in Documentary Film*, 3: 2.

Ci, Jiwei (1994), *Dialectic of the Chinese Revolution: From Utopianism to Hedonism*. Stanford: Stanford University Press.

Corner, John (2009), 'Documenting the political: some issues', *Studies in Documentary Film*, 3: 2, pp. 113–29.

Corner, John (2011), *Theorising Media: Power, Form and Subjectivity*, Manchester: Manchester University Press.

Cover, Rob (2014), 'Becoming and belonging: performativity, subjectivity and the cultural purposes of social networking', in Anna Poletti and Julie Rak (eds), *Identity Technologies: Constructing the Self Online*, Madison: University of Wisconsin Press.

Cuevas, Efrén (2014), 'Change of scale: home movies as microhistory in documentary films', in L. Rascaroli, G. Young and B. Monahan (eds), *Amateur Filmmaking: The Home Movie, the Archive, the Web*, London: Bloomsbury Academic, pp. 139–52.

Czach, Liz (2002), 'Polavision instant movies: Edwin Land's quest for a new medium', *The Moving Image*, 2: 2, pp. 1–24.

Czach, Liz (2014), 'Home movies and amateur film as national cinema', in L. Rascaroli, G. Young and B. Monahan (eds), *Amateur Filmmaking: The Home Movie, the Archive, the Web*, London: Bloomsbury Academic, pp. 27–38.

Damm, Jens, and Simona Thomas (eds) (2006), *Chinese Cyberspaces: Technological Changes and Political Effects*, London: Routledge.

De Bary, Wm. Theodore, and the Conference on Ming Thought (1970), *Self and Society in Ming Thought*, New York: Columbia University Press.

De Bary, Wm. Theodore (1998), *Asian Values and Human Rights: A Confucian Communitarian Perspective*, Cambridge, MA: Harvard University Press.

Denton, Kirk A. (1987), 'Model drama as myth: a semiotic analysis of *Taking Tiger Mountain by Strategy*', in Constantine Tung and Colin MacKerras (eds), *Drama in the People's Republic of China*, Albany: State University of New York Press, pp. 119–36.

Denton, Kirk A. (1998), *The Problematic of Self in Modern Chinese Literature: Hu Feng and Lu Ling*, Stanford: Stanford University Press.

Derk, Bodde (trans.) (1983), *A History of Chinese Philosophy*, Princeton: Princeton University Press.

Dooling, D. Amy (2005), *Women's Literary Feminism in Twentieth Century China*, New York: Palgrave Macmillan.

Dovey, Jon (2000), *Freakshow: First Person Media and Factual Television*, London: Pluto Press.

Edwards, Dan (2015), *Independent Chinese Documentary: Alternative Visions, Alternative Publics*, Edinburgh: University of Edinburgh Press.

Elegent, Simon (2007), 'China's me generation: the new middle class is young, rich and happy. Just don't mention politics', *The Times*, 4 November, pp. 47–51.

Evans, Harriet (1997), *Women and Sexuality in China*, Cambridge: Polity Press.

Evans, Harriet (2008), *The Subject of Gender: Daughters and Mothers in Urban China*, Lanham: Rowman and Littlefield.

Evans, Harriet (2010), 'The gender of communication: changing expectations of mothers and daughters in urban China', *China Quarterly*, 204, pp. 980–1000.

Fei, Xiaotong (1992), *From the Soil: The Foundations of Chinese Society*, trans.Gary G. Hamilton, Zheng Wang and Xiangtu Zhongguo, Berkeley: University of California Press.

Finkelpearl, Tom (2013), *What We Made: Conversations on Art and Social Cooperation*, Durham: Duke University Press.

Fogel, Joshua A., and Peter G. Zarrow (eds) (1997), *Imaging the People: Chinese Intellectuals and the Concept of Citizenship, 1980–1920*, Armonk: M. E. Sharpe.

Fong, Vanessa L. (2006), *Only Hope: Coming of Age Under China's One-Child Policy*, Stanford: Stanford University Press.

Foucault, Michel (1984), 'The subject and power', in Brian Wallis (ed.), *Art after Modernism: Rethinking Representation*, New York: The New Museum of Contemporary Art, pp. 417–60.

Gao, Yuan (1987), *Born Red: A Chronicle of the Cultural Revolution*, Stanford: Stanford University Press.

Giddens, Anthony (1990), *Modernity and Self-Identity: Self and Society in the Late Modern Age*, Stanford: Stanford University Press.

Gladston, Paul (2013), 'Getting Over Ai Weiwei', http://www. randian-online.com/zh/np_feature/getting-over-ai-weiwei/ (accessed 20 November 2010).

Gold, Thomas (1996), 'Youth and the State', in Brian Hook (ed.), *The Individual and the State in China*, Oxford: Clarendon Press, pp. 175–95.

Guo, Yingjie (2004), *Cultural Nationalism in Contemporary China: The Search for National Identity under Reform*, London: Routledge.

Hall, David L., and Roger T. Ames (1998), *Thinking from the Han, Self, Truth, and Transcendence in Chinese and Western Culture*, New York: State University of New York Press.

Hall, Stuart (1992), 'The question of cultural identity', in Stuart Hall, David Held and Anthony McGrew (eds), *Modernity and its Futures*, Cambridge: Polity Press in association with the Open University, pp. 273–326.

Hansen, Mette Halskov, and Rune Svarverud (eds) (2010), *iChina: the Rise of the Individual in Modern Chinese Society*, Copenhagen: Nias Press.

Hara, Kazuo (2009), *Camera Obtrusa: the Action Documentaries of Hara Kazuo*, trans. P. J. Noonan and T. Yasuda, New York: Kaya Press.

He, Baogang (1997), *The Democratic Implications of Civil Society in China*, New York: St Martin's Press.

Hegal, Robert E., and Richard C. Hessney (eds) (1985), *Expressions of Self in Chinese Literature*, New York: Columbia University Press.

Hermes, Joke, and Peter Dahlgren (2006), 'Cultural studies and citizenship', *European Journal of Cultural Studies*, 9, pp. 259–65.

Hirsch, Marianne (ed.) (1999), *The Familial Self*, Hanover: University Press of New England.

Hisashi, Nada (2005), *Self-Documentary: Its Origins and Present State*, https://www.yidff.jp/docbox/26/box26-2-e.html.

Hook, Brian (ed.) (1996), *The Individual and the State in China*, Oxford: Clarendon Press.

Hooper, Beverley (2005), *The Consumer Citizen in Contemporary China*, Working Paper no. 12, Lund: Centre for East and South-East Asian, Lund University.

Howard, Cosmo (ed.) (2007), *Contested Individualisation: Debates about Contemporary Personhood*, New York: Palgrave Macmillan.

Huang, Martin W. (1995), *Literati and Self-re/presentation: Autobiographical Sensibility in the Eighteenth Century Chinese Novel*, Stanford: Stanford University Press.

Huang, Philip C. (1993), '"Public Sphere"/"Civil Society" in China?: The Third Realm between State and Society', *Modern China*, 19: 2, pp. 216–40.

Huang, Xuelei (2016), 'Murmuring voices of the everyday: Jia Zhitan and his village documentaries', *Journal of Chinese Cinemas*, 10: 2, pp. 166–86.

Hwang, K. K. (1995), 'The struggle between Confucianism and legalism in Chinese society and productivity: a Taiwan experience', in K. K. Hwang (ed.), *Easternization: Socio-cultural Impact on Productivity*, Tokyo: Asian Productivity Organization.

Inkeles, Alex. C., Montgomery Broaded and Zhongde Cao (1997), 'Causes and consequences of individual modernity in China', *The China Journal*, 37, pp. 31–59.

Ishizuka, Karen L., and Patricia R. Zimmermann (eds) (2008), *Mining the Home Movie: Excavations in Histories and Memories*, London: University of California Press.

Ivanhoe, Philip J. (2000), *Confucian Moral Self Cultivation*, Indianapolis: Hackett Publications.

Jaffee, Valerie (2006), '"*Every Man a Star*": the ambivalent cult of amateur art in new Chinese documentaries', in Paul G. Pickowicz and Yinjing Zhang (eds), *Underground to Independent*, Lanham: Rowman and Littlefield, pp. 77–108.

James, David E. (1992), 'Film diary/diary film: practice and product in Walden', in David E. James (ed.), *To Free the Cinema: Jonas Mekas and The New York Underground*, Princeton: Princeton University Press, pp. 145–79.

Jenkins, Henry (2006), *Convergence Culture: Where Old and New Media Collide*, New York: New York University Press.

Johnson, Matthew D. (2006), 'A scene beyond our line of sight: Wu Wenguang and new documentary cinema's politics of independence', in Paul G. Pickowicz and Yinjing Zhang (eds), *From Underground to Independent*, Lanham: Rowman and Littlefield, pp. 47–76.

Johnson, Matthew D. (2014), Wu Wenguang and the NGO aesthetic', in M. D. Johnson, K. B. Wagner, T. Yu and L. Vulpiani (eds), *China's iGeneration: Cinema and Moving Image Culture for the Twenty-First Century*, London: Bloomsbury Academic.

Johnson, M. D., K. B. Wagner, T. Yu and L. Vulpiani (eds) (2014), *China's iGeneration: Cinema and Moving Image Culture for the Twenty-First Century*, London: Bloomsbury Academic.

Judge, Joan (2002), 'Citizens or mothers of citizens? Gender and the meaning of modern Chinese citizenship', in Merle Goldman and Elizabeth J. Perry (eds), *Changing Meanings of Citizenship in Modern China*, Cambridge, MA: Harvard University Press, pp. 23–43.

Kahn, R. L., and C. F. Cannell (1957), *The Dynamics of Interviewing: Theory, Technique, and Cases*, New York: Wiley.

Kang, Liu, and Xiaobing Tang (eds) (1993), *Politics, Ideology, and Literary Discourse in Modern China – Theoretical Interventions and Cultural Critique*, Durham: Duke University Press.

Keane, Michael A. (2007), 'Chinese citizenship and globalization', in Wayne Hudson and Steven Slaughter (eds), *Globalisation and Citizenship: The Transnational Challenge*, London: Routledge, pp. 43–51.

Kellner, Douglas (1995), *Media Culture: Cultural Studies, Identity and Politics Between the Modern and Post Modern*, London: Routledge.

King, Ambrose Yeo-chi (1985), 'The individual and group in Confucianism: a relational perspective', in Donald J. Munro (ed.), *Individualism and Holism: Studies in Confucian and Taoist Values*, Ann Arbor: Center for Chinese Studies Publications, University of Michigan, pp. 57–70.

Kipnis, Andrew (1997), *Producing Guanxi: Sentiment, Self and Subculture in a North China Village*, Durham: Duke University Press.

Kogawa, Tetsuo (1996), 'Video: the access medium', in Michael Renov and Erika Suderburg (eds), *Resolutions: Contemporary Video Practices*, Minneapolis: University of Minnesota Press, pp. 51–60.

Krauss, Rosalind (1976), 'Video: the aesthetics of narcissism', *October*, 1, pp. 50–64.

Kuhn, Philip (2002), *Origins of the Modern Chinese State*, Stanford: Stanford University Press.

Lagerkvist, J. (2006), *The Internet in China: Unlocking and Containing the Public Sphere*, Lund: Lund University.

Langman, L. (2005), 'From virtual public spheres to global justice: a critical theory of internetworked social movements', *Sociological Theory*, 23: 1, pp. 42–73.

Lane, Jim (2002), *The Autobiographical Documentary in America*, Madison: University of Wisconsin Press.

Larson, Wendy (1991), *Literary Authority and the Modern Chinese Writers: Ambivalence and Autobiography*, Durham: Duke University Press.

Lash, Scott (1993), 'Reflexive modernization: the aesthetic dimension', *Theory, Culture and Society*, 10, pp. 1–23.

Lebow, Alisa (2008), *First Person Jewish*, Minneapolis: University of Minnesota Press.

Lebow, Alisa (2012), *Cinema of Me: The Self and Subjectivity in First Person Documentary*, New York: Wallflower Press.

Lebow, Alisa (2013), 'First-person political', in Winston Brian (ed.), *The Documentary Film Book*, London: BFI, pp. 257–65.

Lee, Leo Ou-fan (1990), 'In search of modernity: some reflections on a new mode of consciousness in twentieth-century Chinese history and literature', in Paul Cohen and Merle Goldman (eds), *Ideas Across Cultures: Essays on Chinese Thought in Honor of Benjamin I. Schwartz*, Cambridge, MA: Council on East Asian Studies, Harvard University, pp. 109–35.

Levinas, Emmanual (1998), *Totality and Infinity: An Essay on Exteriority*, trans. Alphonso Lingis, Pittsburgh: Duquesne University Press.

Liang, Heng, and Judith Shapiro (1984), *Son of the Revolution*, New York: Vintage.

Lienhardt, Godfrey (1954), 'Modes of thought', in E. E. Evans-Pritchard *et al.*, (eds), *The Institutions of Primitive Society*, Oxford: Blackwell, pp. 95–107.

Lin, G., G. Yang, C. K. Lee and M. Xia (2004), 'Active society in formation: environmentalism, labor, and the underworld in China', *Asian Program Special Report* no. 124.

Lin, Min, and Maria Galikowski (1999), *The Search for Modernity: Chinese Intellectuals and Cultural Discourse in the Post-Mao China*, London: Palgrave Macmillan.

Liu, J. (2009), 'A green virtual space for social changes in China: internet activism and Chinese environmental NGOs', Paper presented at the annual meeting of the International Communication Association, Marriott, Chicago, May 21.

Liu, Lydia H. (1993a), 'Translingual practice: the discourse of individualism between China and the West', *Positions: East Asia Cultures Critique*, 1: 1, pp. 160–93.

Liu, Lydia H. (1993b), 'Narratives of modern selfhood: first-person fiction in May Fourth Literature', in Liu Kang and Xiaobing Tang (eds), *Politics, Ideology, and Literary Discourse in Modern China Theoretical Interventions and Cultural Critique*, Durham: Duke University Press, pp. 102–23.

Liu, Lydia H. (1995), *Translingual Practice – Literature, National Culture and Translated Modernity, China 1900–1937*, Stanford: Stanford University Press.

Liu, Qingping (2003), 'Filiality versus sociality and individuality: on Confucianism as "Consanguinitism"', *Philosophy East and West*, 53, pp. 234–50.

Liu, Xin (2002), *The Otherness of Self: A Genealogy of the Self in Contemporary China*, Ann Arbor: University of Michigan Press.

Lu, Sheldon H. (2007), *Chinese Modernity and Global Biopolitics: Studies in Literature and Visual Culture*, Honolulu: University of Hawaii Press.

Lu, Tonglin (1993), *Gender and Sexuality in Twentieth-Century Chinese Literature and Society*, New York: State University of New York Press.

Lu, Tonglin (1995), *Misogyny, Cultural Nihilism, and Oppositional Politics: Contemporary Chinese Fiction*, Stanford: Stanford University Press.

Lü, Xinyu (2010), 'Rethinking China's new documentary movement', trans. Tan Jia and Lisa Rofel, in Chris Berry, Xinyu Lu and Lisa Rofel (eds), *The New Chinese*

Documentary Film Movement: For the Public Record, Hong Kong: Hong Kong University Press, pp. 15–48.

MacDougall, David (2001), 'Renewing ethnographic film: is digital video changing the genre?', *Anthropology Today*, 17: 3, pp. 15–21.

Mian, Mian (2003), *Candy*, Boston: Little, Brown/Back Bay Books.

Minh-ha, Trinh T. (1991), *When the Moon Waxes Red: Representation, Gender and Cultural Politics*, London: Routledge.

Minh-ha, Trinh T. (1993), 'The totalizing quest of meaning', in M. Renov (ed.), *Theorizing Documentary*, London: Routledge.

Moran, James M. (2002), *There's No Place Like Home Video*, Minneapolis: University of Minnesota Press.

Motrescu-Mayes, Annamaria (2014), 'Uncensored British imperial politics in late colonial home movies', in L. Rascaroli, G. Young and B. Monahan (eds), *Amateur Filmmaking: The Home Movie, the Archive, the Web*, London: Bloomsbury Academic, pp. 95–108.

Muhlhahn, Klaus (2010), '"Friendly pressure": law and the individual in modern China', in M. Halskov Hansen and Rune Svarverud (eds), *iChina: The Rise of the Individual in Modern Chinese Society*, Copenhagen: Nias Press, pp. 226–49.

Munro, Donald J. (ed.) (1985), *Individualism and Holism: Studies in Confucian and Taoist Values*, Ann Arbor: Center for Chinese Studies Publications, University of Michigan.

Nakajima, Seio (2010), 'Watching documentary: critical public discourses and contemporary urban Chinese film clubs', in Chris Berry, Xintu Lu and Lisa Rofel (eds), *The New Chinese Documentary Film Movement: For the Public Record*, Hong Kong: Hong Kong University Press, pp. 117–34.

Ng, Janet (2001), 'A moral landscape: reading Shen Congwen's autobiography and travelogues', *Chinese Literature: Essays, Articles, Reviews*, 23 (December), pp. 81–102.

Ng, Janet (2004), 'The experience of modernity: Chinese autobiography of the early twentieth century', *The Journal of Asian Studies*, 63: 3, pp. 773–5.

Nornes, A. Markus (2002), 'The postwar documentary trace: groping in the dark', *Positions*, 10: 1, pp. 39–78.

Nornes, A. Markus (2003), 'Private reality: Hara Kazuo's films', in Ivone Margulies (ed.), *Rites of Realism: Essays on Corporeal Cinema*, Durham: Duke University Press, pp. 144–63.

Nornes, A. Markus (2009), 'Bulldozers, bibles, and very sharp knives: the Chinese independent documentary scene – reports from the thriving festivals in Songhzhuang and Kunming, China', *Film Quarterly*, 63: 1, pp. 50–5.

Odin, Roger (2008), 'Reflections on the family home movie as document: a semio-pragmatic approach', in Karen L. Ishizuka and Patricia R. Zimmermann (eds), *Mining the Home Movie: Excavations in Histories and Memories*, Oakland: University of California Press, pp. 255–71.

Odin, Roger (2014), 'The home movie and space of communication', in L. Rascaroli, G. Young and B. Monahan (eds), *Amateur Filmmaking: The Home Movie, the Archive, the Web*, London: Bloomsbury Academic, pp. 15–26.

Palmer, Michael (2006), 'The emergence of consumer rights: legal protection of the consumer in the PRC', in Kevin Latham, Stuart Thompson and Jakob Klein (eds), *Consuming China: Approaches to Cultural Change in Contemporary China*, London: Routledge, pp. 56–81.

Phillips, Tom (2016), 'Gone bananas: China bans "erotic" eating of the fruit on live streams', *The Guardian*, 9 May 2016, https://www.theguardian.com/world/2016/may/09/gone-bananas-china-bans-erotic-eating-live-streams (accessed 17 July 2017).

Pickowicz, Paul G. (2006), 'Social and political dynamics of underground filmmaking in China', in Paul G. Pickowicz and Yinjing Zhang (eds), *From Underground to Independent*, Lanham: Rowman and Littlefield, pp. 1–22.

Poletti, Anna, and Julie Rak (eds) (2014), *Identity Technologies: Constructing the Self Online*, Madison: University of Wisconsin Press.

Pratt, Mary Louise (1991), 'Arts of the contact zone', *Profession*, pp. 33–40.

Průšek, Jaroslav, and Leo Ou-fan Lee (eds) (1980), *The Lyrical and the Epic: Studies of Modern Chinese Literature*, Bloomington: Indiana University Press.

Průšek, Jaroslav, and Leo Ou-fan Lee (2001), 'A moral landscape: reading Shen Chongwen's autobiography and travelogues', *Chinese Literature: Essays, Articles, Reviews*, 23, pp. 81–102.

Pye, Lucian W. (1996), 'The State and the individual: an overview interpretation', in Brian Hook (ed.), *The Individual and the State in China*, Oxford: Clarendon Press, pp. 16–42.

Qian, Ying (2014), 'Working with Rubble: montage, tweets, and the reconstruction of an activist cinema', in M. B. Johnson, K. B. Wagner, T. Yu and L. Vulpiani (eds), *China's iGeneration: Cinema and Moving Image Culture for the Twenty-First Century*, London: Bloomsbury Academic, pp. 181–96.

Qiu, Jack Linchuan (1999/2000), 'Virtual censorship in China: keeping the gate between the cyberspaces', *International Journal of Communications Law and Policy*, 4 (Winter), pp. 1–25.

Rascaroli, Laura (2009), *The Personal Camera – Subjective Cinema and the Essay Film*, London: Wallflower Press.

Rascaroli, Laura (2014), 'Working at home: tarnation, amateur authorship, and self-inscription in the digital age', in L. Rascaroli, G. Young and B. Monahan (eds), *Amateur Filmmaking: The Home Movie, the Archive, the Web*, London: Bloomsbury Academic, pp. 229–41.

Rascaroli, L., G. Young and B. Monahan (eds) (2014), *Amateur Filmmaking: The Home Movie, the Archive, the Web*, London: Bloomsbury Academic.

Renov, Michael (ed.) (1993), *Theorizing Documentary*, New York: Routledge.

Renov, Michael (2004), *The Subject of Documentary*, Minneapolis: University of Minnesota Press.

Renov, Michael (2008), 'First-person films. Some theses on self-inscription', in Thomas Austin and Wilma de Jong (eds), *Rethinking Documentary: New Perspectives, New Practices*, Maidenhead: Open University Press, pp. 39–50.

Renov, Michael, and Erika Suderberg (eds) (1996), *Resolutions: Contemporary Video Practice*, Minneapolis: University of Minnesota Press.

Robinson, Luke (2010), 'From "public" to "private": Chinese documentary and the logic of Xianchang', in Chris Berry, Xinyu Lu and Lisa Rofel (eds), *The New Chinese Documentary Film Movement: For the Public Record*, Hong Kong: Hong Kong University Press, pp. 177–94.

Robinson, Luke (2013), *Independent Chinese Documentary: From the Studio to the Street*, Basingstoke: Palgrave Macmillan.

Rofel, Lisa (1999), *Other Modernities: Gendered Yearnings in China After Socialism*, Berkeley: University of California Press.

Rofel, Lisa (2007), *Desiring China: Experiments in Neoliberalism, Sexuality, and Public Culture*, Durham: Duke University Press.

Routt, William D. (1990), 'L'Evidence', *Continuum: The Australian Journal of Media and Culture*, 5: 2, pp. 23–55.

Ruoff, Jeffrey (1993), 'Filming at the margins: the documentaries of Hara Kazuo', *Iris: A Journal of Theory on Image and Sound, Image Theory, Image Culture, and Contemporary Japan*, 16, pp. 115–26.

Russell, Catherine (1999), *Experimental Ethnography – the Work of Film in the Age of Video*, Durham: Duke University Press.

Sikov, Ed (2010), *Film Studies: an Introduction*, New York: Columbia University Press.

Solinger, Dorothy J. (1999), *Contesting Citizenship in Urban China: Peasant Migrants, the State, and the Logic of the Market*, Los Angeles: University of California Press.

Sørenssen, Bjørn (2008), 'Digital video and Alexandre Astruc's caméra-stylo: the new avant-garde in documentary realized?', *Studies in Documentary Film*, 2: 1, pp. 47–59.

Stockman, Norman (2000), *Understanding Chinese Society*, Cambridge: Polity Press.

Svarverud, Rune (2010), 'Individual self-discipline and collective freedom in the minds of Chinese intellectuals', in M. Halskov Hansen and Rune Svarverud (eds), *iChina: The Rise of the Individual in Modern Chinese Society*, Copenhagen: Nias Press, pp. 193–225.

Tang, John C. *et al.* (2017), 'Perspectives on live streaming: apps, users, and research', panel at *CSCW 2017 Companion, 25 February–1 March, 2017, Portland, OR, USA.*

Taylor, Rodney L. (1978), 'The centred self: religious autobiography in the neo-Confucian tradition', *History of Religions*, 17: 3/4, pp. 266–83.

Teets, Jessica C. (2009), 'Post-earthquake relief and reconstruction efforts: the emergence of civil society in China?', *The China Quarterly*, 198, pp. 330–47.

Thelle, Hatla (2004), *Better to Rely on Ourselves: Changing Social Rights in Urban China since 1979*, Copenhagen: Nias Press.

Torchin, Leshu (2012), *Creating the Witness: Documenting Genocide on Film, Video and the Internet*, Minneapolis: University of Minnesota Press.

Trauzettel, Rolf (1990), 'Historical aspects of the individual-society relationship in China', in Carl-Albrecht Seyschab, Armin Sievers and Stawoj Szynkiewicz (eds), *Society, Culture and Patterns of Behaviour*, Unkel/Rhein: Horlemann, pp. 25–70.

Tsagarousianou, R., D. Tambini and C. Bryan (eds) (1998), *Cyberdemocracy: Technology, Cities and Civic Networks*, London: Routledge.

Tyler, Stephen, A. (1986), 'Post-modern ethnography: from document of the occult to occult document', in J. Clifford and G. Marcus (eds), *Writing Culture – the Poetics and Politics of Ethnography*, Berkeley: University of California Press, pp. 122–40.

Un, Siosan (2009), 'Floating as the keyword: independent documentary films in postsocialist China', MA thesis, University of Toronto.

Vinograd, Richard (1992), *Boundaries of the Self: Chinese Portraits, 1600–1900*, Cambridge: Cambridge University Press.

Voci, Paola (2010), *China on Video: Smaller-Screen Realities*, London: Routledge.

Volgel, Ezra (1964), *From Friendship to Comradeship: the Change in Personal Relations in Communist China*, Cambridge, MA: Harvard University Press.

Wagner, B. Keith, and Tianqi Yu (2014), 'Introduction: China's iGeneration cinema', in M. D. Johnson, K. B. Wagner, T. Yu and L. Vulpiani (eds), *China's iGeneration: Cinema and Moving Image Culture for the Twenty-First Century*, London: Bloomsbury Academic, pp. 1–20.

Wang, Hui (2006), 'Depoliticized politics, multiple components of hegemony, and the eclipse of the Sixties', trans. Christopher Connery, *Inter-Asia Cultural Studies*, 7: 4, pp. 683–700.

Wang, Hui (2009), *The End of the Revolution – China and the Limits of Modernity*, London: Verso.

Wang, Lingzhen (1998), 'Retheorizing the personal: identity, writing, and gender in Yu Luojin's autobiographical act', *Positions: East Asia Cultures Critique*, 6: 2, pp. 394–438.

Wang, Lingzhen (2004), *Personal Matters: Women's Autobiographical Practice in Twentieth-Century China*, Stanford: Stanford University Press.

Wang, Lingzhen (2005), 'Reproducing the self: consumption, imaginary, and identity in women's autobiographical practice in the 1990s', in Charles A. Laughlin (ed.), *Contested Modernities in Chinese Literature*, New York: Palgrave Macmillan, pp. 173–92.

Wang, Qi (2014), *Memory, Subjectivity and Independent Chinese Cinema*, Edinburgh: University of Edinburgh Press.

Wang, Yiman (2005), 'The amateur's lightning rod: DV documentary in postsocialist China', *Film Quarterly*, 58: 4, pp. 16–26.

Wang, Zheng (1999), *Women in the Chinese Enlightenment: Oral and Textual Histories*, Berkeley: University of California Press.

Wedell-Wedellsborg, Anne (2010), 'Between self and community: the individual in contemporary Chinese literature', in M. Halskov Hasen and Rune Svarverud (eds), *iChina, the Rise of the Individual in Modern Chinese Society*, Copenhagen: Nias Press, pp. 164–92.

Wei Hui (2001), *Shanghai Baby*, trans. B. Humes, London: Robinson.

Wei Hui (2005), *Marrying Buddha*, London: Robinson.

Whiteman, D. (2004), 'Out of the theaters and into the streets: a coalition model of the political impact of documentary film and video', *Political Communication*, 21: 1, pp. 51–69. (doi: 10.1080/10584600490273263-1585)

Woesler, Martin (ed.) (2000), *The Modern Chinese Literary Essay: Defining the Chinese Self in the 20th Century*, Bochum: West German University Press.

Wolf, Margery (1985), *Revolution Postponed: Women in Contemporary China*, Stanford: Stanford University Press.

Woolf, Virginia [1925] (2003), 'Montaigne', in V. Woolf, *Common Reader*, London: Vintage, pp. 64–5.

Wu, Pei-Yi (1992), *The Confucian's Progress: Autobiographical Writings in Traditional China*, Princeton: Princeton University Press.

Xiao, Qiang (2003), 'Cyber speech: catalyzing free expression and civil society', *Harvard International Review*, Summer, pp. 70–5.

Xiao, Qiang (2004), 'The rising tide of Internet opinion in China: online discussions "now actually drive the agenda of official media"', *Nieman Reports*, 58: 2 (Summer), pp. 103–4.

Yan, Yunxiang (2003), *Private Life Under Socialism – Love, Intimacy, and Family Change in a Chinese Village 1949–1999*, Stanford: Stanford University Press.

Yan, Yunxiang (2009), *The Individualization of Chinese Society*, London: London School of Economics.

Yan, Yunxiang (2010), 'Introduction: Conflicting images of the individual and contested process of individualisation', in M. Halskov Hansen and Rune Svarverud (eds), *iChina: The Rise of the Individual in Modern Chinese Society*, Copenhagen: Nias Press, pp. 1–38.

Yang, Guobin (2002), 'Civil society in China: a dynamic field of study', *China Review International*, 9: 1 (Spring), pp. 1–16.

Yang, Guobin (2003a), 'The co-evolution of the Internet and civil society in China', *Asian Survey*, XLIII: 3, pp. 405–22.

Yang, Guobin (2003b), The Internet and the rise of a transnational Chinese cultural sphere', *Media, Culture & Society*, 25, pp. 469–90.

Yang, Guobin (2003c), 'The Internet and civil society in China: a preliminary assessment', *Journal of Contemporary China*, 12: 36, pp. 453–75.

Yang, Guobin (2006a), 'Between control and contention: China's new Internet politics', *Washington Journal of Modern China*, 8: 1 (Spring/Summer), pp. 30–47.

Yang, Guobin (2006b), 'Activists beyond virtual borders: Internet-mediated networks and informational politics in China', *First Monday*, 11: 9 (September).

Yang, Guobin (2009), *The Power of the Internet in China: Citizen Activism Online*, New York: Columbia University Press.

Yang, Mayfair (1994), *Gifts, Favors, and Banquets: the Art of Social Relationships in China*, Ithaca: Cornell University Press.

Yang, Rae (1979), *Spider Eaters*, Los Angeles: University of California Press.

Yin, Zhiguang (2011), 'The politics of art, the intellectual configuration of individual and nation-building under Marxist discourse in China, 1918–1930', Ph.D. dissertation, University of Cambridge.

Yu, Haiqing (2006), 'From active audience to media citizenship: the case of post-Mao China', *Social Semiotics*, 16: 2, pp. 303–26.

Yuan, Ji Feng, Koenraad Kuiper and Shaogu Shu (1990), 'Language and revolution: formulae of the Cultural Revolution', *Language in Society*, 19: 1, pp. 61–79.

Zarrow, Peter (1998), 'Citizenship and human rights in early twentieth-century Chinese thought: Liu Shipei and Liang Qichao', in Wm. Theodore De Bary and Tu Weiming (eds), *Confucianism and Human Rights*, New York: Columbia University Press, pp. 209–33.

Zhang, Xudong (1997), *Chinese Modernism in the Era of Reforms. Cultural Fever, Avant-garde Fiction, and the New Chinese Cinema*, Durham: Duke University Press.

Zhang, Yingjin (2004), 'Styles, subjects, and special points of view: a study of contemporary Chinese independent documentary', *New Cinemas: Journal of Contemporary Film*, 2: 2, pp. 119–35.

Zhang, Yingjin (2006), My camera doesn't lie? Truth, subjectivity, and audience in Chinese independent film and video', in Paul G. Pickowicz and Yingjin Zhang (eds), *From Underground to Independent*, Lanham: Rowman and Littlefield.

Zhang, Yingjin (2007), 'Rebel without a cause? China's new urban generation and postsocialist filmmaking', in Zhang Zhen (ed.), *The Urban Generation: Chinese Cinema and Society at the Turn of the Twenty-first Century*, Durham: Duke University Press, pp. 49–80.

Zhang, Yingjin (2010), *Cinema, Space, and Polylocality in a Globalizing World*, Honolulu: University of Hawai'i Press.

Zimmermann, Patricia (1995), *Reel Families: A Social History of Amateur Film*, Bloomington: Indiana University Press.

Zimmermann, Patricia (2008a), 'Introduction: the home movie movement: excavations, artifacts, minings', in Karen L. Ishizuka and Patricia R. Zimmermann (eds), *Mining the Home Movie: Excavations in Histories and Memories*, Oakland: University of California Press, pp. 1–28.

Zimmermann, Patricia (2008b), 'Morphing history into histories: from amateur film to the archive of the future', in Karen L. Ishizuka and Patricia R. Zimmermann (eds), *Mining the Home Movie: Excavations in Histories and Memories*, Oakland: University of California Press, pp. 275–88.

Chinese Publications

Books/journals

De Bary (1893), *Zhongguo de ziyou chuantong* (*Chinese Tradition of Freedom*), Hong Kong: Chinese University Press.

Dong, Zhongshu (1879), *Chun Qiu Fan Lu*, 17 vols, Taipei: Yiwen Yinshuguan.

Feng, Youlan (1934), *Zhongguo Zhexue Shi* (*The History of Chinese Philosophy*), Shanghai: Commercial Press.

Han, Yanbin (2005), 'On the tendency towards creating individualized fiction in the 1990s', *Nei Menggu University Journal*, 37: 1, pp. 31–5.

Jiao, Guocheng (1991), *Zhongguo Gudai Renwo Guanxi (On the Relation between Others and Self in Ancient China)*, Beijing: China People's University Press.

Jin, Guantao, and Liu Qingfeng (2009), *Guannian shi yanjiu: zhongguo xiandai zhongyao zhengzhi shuyu de xingcheng (May Fourth Movement 1999 as a historical term)*, Beijing: Falü chuban she.

Jing, Li (2002), *Renqing Shehui: Renji Guanxi yu Ziwoguande Jiangou (Society of Favours: Interpersonal Relationships and the Structure of Self)*, Bentu Shehui Yanjiu Yeshu Zhi Wu (Nativist Social Research Series) No. 5, River Edge: Global Publishing Co.

Li, Yulin (2009), Fanyi Kunjing, Zhuti, Luli, Meixne (*Liminality of Translation: Subjectivity, Ethics and Aesthetics*), Taibei: Shu lin chu ban gong si.

Liang, Qichao (1998), *Xinmingshuo (China's New Revolution)*, Zhongzhou: Zhongzhou Ancient Book Press.

Liang, Qichao (1999), 'Ouyou Xinying Lu (The Records of Travels in Europe)', in *Liang Qichao Quanji*, vol. 5, Beijing: Beijing Press.

Liang, Shuming (1990), 'Zhongguo Wenhua Yaoyi (The essentials of Chinese culture)', in *Liang Shuming Quanji*, vol. 3, Jinan: Shangdong People's Press.

Lu, Xinyu (2003), *Jilu Zhongguo, Dangdai Zhongguo Xin Jilu Yundong (Recording China: Contemporary Chinese New Documentary Movement)*, Beijing: Sanlian Press.

Luo, Xiaojing (2007), *Xunzhao Geren (Searching for the Individual)*, Beijing: China's Social Science Press.

Wanguo gongfa (Public Law of all Nations) (1864), Beijing: Chongshiguan Press.

Wu, Wenguang (2009), 'Me and these peasants that I know', unpublished manuscript.

Wu, Wenguang, Xinyu Hu and Tianqi Yu (eds) (2016), 'Special issue: First person documentary and private image', *Film Auteur*, March.

Yang, Guoquan (2004), *Zhongguoren de Xinli yu Xingwei: Benduhua Yanjiu (The Psyche and Behaviour of Chinese People: Indigenous Research)*, Beijing: China People's University Press.

Yang, Zhende (2009), *Zhuanxiang Ziwo: Jindai Zhongguo Zhengzhi Sixiang Shang de Geren (Turning Inward to the Self: Political Thoughts on Individualism in Modern China)*, Taibei: Zhongyang yanjiuyuan zhongguo wenzhe yangjiusuo.

Yao, Daimei (2010), 'Self portrait: women's art in China 1920–2010', in Exhibition Catalogue, *Self Image Woman Art in China 1920–2010*, Beijing: Art Museum of Central Academy of Fine Arts Publishing.

Yu, Yingshi (1989), 'Cong Jiazhi Xitong Kan Zhongguo Wenhua de Xiandai Yiyi (The modern meaning of Chinese culture – approach from the value system)', in *Zhongguo Sixiang Chuantong de Xiandai Quanshi*, Jiangsu: Jiangsu People's Press, pp. 1–48.

Yu, Yingshi (1998), 'Qunji Zhijian: zhongguo xiandai sixiangshi shang de liangge xunhuan (Between the self and the collective: two circles in the history of modern Chinese thoughts)', in *Xiandai shuxuelun (Modern Confucianism)*, Shanghai: Shanghai People's Press, pp. 236–40.

Zhang, Zhen (2012), 'Yishu, Gandongli, he Xingdong Zhuyi Jilupian (Art, affect, activist documentary)', *Zhongguo Duli Yingxiang (Chinese Independent Cinema)*, 11.

Zhu, Jingjiang, and Mei Bing (2004), *Zhongguo Duli Jjilupian Dang'an* (*A Record of Independent Chinese Documentary*), Shanxi: Shanxi Normal University Press.

Zhu, Qingsheng (2010), 'Preface I', in Exhibition Catalogue, *Self Image Woman Art in China 1920–2010*, Beijing: Art Museum of Central Academy of Fine Arts Publishing.

Zhu, Rikun, and Xiaogang Wan (2005), *Independent Record*, Beijing: China Ethnic Photo and Art Press.

Online resources

Hu, Xiao, *Nüshiran Tang Danhong Jiemi Guanbi Kafuka Shudian yinqing* (*The Female Poet Tang Danhong Reveals the Hidden Secrets of the Close-down of Kafuka Bookshop*), http://news.xinhuanet.com/book/2008-03/05/ content_7720029.htm (accessed 17 February 2010).

Li, Zhengqi, *Huizhibuqu de Xiangchou* (*The Lingering Nostalgia*), http://xinmin.news365.com.cn/ygb/200806/t20080608_1902418.htm (accessed 3 April 2010).

Liu, Mengxi, *May Fourth and the Anti-tradition Thoughts*, http://blog.sina.com.cn/s/blog_4a169fd50100d7rx.html (accessed 20 October 2009).

Wang, Xiaolu (2010), 'Zhuti Jianxian – 20 Nian Zhongguo Duli Jilupian de Guancha (The gradual reveal of subjectivity – an observation of 20 years' development of independent documentary)', *Dianying Yishu* (*Cinema World*), 6, http://www.indicine.org/cntextdetails.aspx?id=23 (accessed 5 July 2011).

Wang, Zhifu (2016), 'Wenhuabu chachu douyu deng 26 ge zhibo pingtai, Beijing shixing zhubo heimingdan (Cultural Bureau investigate more than 26 zibo platforms, including Douyu, Beijing create a black list), *Everyday News*, 13 July 2017, http://www.nbd.com.cn/articles/2016-07-13/1021476.html (accessed 17 July 2017).

Weishi, Yangguang (2011), *Sun TV's interview with Ai Weiwei*, http://loveaiww.blogspot.com/2011/09/blog-post_2825.html (accessed 30 September 2011).

Wu, Mei (2003), *Yibu Jilupian he Yiwei Yishujia de Shenjingzheng Shi* (*A Documentary and the Neurological Disease History of an Artist*), http://www.filmsea.com.cn/newsreel/archives/200304160022.htm or http://blog.sina.com.cn/ s/blog_485b1a4201008kjh.html (accessed 17 February 2010).

Wu, Mukun (2010), *Daoyan Fangtan: Yang Lina* (*Director's interview: Yang Lina*), http://zgushu.blog.163.com/blog/static/43270469200842412759536/ (accessed 17 February 2010).

Xu, Jilin (2009), 'Dawo de Xiaochu: Xiandan Zhongguo Geren Zhuyi Sichao de Bianqian (The disappearance of 'big self': the change of modern Chinese individualism)', *Zhongguo shehui kexue jikan*, 26, http://www.bianlunchina.com/thread-600-1-1.html (accessed 15 March 2010).

Xu, Linling (2008), *Daoyan Shu Haolun: Shanghai Bushi Zheyang de* (*Director Shu Haolun: Shanghai was not like this*), http://news.sina.com.cn/s/ 2008-06-13/110215738621.shtml (accessed 3 April 2010).

Zhang, Tielin, *Hanhan de Guang* (*The Light of Hanhan*), http://www.my1510.cn/article.php?id=f4f64ac2869c5e0d (accessed 18 October 2011).

Zhao, Ying (2010), *Zuonv Tang Danhong: Wode Huai Zai Aiqiu Wode Hao* (*Female Writer Tang Danhong: My Evilness is Entreating My Goodness*), http:// mochou.cn/542.html (accessed 17 February 2010).

Zhu, Rikun (2010), *Ai Weiwei: Zuo Jilupian Meishenme Jihua, Zhishi hen Shunshou de Yige Xingwei* (*Ai Weiwei: Making Documentary Does Not Need Plans, it is just a Handy Act*), http://art.m6699.com/content-11362-4.htm (accessed 18 October 2011).

Zuo, Xiaoming (2010), *Tang Danhong: Zhongshi Ziwo* (*Tang Danhong: Loyal to the Self*), http://people.com.cn/GB/wenyu/ 66/134/20010621/493565.html (accessed 17 February 2010).

Index

CPSIA information can be obtained
at www.ICGtesting.com
Printed in the USA
JSHW020452280920
8208JS00001B/20

9 781474 474122